9.6t

D0793787

917.8   Drago, Harry Sinclair
Dra   The legend makers: tales of the old-
c.3   time peace officers and desperadoes of the
         frontier.   Dodd, Mead [c1975]
             239 p.   illus.

THE LEGEND MAKERS

Also by Harry Sinclair Drago

ROAD AGENTS AND TRAIN ROBBERS

THE GREAT RANGE WARS

NOTORIOUS LADIES OF THE FRONTIER

ROADS TO EMPIRE

THE STEAMBOATERS

LOST BONANZAS

GREAT AMERICAN CATTLE TRAILS

OUTLAWS ON HORSEBACK

RED RIVER VALLEY

WILD, WOOLLY AND WICKED

WHERE THE LOON CALLS

FOLLOWING THE GRASS

MONTANA ROAD

THE WILD BUNCH

BUCKSKIN EMPIRE

STAGECOACH KINGDOM

RIVER OF GOLD

For Younger Readers

MANY BEAVERS

THE LEGEND MAKERS

WITHDRAWN

Tales of the Old-Time Peace Officers
and Desperadoes of the Frontier

HARRY SINCLAIR DRAGO

Illustrated with Photographs

917.8
Dra
c. 3

DODD, MEAD & COMPANY

NEW YORK

Copyright © 1975 by Harry Sinclair Drago

All rights reserved

No part of this book may be reproduced in any form
without permission in writing from the publisher

ISBN: 0-396-07003-5
Library of Congress Catalog Card Number: 74-10005

Printed in the United States of America
by The Cornwall Press, Inc., Cornwall, N. Y.

Foreword

WHO COINED the pleasant expression "the American West" has been lost to history. I first encountered it in 1903, in Hiram Martin Chittenden's *History of Early Steamboat Navigation on the Missouri River*. Several years later it was in general use. By then the time had passed when everything beyond the Alleghenies was referred to as "West"; when you spoke of the American West, you were speaking of that vast sweep of plains, prairies, and mountains beyond the Missouri River, extending north and south from the Canadian boundary to the Mexican border. It did not include the region beyond the Rockies, which was commonly identified as the Far West.

Beginning with the Lewis and Clark Journals, the discovery and publication of numerous personal accounts of frontiersmen engaged in the fur trade have made us better acquainted with that particular area than any other within the continental limits of the United States. But the trappers, the so-called mountain men, the buffalo hunters, and the cattlemen of the free-range era did little to advance the settling of the American West. For selfish but understandable reasons, they wanted the country kept as it was.

Who was it then who herded the Indians on reservations, eliminated the buffalo that had been their sustenance, and began turning under the prairie sod? Certainly it was the white man—the dirt farmer, the homesteader, the range cattle industry and its ally, the railroad. In the absence of organized law, the American West became an armed camp, "the good guys fighting the bad guys."

In a world where all men—or nearly all—went armed, gun law became the only law, at least the only enforceable law. It was argued, and events often proved it, that the more horrendous a man's reputation as a gunman, the better a peace officer he made. When he rode forth with a sheriff's badge pinned to his vest, he was the law, and he could count on its protection no matter how the chips might fall.

Among the men who put their outlawry behind them and became efficient peace officers, only one achieved fame before he backslid into bank robbery. He was Hendry Brown, town marshal of Caldwell, Kansas, when it was a booming cowtown. Beyond question he was the best marshal Caldwell ever had. His leadership of the bungled attempt to rob the Medicine Valley Bank at Medicine Lodge, Kansas, some fifty miles west of Caldwell, cost him his life and took the lives of five others. His last moments have always been highlighted in my mind by the fact that, having been captured, he attempted to break away, preferring death by gunfire to dangling at the end of a rope.

In half a century of delving into the characters and lives of the so-called outlaws on horseback, I have found very little to admire. To a man they were fatalists, which gave them an audacity that was often mistaken for courage. It was the goal of all outlaw gangs to make a big stake and get away to the banana republics to enjoy it. Presumably Frank and Jesse James did, and the inept Jennings Gang as well. But they soon ran through their money and returned to the States for more, which was their undoing.

"It isn't only the lure of money that takes a man into outlawry," Henry Starr, the last of the horseback outlaws, told a reporter for the St. Louis *Globe*. "There's the thrill of dashing into a town after an all-night ride, guns blazing, and cowing it for half an hour. From every window across the street rifles and shotguns are spitting lead at you. The boys who had gone into the bank come running out with a grain sack bulging with loot. It's time to leave. One of your boys is down, stretched out in the dust. You realize there is nothing you can do for him. You vault into the saddle and roar out of town, guns bucking. You think of the boy you left lying back there in the dust. It's tough, but you realize that it may be you the next time. That helps some."

I have never been able to overcome the feeling that Henry Starr was the sort that should have escaped the burning. But he didn't. On February 18, 1921, he was killed in the attempted robbery of the Harrisonville, Arkansas, State Bank.

Henry Starr was a handsome man, all Cherokee in appearance, although there was a Scottish-Irish strain in him, as in all the numerous Starr clan. He was related to Belle Starr by marriage only, his father being the brother of Belle's husband, Sam Starr.

No one can say with certainty who originated the title The Three Guardsmen for United States Field Marshals Bill Tilghman, Heck Thomas, and Chris Madsen. Very likely it was someone in the editorial room of the *Oklahoma State Capital* in Guthrie. Because it was offered in richly deserved recognition of the services they had rendered Oklahoma, it has endured. Among Western lawmen they take second place to none. They scored their greatest triumph when they broke up the notorious Doolin Gang and eliminated its remarkable leader, Bill Doolin, the son of a poor Arkansas dirt farmer.

I have written many pieces about Doolin, perhaps because I long ago detected that what was true of Doolin the bandit was not necessarily true of Doolin the man. Although his life, inside the law and out, was spent among rough, ignorant men, he had the instincts of a gentleman. They had a way of surfacing unexpectedly, which I do not offer as an excuse for him. By choice he was an outlaw, and he was hunted down and killed as he deserved to be.

Marshal Tilghman supplied him with a fitting epitaph when he said: "There was a wide streak of decency in Bill Doolin."

HARRY SINCLAIR DRAGO

Contents

Contents

Illustrations

THE LEGEND MAKERS

I

The Shaping of the West

BEFORE 1787, when Congress organized the vast and fertile North-west Territory and opened it to settlement on very generous terms, few Americans had ventured beyond the Alleghenies. Approximately thirty-five years later the United States established its west-ernmost post office at Independence, Missouri. In those few, brief years the frontier had advanced almost halfway across the conti-nent. What the nation was witnessing was the greatest mass move-ment of its people in history, dwarfing even the covered-wagon exodus to Oregon and the stampede to the goldfields of California.

In the beginning it was the farmers of New England who sparked the great movement westward. By the thousands they put their family and belongings in a wagon and deserted their rocky hillside acres, sustained by the conviction that in a new land they could better their lot. In the towns, factory and mill workers, daily exposed to the sight of passing emigrant wagons bound for Ohio or beyond, began to catch fire. Putting down their tools, they organized themselves into colonization companies and joined the great migration, their eventual destination loosely defined as "the Ohio country."

In several Connecticut and Rhode Island towns so many trained workers left their jobs that the mills were compelled to close down

1

temporarily. But it was not only in the North, in New England and New York State, that the local economy was disrupted by the mass movement to the West; far to the south other thousands of movers were making their way up the Potomac River to Cumberland and picking their way through the mountains to the Ohio River at today's Wheeling, West Virginia. In time, the route they hacked out was to become the great National Road, the first internal improvement undertaken by the federal government. It cost $6 million, a staggering sum in its day.

Out of the original Northwest Territory were to be carved the states of Ohio, Indiana, Illinois, Michigan, Wisconsin, and the eastern half of Minnesota, always mentioned mellifluously by aspiring nineteenth-century politicians as "the heartland of America." Ohio was the first to be admitted to the Union, in 1803, Indiana followed in 1816, and Illinois in 1818. By then steamboats were crossing Lake Erie and plying the Ohio, Mississippi, and other navigable rivers, providing a reasonably safe and fast means of transportation. By way of New Orleans a world market had been opened for the Midwest. What was to prove even more important, construction of the Erie Canal, which was to connect the Hudson River with Lake Erie, was being pressed with all possible haste by the state of New York.

If, as most estimates have it, 160,000 whites had taken up permanent residence in the original Northwest Territory by the close of 1818, it must be assumed that among them were persons of all character, including thieves, robbers, and outlaws, and that sheriffs and other peace officers were engaged in running them down. There is very little in the record to prove it: plenty of crime but no notorious criminals, and no outstanding or famous lawmen. River piracy had flourished back in the beginning, when hundreds of flatboatmen had floated down the Ohio in their unwieldy craft.

Most notorious of the river pirates was Colonel Pfluger, commonly known as Colonel Plug. He made his headquarters in a house at the head of Cash Creek, just above Cairo, where he conducted a low groggery and commanded a gang of robbers and cutthroats who preyed on the rivermen—getting them helpless with whiskey, then splitting their throats before confiscating their goods and sinking their boats. Plug's career ended when he became trapped in a boat he was sinking and went to the bottom with it.

A thug named Wilson took command of the gang and moved up the Ohio to Cave-in-Rock, on the Illinois shore. When they caught one of the big flats tied up to the bank for the night, they drove the crew off at gunpoint and helped themselves to the cargo. If they met resistance, they used their guns. After suffering a number of such incidents, the boaters banded together, came ashore several miles above Cave-in-Rock, and closed in on the pirate hangout by land. The thugs were taken by surprise, but the ringleaders—Wilson and Micayah and Wiley Harpe—escaped and reached the Kentucky shore. Eleven others were beheaded at daylight.

If the Harpe brothers, known to folklore and history as Big and Little Harpe, were guilty of only half the crimes with which they were charged, they would have been infamous. Putting river piracy behind them, they became the scourge of the forest trails of Kentucky and the Carolinas until pioneer vengeance caught up with them. Posing as itinerant preachers and accompanied by several female "gospel singers," they induced Moses Stigall, a prosperous farmer, to offer them the hospitality of his home, and they moved in with Stigall, his wife, their young daughter, and a nephew named Love. During Stigall's absence on a business trip to the county seat, the Harpes murdered his wife and child and young Love, then stole all they could carry before fleeing.

The crime was not discovered until Stigall's return the following day. A posse was hastily organized and set off in pursuit of the Harpes and their consorts. Obviously fearing that he and his brother were being pursued, Little Harpe broke away from the others and made good his escape. No further mention of him is found in the folklore of the region.

With the posse in sight, Big Harpe deserted the women and rode for his life. He had waited too long. A rifle shot toppled him from the saddle. Stigall rode up to him and, beside himself with grief and rage, blasted the remaining spark of life out of the notorious thug. Severing the head from the body, he climbed a pine, ripped away the crown, and affixed the head to the sharpened stem.

Admittedly this is largely legend, but it gains credence from the fact that when a village came into being there, it named itself Harpe's Head, Kentucky.

There were other such desperadoes. James Girty, the cousin of the notorious Major Simon Girty, was one, and far down the Mississippi, twenty-seven miles north of Natchez, at Stack Island and the Crow's Nest, was gathered the largest and most formidable gang of river pirates and cutthroats of their time. It was there that John A. Murrell, Public Enemy No. 1 of his day, held forth. A Tennesseean by birth, rather handsome and better educated than his followers, he ruled them with an iron hand. A man who differed with him usually soon disappeared, and no questions asked. He disemboweled the men he killed before tossing the bodies into the river. It was his boast that they never came to the surface.

After the crew of a flatboat had succeeded in drifting down the Mississippi to New Orleans and had disposed of their cargo and sold their craft for its value as lumber (since it was impossible to pole it the hundreds of miles back north), it was the custom to enjoy a carouse before beginning the long trek home. The shortest and most direct route was up the Natchez Trace. Murrell made it the most dangerous. The trailside inns and groggeries operated by his confederates, where travelers laid over for the night, made excellent observation posts for determining which of the wayfarers were carrying gold or "dixies" (the ten-, twenty- and fifty-dollar notes issued by the Bank of New Orleans and accepted everywhere at face value).

This relieved the thugs of the embarrassment of holding up a wayfarer only to discover that he had nothing on him that could be turned into cash. They didn't run that risk with the boaters who were trudging homeward with the proceeds of three months' hard labor in their jeans. Since that was where the pickings were the best, Murrell and his followers leveled their attention on them. Men disappeared mysteriously and were never seen again. Stories multiplied that they had been robbed and murdered by the Murrell Gang and their lifeless bodies disposed of in the most convenient of all graveyards, the Mississippi.

Rivermen believed the tales. Down in New Orleans boaters organized themselves into armed parties of twenty or more before setting out on the long journey north. Thirsting for revenge, they marched into the den of thieves and cutthroats at Under-the-Hill at Natchez, did some killing of their own, scattered the rest, and put the torch to the district.

Murrell read the handwriting on the wall. The age of the steamboat was at hand and he was smart enough to realize that it would spell the end of river piracy. Putting his criminal talents to work in other directions, he organized a slave-stealing ring. Although successful for a time, it led to his downfall and he died in prison in 1847. He was only forty-three.

We know the names and something about the savagery of the "half-man half-alligator" river pirates and outlaws of the period. But really we know very little. Of the lawmen who hunted them down and eliminated them we know nothing. Even their names have escaped written history.

On a May morning in 1823, Captain William Becknell, riding at the head of his little train of five heavily laden wagons, left the cluster of villages that had taken root at the big bend of the Missouri River and struck off to the southwest across the untracked plains of Kansas. It set in motion a series of related events that were to anchor the frontier at Independence for the next thirty years.

Becknell was a respected and prosperous Indian trader. In the parlance of the day, he had "been to the mountains," meaning the Rockies. In the past year, accompanied by several of his fellow frontiersmen, he had ventured as far as the Spanish-speaking settlements of New Mexico with a sizable pack train. He had been welcomed by the Mexicans and disposed of his trade goods at a handsome profit. Mexico had just won its independence from Spain and opened its northern border to commerce with the United States.

Although this open-door policy was destined to be short-lived, it touched off a stir of activity in the Missouri river towns. Several companies were organized for trading with the New Mexicans. The pack train of Colonel Benjamin Cooper and his cousins Braxton and Stephen was the first to take off. In the packs was merchandise valued at $8,000, Missouri prices. A second party, led by Captain Joseph Walker, overtook the Coopers before they reached the Arkansas River. For greater safety, they joined forces and proceeded together.

Becknell, still back at his home village of Arrow Rock, where he had been outfitting for his second journey to Santa Fe, was not disturbed at being left so far behind. He took it for granted that Captain Walker would lead the combined Cooper-Walker party up the Arkansas to the Purgatoire, ascend that stream to its headwaters, and go through Raton Pass into New Mexico. Becknell had been over Raton Pass. He knew that wagons could not be put through it. And that was the rub: he was going to open a wagon road to Santa Fe.

Men whose judgment he respected shook their heads in disbelief. How could heavily laden wagons be taken across 780 miles of savage land, cut up by countless small streams, dry washes, treacherous beds of quicksand, and inhabited only by roving bands of Plains Indians?

The course Becknell proposed to take can be traced on most maps of the region. From the cottonwoods on the Neosho River (Council Grove), he planned to continue on to the southwest until he reached the Arkansas River at Cow Creek. Moving up the river past Walnut Creek and the future site of Fort Zarah, it was his intention to ascend the Arkansas until he passed Pawnee Rock.

From there he would be reaching for Cimarron Crossing, five miles west of today's Dodge City, where he intended to cross the Arkansas and, pointing south, challenge the sixty sandy, waterless miles stretching away between him and the shallow Cimarron River.

Men and animals survived the ordeal and the train paused to recuperate for a week in the New Mexican village of San Miguel before pushing on the final fifty-eight miles to the capital.

William Becknell has justly been hailed as the Father of the Santa Fe Trail. He left Arrow Rock, Missouri, on May 22, and rolled into the New Mexican capital with his cavalcade of wagons on November 16. He had opened the greatest of all American trade routes. Josiah Gregg, the trail's recognized historian, places the value of goods moved over it in 1828, five years later, at $150,000. In 1831 the figure had swelled to a quarter of a million dollars.

It was only the beginning, for the Mexicans, expert horsemen and inured by long experience to the rigors of the trail, were sending their own caravans north in competition with the Americans. Independence, favorably situated at the head of the great trade route, was rapidly establishing itself as the undisputed metropolis of the frontier. Despite the shifting snags and sandbars, steamboats were navigating the Missouri, arriving and departing from rival Westport. When a spring flood swept away its wharf, Independence built its own facility, named it Westport Landing and captured the trade.

In 1829, a few miles up the Missouri on the Kansas shore, the United States established Fort Leavenworth. Its dual purpose was to protect the frontier and prevent Indian raids on the caravans moving over the Santa Fe Trail. It proved to be an impossible task, but it established Independence as the jumping-off place for the Far West. When parties of shaggy-haired, greasy-looking trappers rode into town, after spending five months on the mountain streams of Colorado, they announced their return by firing their guns. After disposing of their peltries they caroused in the dram shops in drunken revelry. But Independence was never distinguished for its lawlessness until 1838, when a campaign to eject all Mormons from the state, by force, if necessary, swept Missouri. The charge against Prophet Joseph Smith, Jr., and his followers was that they were preaching, and living in, polygamy.

Fleeing religious persecution in the Midwest, over fifteen thousand Latter-Day Saints had settled in their New Zion at the towns of Far West, Haun's Mill, and other Missouri villages, all in the vicinity of Independence. It pitted neighbor against neighbor, and put the lives of suspected Mormon sympathizers in jeopardy. Some men were shot. Governor Lillburn Boggs, acceding to the wishes of the majority, dispatched three thousand militiamen to Far West under orders to "drive the Mormons from the state or exterminate them." The latter, realizing it was useless to resist, fled across the Mississippi into Illinois, where they were to suffer new harassment and persecution.

In the spring of 1843 the deck of every steamboat arriving at Independence (Westport Landing) was crowded with the covered wagons of pioneers bound for Oregon. Singly and in groups, other trains of settlers, making their way over Missouri's primitive roads, arrived and found places for themselves in the sprawling prairie bivouac at the edge of town. There, as their animals recuperated, a semblance of order emerged from chaos; trains were organized for the long and dangerous journey across the plains, captains elected and guides engaged, supplies replenished.

Before it was largely over in 1847, the great migration to Oregon had further enhanced the prosperity and preeminence of Independence. In the meantime, however, other events had transpired that were of even greater importance. Texas had won its independence from Mexico in 1836. In 1845 it was annexed by the United States and entered the Union as its twenty-eighth state, which made war with Mexico inevitable.

Stripped of its heroics, it was an unequal, thinly disguised war of conquest. It closed the Santa Fe Trail, and Independence turned from its peaceful pursuits to supplying the troops marching on the border with sustenance and ammunition.

The outcome of the war was never in doubt. When the smoke of battle drifted away in 1848, New Mexico, the future Arizona, and California were American territory. The nation scarcely had time to catch its breath when it was rocked by the electrifying news that gold had been discovered on the mountain streams of the distant Sierra Nevada. As has been said a thousand times, it touched off the greatest stampede for gold in recorded history.

It was June, 1849, before the chaos produced at Independence by the arrival of thousands of California-bound argonauts was reduced to a semblance of order, and wagon trains began rolling out of town. They were pointing for the old Oregon Trail up the North Platte, which the forty-niners, with little respect for history, promptly renamed the Overland Trail.

They did not have the trail up the North Platte to themselves; separated by only the mile-wide bottoms, thousands of Mormons, forced out of Illinois, were again on the move, their destination the remote sanctuary on the shore of Great Salt Lake that Brigham Young, their new and dynamic leader, the "Lion of the Lord," was carving out of the wilderness.

Missouri had entered the Union as a slave state in 1821, under the terms of the Missouri Compromise, which stipulated that all future states west of the Mississippi and north of latitude 36° 30′ N. should be free. It settled nothing, and in 1860 it exploded into the bloody and bitter "border" war between the Free-Soilers of Kansas and the pro-slavery radicals of Missouri, captained by such notorious guerrilla leaders as William Clarke Quantrill, Bloody Bill Anderson and Jim Lane and his Kansas "Redlegs."

Both sides were swept into the great War Between the States. When that long and costly struggle was over, the series of events with which this narrative is primarily concerned—the emergence of the Western peace officer and the establishment of law and order— had yet to be resolved.

Hopefully, however, railroads, spurred by government land grants, were opening up new country. The Missouri Pacific, stalled halfway across the state at Tipton during the war, was pushing on

9

again for what had been Westport Landing and was now Kansas City, the future metropolis of the Missouri Valley. From St. Joe, the Hannibal and St. Joseph Railroad, connecting the Mississippi with the Missouri, was extending its tracks southward. In Wyoming, the Union Pacific, America's first transcontinental, had passed Cheyenne and was laying a mile of track a day. The Kansas Pacific, its Eastern Branch, was building up the Valley of the Kaw.

It reached the confluence of the Smoky Hill and the Republican rivers in May. Pausing only long enough to put up a signboard identifying the place as Junction City, the graders and tracklayers hurried on, their next immediate goal the cluster of dirt-roofed cabins on Turkey Creek, some twenty miles to the west, which the hardy souls who dwelt there had named Abilene.

Few others had ever heard of the place. Three years later, however, its reputation was nationwide. The Kansas prairies had been invaded by thousands of Longhorn cattle and the swarm of Texans who had driven them up the Chisholm Trail. Abilene, an island in a sea of cattle, was reeking with prosperity and notorious for its violence and lawlessness.

Among the Texans were many who had worn Confederate gray. To them Kansas was foreign soil. Riding tall in the saddle, they regarded it with contempt and recognized no law but their own. But even among those who went wrong—and many did—men found something in them to admire, for it was out of such rough material that the legendary, half-mythical cowboy and Western peace officer were created. They were a breed apart, and they left their mark on their time and place.

II

The Law Comes to Abilene

When Joseph G. McCoy, only thirty-two at the time, opened his "northern cattle market" at Abilene, Kansas, in the fall of 1867, the success of the venture was regarded dubiously even by his brothers, John and James McCoy, the prosperous livestock dealers of Springfield, Illinois. At the time—aside from the several military posts in Indian Territory—there were no established settlements between Abilene and Red River, on the Texas border, nor was there an established north-south trail over which cattle could be driven from Red River Station to the Kansas market.

Jesse Chisholm, the Scottish-Cherokee Indian trader, had located what he referred to as his "wagon road," running from his home on Chisholm Creek, at the confluence of the Little Arkansas and the Arkansas River, to his trading post on the North Canadian, a scant 220 miles. This, of course, was to become the nucleus of the famous Chisholm Trail.[1] For years Texans had been swimming their cattle across Red River at Rock Bluff Crossing (Preston) and trailing them north to Missouri over what they called the Shawnee Trail, the forerunner of the famous Texas Road, up and down which the skirmishes and battles of the Civil War were to be fought.

By midsummer of 1867, an estimated hundred thousand Long-

horns had been trailed north over the Texas Road, when an outbreak of Spanish, or "tick," fever, to which the Longhorns were
immune but which was fatal to domestic livestock, led Missouri to
clamp down a statewide embargo on the entry of all Texas cattle.
Two weeks later Kansas took similar action, the hastily passed
legislation stipulating that "longhorn cattle shall not be permitted
to enter or pass through that part of Kansas lying east of 96
degrees of longitude."

Abilene was some sixty miles to the west of the proscribed area.
McCoy could scarcely have devised anything more favorable to
his prospects than the situation that now presented itself. Texas
herds, stopped by the embargo, would have to turn back and be
put on grass in Indian Territory and pay toll.

Making the most of his opportunity, McCoy dispatched several
scouts into the Great Osage Reservation and the Cherokee Outlet
to inform the frustrated Texans that his cattle market at Abilene
was open for business.

After some aimless wandering, the first herd was received early
in September. Although it was already late in the season, before
it was over, some forty thousand cattle had been sold and shipped.
The following year saw that figure tripled. And it was only the
beginning. In May, 1870, it was said that half a million Longhorns
would reach Abilene that year.[2]

In the meantime Abilene had become a wild, brawling town
without any semblance of law and order. Between the cow outfits camped out on the surrounding prairie, waiting to get their
turn at the shipping pens, and the trail crews about to head home
for Texas, it had a daily cowboy population numbering between
three and four thousand. Gathered there to prey on them were a
hundred assorted saloonkeepers, gamblers, thugs, pimps, and the
painted denizens of "McCoy's Addition," the red-light district at
the eastern edge of town. They closed up shop at the end of the
shipping season and departed for St. Louis or New Orleans, only
to be back the following spring.

Abilene was now an incorporated town with a permanent population of six hundred or more, who, with good reason, lived in fear of their lives and were demanding that the nightly shootings and the lawlessness of Texas Street be curbed. Mayor T. C. Henry induced Tom Sheran, the grocer and sheriff of Dickinson County, to assume the added responsibility of acting town marshal. Jim McDonald was put on the town payroll as deputy marshal.

Sheran had no great difficulty collecting license fees, but his proclamation that it was forbidden to pack a gun within the town limits went unheeded. He built a calaboose on Texas Street, which infuriated the Texans, who had to pass it as they trooped from saloon to saloon. To express their displeasure, they riddled the planks with their bullets. The first offender to be lodged in the jail was the Negro cook of an outfit camped on the prairie. A score of Texans attacked the building, ripped off the roof, and freed the prisoner, which was something of a switch—Texans coming to the aid of a black man. Then a score of them thundered up Railroad Street, guns blazing, and riddled the little building in which the mayor had his office.

Mayor Henry ordered the roof replaced and bolted down, and he had the jail put under armed guard, day and night. But Sheran had had enough and turned in his badge. When Deputy Marshal McDonald resigned a week later, the mayor communicated with the St. Louis Police Department, requesting the Chief to send him two reliable men who could handle the situation in Abilene.

Several days later, two of the Mound City's finest arrived in Abilene. Somehow, the Texas Street crowd discovered why the officers were there, and for their benefit staged a wild mock shootout that must have been convincing, for the visitors took the next train back east.

Bear River Tom Smith had distinguished himself in the so-called Bear River Riot, in which Union Pacific construction workers had risen up against the human parasites who had been robbing them blind in the tent towns along the right-of-way. He had been

13

wounded in that bloody fracas, but when hale and hearty again had been made marshal of new camps as the rails advanced. A year later he was in Ellsworth, Kansas, fifty miles west of Abilene. An item in the Topeka *Commonwealth* caught his attention. "We understand," said the *Commonwealth*, "that Hell is again in session at Abilene. Anyone interested in the job of town marshal should contact Mayor Henry."

It did not take Tom Smith long to decide that he was interested. In the morning, mounted on his big gray horse, Silverheels, he set out across the prairie for Abilene.

Apparently there is only one photograph of Thomas J. Smith. It has been reprinted countless times. It shows him as a compact, brawny man with a pleasing Irish face. His broad, muscular shoulders give him the appearance of being shorter than he is known to have been. That he was born in New York in 1840 and had been a member of the New York City Police Department is fairly certain. No one knows why he suddenly left New York and headed west. Romanticists say it was because of an unhappy love affair. This was the man who had come to Abilene seeking the job of town marshal. Of him, Mayor Henry was one day to write:

"Tom Smith was fairly well educated, reared a Catholic, and was clean of speech. I never heard him offer a profane word or employ a vulgar phrase. He neither gambled, drank, nor was in the least dissolute otherwise. I recall our first meeting. 'You better look the town over,' I told him, when he informed me that he was there to apply for the job of town marshal. 'You may change your mind.'

" 'I've looked it over,' he replied calmly. 'It's about what I expected.'

" 'And you believe you can control it?'

" 'I believe I can.'

"When I inquired if he still wanted the job, he replied quietly, 'That's what I'm here for, Mr. Henry.' "

The town board met that afternoon, and Tom Smith was hired for a month on a trial basis at a salary of $125, plus a fee of $2 for every arrest he made.[3]

14

For almost a quarter of a century it was popularly believed that if a town wanted law and order, the best way to get it was to import a gunman whose reputation was such that it would cause lesser fry to pull up stakes and remove themselves to a healthier climate. Of course, arming a desperado with a law badge was tantamount to giving him a license to kill. It was so interpreted and increased the population of various boot hills.

Tom Smith did not belong to that breed. He didn't kill anyone. Beneath his coat, in shoulder holsters, he wore a brace of pistols, but he didn't find it necessary to display them in order to throw fear into the men with whom he had to deal; the only weapons he used were his fists. He was a new type of peace officer; instead of making his rounds on foot, he patrolled the streets of Abilene on horseback.

He had signs printed proclaiming that it was unlawful to carry a gun in the town limits. They were defaced or torn down almost as soon as he put them up. "I expected they would be," he told the mayor. "I'll put up new ones this morning and keep on putting them up until they are respected."

That afternoon he caught a young Texan tearing down the sign that had just been nailed up on the wooden lamppost in front of the Old Fruit Saloon. Slipping from the saddle, he knocked the cowboy cold and, with a crowd watching, flung him over his shoulder and carried him across Texas Street to lock him up in the calaboose.

The incident had repercussions, but after three or four men had been taken before the justice of the peace and fined for carrying firearms, the signs began to stay up. The marshal enlisted the support of merchants and saloonkeepers and got them to put up gunracks. When a cowpuncher turned his gun over to a clerk or bartender, he was given a check for it and reclaimed his weapon when he was ready to leave town. The argument Smith advanced was a sound one: they all wanted to do more business, and there was no better way that could be done than by curtailing the senseless gunfighting.

Coming up the Chisholm Trail with a herd of cattle from the mesquite country of south Texas, lanky Wyoming Frank McGee heard how things were going in Abilene and declared long and loudly that no Yankee badge wearer was going to make him hand over his gun while he was in town doing a little celebrating. Eventually his outfit reached the end of the trail and made camp on a branch of Chapman Creek. Wyoming Frank had boasted so violently that no town marshal was going to make him hand over his gun that the rest of the crew watched to see what he would do. He knew it. But it was too late to back down now. On Sunday morning he and four or five members of the crew rode into Abilene. The town was crowded, even though the hour was early, Sunday on Texas Street being considered no different from any other day. Wyoming Frank tethered his bronc and took up a position at the corner in front of the Lone Star Saloon.

For some unknown reason the marshal was late making his rounds this morning. But finally Wyoming Frank saw him coming, his big gray horse moving at a slow walk.

On turning the corner, Marshal Smith was instantly aware of the lanky Texan standing there, his holstered gun prominently displayed. Suspecting at once that this was a planned confrontation, he slipped out of the saddle and demanded the weapon.

"No, you don't" was the surly response. "I ain't breaking the peace. If you want my gun, you'll have to take it."

But the steely glitter in Smith's eyes made him back off a step. The marshal followed him up through the open door of the Lone Star and into the saloon. The crowd drinking at the bar got out of the way.

Wyoming Frank tried to get his gun out of the holster, but Smith crowded him so closely that he couldn't get arm room. Fetching up against the bar gave the marshal his opportunity. His fist flashed out and a blow flattened the cowboy to the floor. Yanking the man to his feet, he gave him a pistol-whipping that laid his head open.

16

"I'm giving you five minutes to get out of town," he told Wyoming Frank, "and don't ever let me set eyes on you again."

By such methods Abilene was being brought to heel. Violence did not end, but the Texans began to respect Tom Smith. He had never tried to police the red-light district, but when a feud erupted among the inmates that resulted in the killing of one, he marched in and compelled the several hundred prostitutes to hand over their derringers. Mayor Henry reported that the marshal collected a basketful of weapons.

The town board registered its appreciation of the job Smith was doing by building a little office for him, adjacent to the mayor's, and increasing his salary to $225 per month, retroactive to July 4. With the peak of the season at hand, a man named Scott and the aforementioned Jim McDonald were hired as policemen on a temporary basis. According to the record, their only contribution to maintaining the peace of the town was arresting drunks.

Abilene had never been busier. From early morning until long after sundown, panting locomotives were shunting empty stock cars up to the loading chutes and switching loaded ones into position for the journey east. No fewer than four loaded stock trains a day were being dispatched down the Valley of the Kaw. The Drovers' Cottage, McCoy's famous hotel for owners and stock buyers, now in its second year, was filled to overflowing. No crime had occurred there until a wealthy Texan awakened one night in time to see a thief fleeing down the hall with his money belt. He pursued the intruder and shot and killed him. Marshal Smith investigated the matter and dismissed it as a justifiable homicide.

Abilene got its first newspaper in September, 1870, the four-page weekly *Chronicle*. Its politics were Republican, and like so many Kansas newspapers, its editorial policy was slanted in favor of the tillers of the soil. Theodore Henry was doing a prosperous business buying and selling land to prospective grangers. Realizing that the newspaper would provide him with an excellent means of addressing the men he wanted to reach, he had invested in the

17

Chronicle. Its first issue carried an article by him that was so critical
of the Texas cattle trade that he and Joe McCoy never again were
friends. "Vast sums of money change hands here every day but
very little remains in Abilene. The cattle trade builds no roads, no
schoolhouses, no churches. When the present madness passes, the
farmers of Dickinson County will be its salvation."

When a trail boss found a brush fence blocking his way, he
seldom turned aside to avoid it. Oftener than not, he sent his herd
crashing through it, scattering brush and trampling the crop it was
protecting. But now having found a spokesman, the grangers began
to organize. Armed clashes were reported in which trail herds were
turned aside by gunfire.

Officially it did not concern the marshal, but he sensed that the
climate of Abilene had changed. Several days after the last herd
of the year arrived, the Drovers' Cottage closed for the season and
the annual migration of the sporting fraternity began. Jake Karatofsky boarded up his Great Western Store, the town's leading
mercantile establishment; the Novelty Theatre padlocked its doors,
and the saloons, including the elegant Alamo, boarded up their
plate-glass doors and windows. The town board economized by
dismissing Deputy Marshals Scott and McDonald.

Expecting to be informed that his services were no longer required, Smith endeavored to end the uncertainty by submitting his
resignation, only to have it unanimously rejected. It was to result
in unexpected tragedy. The facts are well known.

Andrew McConnell, a Scotsman living in a dugout on Chapman
Creek, had been out deer hunting on Sunday, October 23. When
he returned home, he found cows belonging to his neighbor John
Shea trespassing on his unfenced land. It had happened before and
caused bad blood between them. Carrying his deer gun and accompanied by his friend Moses Miles, also a Scot, he marched over
to Shea's farm for an accounting. They had a violent argument that
ended when Shea drew his pistol and tried to snap a shot at Mc-
Connell. For some reason the gun failed to fire.

Moses Miles, standing only a few feet away, later testified that Shea snapped his pistol three times before McConnell killed him.

The investigation that followed resulted in the acquittal of McConnell on his plea of self-defense. Neighbors were not satisfied with the outcome. Shea's gun was examined and found to be in excellent working order. Indictments for murder were voted against McConnell and Miles. Warrants for their arrest were placed in the hands of Sheriff Joseph Cramer.

Cramer was a spineless nonentity, and so was Jim McDonald, his recently appointed deputy. Neither had any appetite for taking McConnell and Miles into custody. Whether it was Cramer's idea or McDonald's to get Marshal Smith to accompany them to Chapman Creek to make the arrests, is unknown. However, it was definitely McDonald who requested the marshal's assistance. The latter's jurisdiction ended at the town line, and he therefore was under no official obligation to assist Cramer in making the arrest. However, he readily volunteered to accompany the sheriff and his deputy.

On the morning of November 2, as the men were about to set out for the dugout on Chapman Creek, Cramer found a convenient excuse for not accompanying them. When they reached the creek, a neighbor, William Stambaugh, informed them that McConnell and Miles, having heard that warrants were out on them, had forted up in the dugout and were prepared to resist arrest. There are several accounts of what followed. Two that have stood the test of time appeared in the *Chronicle*, one by John Edwards, Abilene's celebrated grass-roots historian, and the other by Stambaugh, who was almost an eyewitness. First Stambaugh:

"It was no later than ten o'clock when they [Marshal Smith and McDonald] arrived at McConnell's place. They tethered their horses at the rail fence and walked toward the entrance. Moses Miles was in the yard splitting firewood with an axe. Marshal Smith passed him and entered the dugout. Presently two shots were heard from within. McDonald was so panic stricken that he ran out of the yard and across the fields to my claim.

"McConnell was shot through the hand, the marshal in the breast. They grappled and struggled into the open air, Smith, with a mortal wound, giving McConnell a fearful battle. Smith got McConnell down and was either getting the handcuffs out of his pocket or attempting to put them on his prisoner when Miles, who was McConnell's partner, came up behind and buried the blade of his axe in Smith's head, striking three blows and almost severing the head from the body. I let McDonald have a pony and he raced into town with his dreadful news." [4]

"Abilene was stunned by the news that Marshal Smith had been killed," Edwards wrote. "Feeling ran high against Sheriff Cramer and Deputy Sheriff McDonald. In a very few minutes a posse (including myself) was off for the scene of the conflict. On arriving there we found Smith's body lying some ten yards from the dugout with his head severed from the body excepting the skin on the back of the neck. McConnell and Miles had fled. Judge Kuney and James Gainsford, who were with the posse, took up the pursuit of McConnell and Miles and continued on the trail, traveling day and night until the two men were captured on Saturday morning, just before sunrise, some fifteen miles northwest of Clay Center, on the Republican River. By telegraph from Junction City, Abilene was informed that the prisoners were being brought to town on the Sunday-morning train. A great crowd gathered and threats of lynching were heard. The two prisoners were taken to the courthouse and placed in a room on the second floor under continuous guard." [5]

With such an outpouring of grief and respect as frontier Abilene was not to see again, Marshal Smith was buried the following day. It was expected that McConnell and Miles would quickly be found guilty and sentenced to be hanged, but when they were placed on trial, an impartial jury could not be impaneled. A change of venue to Riley County was granted, and the defendants were lodged in the Riley County jail at Manhattan. They were found guilty but instead of being sentenced to death, they received long prison terms.

With the spring elections at hand, Mayor Henry announced that he would not be a candidate himself. McCoy got into the race and was elected mayor, even though Henry campaigned against him.

Abilene was coming back to life; the saloons were reopening and the birds of passage, male and female, were returning for the expected bonanza.

Among his problems the new mayor faced the urgent need to find someone to replace the lamented Tom Smith. His quest appeared to have ended when tall, blond, dandified James Butler Hickok, he of the fearsome reputation of Wild Bill, the Prince of Pistoleers, stepped down from an eastbound train at Abilene and took up his headquarters at the Alamo Saloon.

III

Wild Bill Takes Charge

WHEN THE Kansas-Pacific Railroad, building westward for the Colorado line, intersected the Jones and Plummer (Texas) Trail in the vicinity of Fort Hays, the cluster of shacks, sod shanties, and saloons that stood there became the town of Hays City. Thousands of Texas stock cattle were being driven up to Ogallala, Nebraska, and sold north to populate the empty ranges of Wyoming and Dakota.

Trail drivers found Hays City a convenient and agreeable point at which to stop over while permitting their herds to recuperate. The town's resident buffalo hunters and the troopers from the fort contributed to its prosperity.

There was no law in Hays City. When things began to get out of hand, Jim (Hound) Kelley, Tommy Drumm, and other saloon-keepers decided that Hays City had to have a town marshal. George A. Custer, then a lieutenant colonel, who commanded at Fort Hays, suggested to Kelley that his favorite scout and friend, Wild Bill Hickok, be appointed. That was done, and while they were about it, they "elected" him sheriff of Ellis County.[1]

Hickok shed his frontier garb of fringed buckskins and strode about Hays City resplendent in skirted frock coat, frilled silk shirt, and red silk sash, a brace of pistols at his waist. The bloody incident at the Rock Creek (Nebraska) station of the Overland Express, in which he had killed—murdered, his critics have it—Dave Mc-Canles, the former station owner, and two others, an incident that had brought him wide attention, was almost ten years behind him. In the interim he had been bodyguard to General (Senator) Lane in the Kansas-Missouri border war, Army scout, stage driver, and deputy marshal at Fort Riley.

Recently he had been featured briefly in what must have been the first outdoor Wild West show presented in America, at Niagara Falls, New York. The exhibition had been a financial disaster, and he was supporting himself by gambling. As marshal of Hays, he continued to gamble, making Tommy Drumm's saloon his unofficial headquarters.

Being a vain man, he never bothered to deny the countless tales of his expertise with a handgun or that his pistols were so covered with "credits" that he had lost count of them. No one knows how many men were cut down by his guns. However, the statement that "not including Indians, Hickok killed more than twenty-five men" has been widely accepted. Presumably that figure includes the killing of Whistler, Badger, and Handsmeller, the three Oglala chiefs, of which he was accused but never proved guilty. On the other hand, court records reveal that he was responsible for the death of eleven white men and absolved of responsibility in each instance by reason of self-defense or accident. Five of these killings occurred in his brief tenure as marshal of Hays City.

He was in Drumm's place, early one evening, talking with the proprietor, when a man ran in with word that two drunks were shooting up the Santa Fe Saloon, a groggery patronized by buffalo hunters. It took Hickok only a moment or two to reach the scene of the shooting. As he pushed through the door of the Santa Fe, the drunks turned their guns on him. He did not hesitate; his pistols spurted flame and the two fools were dead when they hit the floor.

The slaying of the two men in the Santa Fe Saloon was impersonal as far as Wild Bill was concerned, unless, as some accounts have it, one of the slain men was Bill Mulvey (or Mulrey), a saloon character of dubious reputation with whom Hickok had become acquainted in previous days in Ellsworth, Kansas. If so, it would suggest that the shoot-out in the Santa Fe was not unconnected with the slaying of Sam Strawhorne in Tommy Drumm's saloon several weeks later.[2]

Strawhorne, a professional gambler, had recently come over to Hays from Ellsworth, where he had been in local politics, and where his trail had first crossed Wild Bill's. They never were friends and soon were bitter enemies, both of them vying for the favor of the same woman.

On his rounds as marshal of Hays City, Hickok had become accustomed to seeing Strawhorne in the saloons. Neither of them made any secret of the enmity he bore the other. Following the shooting in the Santa Fe, Strawhorne expressed his contempt for Bill with increased venom. A showdown appeared inevitable. But nothing came of it, at least not immediately. And then, several weeks later, and quite by chance, the two of them took the morning train to Ellsworth to spend the day. The nature of their business there has never been explained.

They returned to Hays that afternoon, again on the same train. With Hickok and Strawhorne sharing a small railroad coach for more than three hours, a violent eruption might have been expected. "There wasn't any trouble," a fellow passenger was later quoted as saying in the Hays City *Advance*. "Strawhorne had been drinking and was soon asleep. The conductor had to wake him up when the engineer blew for Hays."

That evening, shortly before midnight, Strawhorne, who appeared to have his wits about him, strolled into Tommy Drumm's place. Walking to the bar, he stood there, talking with Tommy. Over the heads of the crowd he saw Hickok push in through the batwing doors. Before the marshal's sweeping glance got around to him, he jerked his pistol out of the holster. He was much too slow. Before he could squeeze the trigger, Bill had blasted him into eternity.

There was a coroner's inquest the following morning. The official verdict was that Marshal Hickok had acted in self-defense. Unofficially it widened the breach between him and the lawless element, who wanted Hays City kept a wide-open town, and that included the troopers from the fort, who spent their money in Hays and felt that it gave them the right to do as they pleased.

Unquestionably Wild Bill's friendly relations with Lieutenant Colonel and Mrs. Custer had something to do with the resentment the troopers bore him. Captain Tom Custer also did not share his brother's regard for Wild Bill, and when he was on one of his frequent drinking bouts, he would dismiss Bill contemptuously as a "dime novel character of little consequence."

Although police court records reveal that Hickok, on numerous occasions, arrested soldiers for being drunk and disorderly, he appears to have acted with great restraint in his relations with Tom Custer, until that April afternoon when the captain, uproariously drunk, raced up and down Fort Street, hallooing the town with his guns. Bill arrested him and later escorted him to the fort. Custer swore to be revenged for the humiliation he had suffered.

It was only several evenings later that he marched into Tommy Drumm's place seeking redress. He had a number of troopers with him. There is no agreement as to how many. Some accounts say as many as five. I can account for only three. Were they there to kill Wild Bill, or just to rough him up and put the crawl on him? Only Tom Custer could have answered that question, and he never did. Certainly Bill believed they were there to gun him down. He was standing at the bar with his back to them as they closed in. Without turning, his right hand flashed to a holster and in what witnesses described as one motion, fired over his left shoulder, killing the man at his back. Whirling then, his second shot sent another member of Custer's party crumbling to the floor mortally wounded. Friends closed in on Bill and prevented further carnage.

It couldn't have taken much persuasion to convince Hickok that the incident would have serious repercussions. His loyal supporters concealed him for the night and smuggled him aboard the morning train for Ellsworth, where he hid out in the home of his old friend Harry Pestana. Later, when the storm had blown over, he surfaced at Topeka. Asked why he had fled Hays City, he is reputed to have replied, "I couldn't fight the whole Seventh Cavalry."

That Wild Bill arrived in Abilene from Fort Harker (Ellsworth) on the tenth or eleventh of April, 1871, seeking the job of town marshal, is undoubtedly true. I do not accept Joseph Rosa's account that Charles Gross, Mayor McCoy's favorite lackey, had Hickok in tow and that Bill had already been assured that the job was his. Mayor McCoy sheds some light on it. "I hesitated about turning the town over to Wild Bill," he wrote. "Did we want the same kind of gun rule he had enforced on Hays City? I called a special meeting of the Council [formerly the town board] to discuss the matter. Seeing that a majority favored appointing Wild Bill, I withdrew my objections. With T. C. Henry abstaining from voting, the motion carried and I was instructed to confer with Hickok, the City agreeing to pay him a salary of $150 a month, supplemented by 25% of the fines imposed in court. It was further agreed that the City would supply him with three deputies. At my invitation Hickok came to the office that afternoon. After a brief conversation he accepted the City's offer, his employment as town marshal to begin the following day, April 15th."

The salary Hickok was to receive was little more than half what Abilene had paid Tom Smith. Many of his critics profess to see in this evidence of the council's at-best lukewarm confidence in him. They also have it that it was only because he was temporarily strapped for money that Bill agreed to police Abilene for such niggardly wages. He may have needed money, but $150 a month, plus a percentage of the fines levied, could hardly be called "niggardly wages" at a time when skilled mechanics toiled for a dollar a day.

It did not take Abilene long to realize that its new marshal did not intend to police the town in the manner Tom Smith had employed. He had rented a cabin down the alley at the rear of the Alamo, took his meals at the Gulf House, and made his headquarters in the Alamo, from where, seated in a corner, his back to the wall, he could observe Texas Street through the triple front windows. Punctually, three times a day, he stepped out of the Alamo, and, keeping to the middle of the road, strode down the length of Texas Street and back. His other leg work he left to his deputies.[3]

Abilene had finished its refurbishing and was waiting for the first rail herd to arrive, when fire broke out in the Novelty Theatre. It was extinguished before it could do much damage. No one was injured, which very likely would not have been the case had the theatre been crowded, as it usually was. The town council asserted its authority by refusing to renew the theatre's license. Marshal Hickok solved the impasse by getting the management of the Novelty to hire a private policeman to guard the premises. He saw to it that Mike Williams, a friend of his Fort Riley days, got the job. It was a favor that was to result in tragedy for Williams.

It would be silly to regard seriously the charge of the rabid anti-Hickok faction that he was a hermaphrodite, half male, half female. He had too many women in his life to leave any doubt about his masculinity. One of them, Susanna Moore, over whom he had killed Dave Tutt, in Springfield, Missouri, in 1865, had hurried to Abilene and moved in with him upon learning where he was located.

It was the second time around for them, and they soon found that the old flame could not be reignited. Susanna went back to Springfield, and Bill focused his attention on beautiful Jessie Hazel, Madame Mattie Silk's star "boarder."

By early June, Abilene was beginning to roar. There was some shooting, some violence, but very few arrests. Wild Bill seldom exerted himself beyond stepping from one saloon to the next and taking his turn up Texas Street. But he had his fearsome reputation as master of the six-gun working overtime for him. "The run of ordinary cowboys and two-bit desperadoes walked wide of Bill. They had heard about his basilisk eyes that gleamed like two devils and held a man helpless while he drew and fired." [4] It almost justified McCoy's saying, "Talk about a rule of iron! We had it."

But there were other visitors from Austin, San Antonio, and the *brasada* of Texas, men made of sterner stuff, such as young Wes Hardin, with a score of "credits" on his guns, and his fighting cousins; Manning Clements and his brothers; and Simp, Bud, and Tom Dixon. And there was Ben Thompson, "the most dangerous killer in the Old West," as the redoubtable Bat Masterson called him. "The very name of Ben Thompson was enough to cause the general run of man-killers . . . to seek safety in flight." Proud of their prowess with the gun, such men were drawn to Abilene by Wild Bill's reputation as the Prince of Pistoleers as flies are drawn to molasses.

Ben had just finished serving a prison term for killing a Reconstruction official when he came up the trail to Abilene. He was almost broke, but a phenomenal run of cards netted him a huge stake, and when his friend, big, handsome, blond Phil Coe, the Austin gambler, arrived in town a few days later, well supplied with money, they pooled their funds and purchased a saloon, which they renovated, put in new fixtures, and renamed. This was the famous Bull's Head Saloon. It had a false front, which gave it the appearance of being two stories high. On it they had painted not only the name "Bull's Head" but a garish picture of an old mossy-horned bull, its masculinity prominently displayed.

The *Chronicle* was outraged that schoolchildren and decent women had to view such obscenity and demanded that the town council should have the offensive picture removed. The city fathers agreed and ordered Marshal Hickok to have it taken down or painted out.

When Wild Bill walked into the saloon and informed Thompson of the council's decision, Ben, notorious for his low boiling point, standing on what he called his "constitution rights," indignantly refused to do anything about the sign.

"Then I'll have it done," said the marshal.

Buying a can of paint, he ordered Deputy Marshal Tom Carson to put up a ladder and paint out the offensive section of the bull's anatomy. This tampering with "art" backfired on Wild Bill, for when the fresh paint dried out, the original depiction of the offensive part of the bull's anatomy began to show through and attracted more attention than ever.

Young John Wesley Hardin had arrived in Abilene and, as Wild Bill's detractors would have it, was "strutting about town and making Hickok talk small." In the trail crew in which Hardin had come north were the Clements boys and the Dixon brothers. If he felt any need of backing, he certainly had it, for it wasn't their style to walk wide of any man. There is nothing in the record, however, to indicate that in the months Wes spent in Abilene in the summer of 1871, he had to turn to them for support. Perhaps just their presence was enough to keep him out of trouble.

Back in Texas, five years later, Wes Hardin, "the man with forty notches on his gun," was convicted of killing a Gonzales County deputy sheriff and sentenced to twenty-five years in the state penitentiary at Huntsville. He had served fifteen years of his sentence when Governor Jim Hogg granted him a full pardon. Wes had studied law in the years he spent in prison (he was later admitted to the bar) and had produced a book: *The Life of John Wesley Hardin. As Written by Himself.*

It is a crude, unbelievable, self-laudatory book, filled with incidents of which no echo can be found elsewhere. He relates his first meeting with Wild Bill. When the marshal asked him to hand over his guns, he presented them to him, butts first, but keeping a forefinger on the trigger guards. Suddenly giving the pistols an upward flip, he had the marshal at his mercy. This was the well-known "road agent's spin." "I kept my pistols," says Hardin, "and I continued to wear them all the time I was in Abilene."

This is nonsense. Chances are that Wild Bill was better acquainted with that bit of triggernometry than Hardin.

Very likely Ben Thompson bore Hickok some animosity over the manner in which the incident of the painting of the bull had been handled. Hardin, always a plausible liar, says that Ben was so incensed that he tried to hire him to kill Wild Bill. "I told him," he says, "I'm not doing anybody's fighting just now except my own. . . . If Bill needs killing, why don't you kill him yourself?"

"I would rather get someone else to do it," was Ben's answer.

This is preposterous. There is nothing in Ben Thompson's record to suggest that he ever asked any man to do his fighting. Of course, Ben had been in his grave for seven years when Hardin's book appeared, leaving its author free to write what he pleased without fear of rebuttal.

Hickok is often accused by his detractors of having had Texas warrants on Hardin in his possession, which he made no effort to serve. They take their cue from Hardin himself, who wrote: "Bill had requisitions on me. He told me he wasn't inclined to do anything about them; that his job was to police the town."

This is transparent nonsense. Had a Texas court asked for the arrest and detention of a wanted man, pending extradition, the request would have been made to the governor of Kansas, not to any county or town official. There is nothing in the minute book of Governor Harvey's office to indicate that such a request was ever received.

Colonel Dan Wheeler's trail herd, with which Hardin had come up from Texas, was being held on the North Cottonwood, some forty miles south of Abilene, waiting for a rise in the market. On July 5, 1871, word reached town that popular Billy Chorn (or Coran), Colonel Wheeler's trail boss, had been killed by a disgruntled Mexican cowboy named Bideno. Chorn was Hardin's friend, and he was urged to go after Bideno. "I said I would if I was made a deputy sheriff for a few days and given a warrant," he said. "I wanted to be in the clear if I was not able to bring Bideno in alive."

His request was granted, and accompanied by Jim Rodgers, he headed south. In a cow camp on the Newton Prairies he and Rodgers were joined by Chorn's brother and Hugh Anderson. They were two hundred miles south of Abilene when they caught up with the Mexican in a restaurant in Bluff City, a settlement of fifty people on Bluff Creek. Bideno attempted to draw his pistol, which was all the excuse Hardin needed for killing him.

On returning to Abilene, Wes found himself something of a hero. Cattlemen took up a purse for him, amounting to six hundred dollars, he says. He disappeared from Abilene several weeks later and was not seen there again. The following year he was in the new camp of Wichita—why, has never been explained, for Wichita had not yet shown signs of becoming the booming cow town that dominated the Texas cattle trade several years later.

The story of how Agnes Thatcher Lake, the buxom young widow of old man Lake, the showman, brought her circus to Abilene in 1871 and fell madly in love with Wild Bill has been told a hundred times. He helped her pitch her tent in the vicinity of the Drovers' Cottage and otherwise danced attendance on her. Although he certainly was interested, she failed in her efforts to get him to turn in his badge and travel with her as the star of her circus. He had had a brief theatrical experience in one of his friend Bill Cody's Wild West spectaculars and wanted no more of it. He married Agnes Lake five years later, in Cheyenne.

Any attempt to arrive at an honest evaluation of James Butler Hickok, a century after he set out on his last trail to Deadwood and the Black Hills, confronts the writer with the inescapable fact that there were two Wild Bills; one the mythical, superefficient master of the six-gun and defender of law and order; the other the consort of criminals and the lawless, of whom Stuart Henry, the ex-mayor's brother, wrote: "He lived outside the civil life. Abilene civilians regarded him as a desperado. How could Hickok establish a respectable peace while encouraging the very difficulties he should surmount?" [5]

For how the young Texans, trooping back and forth from one

31

saloon to the next, trying to buy some fun for the money they were tossing away, regarded Wild Bill, no one ever expressed it more vividly than Brown Paschal, who in his old age was still chasing Longhorns out of the mesquite thickets along the Rio Grande.

"He came out of Ben Thompson's Bull's Head Saloon," the old puncher recalled. "He wore a low-crowned, wide black hat and a frock coat. His hair was yellow and it hung down to his shoulders. When I came along the street he was standing there with his back to the wall and his thumbs hooked in his red sash. He stood there and rolled his head from side to side looking at everything and everybody from under his eyebrows—just like a mad old bull. I decided then and there that I didn't want any part of him."

" 'A mad old bull . . .' " Eugene Cunningham, the well-known Western historian, wrote some time later. "The phrasing seems to me particularly happy. For by the time he came to the hellroaring Kansas trail town, to police the wild cowboys, the crooked gamblers and prostitutes who preyed upon them he was very much like a bull—the biggest and proudest of the herd."

I have mentioned Jessie Hazel. Bill believed that beyond her professional chores he had established his rights to her. He learned his mistake one afternoon when his friend Mike Williams came running to tell him that Jessie and Phil Coe were drinking together in the private wine room of the Gulf House. Bill burst in on the surprised couple a few minutes later. Coe never went armed, but there was a brief scuffle, with Coe getting the better of it. By evening, news of the encounter was all over town, and, much to Bill's embarrassment, that he had been worsted. Knowing the two men, it was freely predicted that a head-on collision would follow. The big blond gambler from Texas added fuel to the fire by taking the fair Jessie out of Mattie Silk's house and establishing her in his cabin as his mistress.

Ben Thompson made light of it. The Bull's Head had proved to be a gold mine. Better off financially than he had ever been, he left it to Coe and Tom Sharon, their silent partner, to close the saloon for the winter and took off for Kansas City to join his wife and from there go on to Joplin and make the long drive home to Austin.

Somewhere going down the Texas Road, the spirited team Ben had purchased ran away, upsetting the rig. Both Ben and his wife were seriously injured. Weeks passed before Ben learned that Phil Coe, his friend and partner, had been killed.

The circumstances leading up to the death of Coe are well known. It is over the last few moments preceding the shooting that the Hickok faction and the Texans disagree so violently, with Wild Bill's adherents calling it an accidental killing and the Texans branding it murder.

With the end of the 1871 season at hand, Abilene was so quiet that the city council dismissed Wild Bill's deputies. The annual exodus of the undesirables was under way. Many of the saloons were already boarded up. Phil Coe had shipped his Jessie off to St. Louis for the winter and arranged to travel home to Austin with a large party of Texans. On Saturday evening, October 5, their plans for leaving Abilene the following morning completed, they trooped up and down Texas Street, crowding into the saloons that were still open and indulging in some noisy, though innocent, high jinks. Coe was with them, and, as was not his habit, he was armed.

Wild Bill watched them through the plate-glass windows of the Alamo and did not attempt to interfere with their fun. They "captured" Jake Karatofsky and marched him into the Applejack and made him buy drinks for the crowd. It was so much fun that they came looking for the marshal to make him stand treat. They found Hickok in a restaurant around the corner, eating his supper. He told them to go to the bar in the Novelty Theatre and have some drinks at his expense.

Hickok partisans point to this as proof that Bill wanted no trouble with Coe and his friends.

It got to be nine o'clock. By then the revelers were well liquored. They were passing the Alamo again when a shot rang out.

33

Bill stepped through the open doors and demanded an explanation. Standing at the edge of the sidewalk, his gun still in his hand, Coe said, "I just fired at a stray dog." He laughed. So did his friends. No one had seen a dog.

Hickok understood. He recognized the challenge and surely realized that the odds were twenty-to-one against him. He was turning away, his decision made, when he whipped around, a gun in either hand, and fired. Clutching his stomach with one hand, Coe, mortally wounded, brought up his pistol and squeezed the trigger, the slug splintering the door jamb a few inches from Wild Bill's head. Hearing someone running up in back of him, Bill fired again and the man dropped. It was his friend Mike Williams, who had come to his aid.

Phil Coe died on the following Monday. His friend Bud Cotton took the body back to Austin. Williams was buried in the Abilene cemetery. They were the only men Wild Bill killed in Abilene.

The City Council passed a resolution on December 12 discharging "William Butler Hickok as marshal for the reason that the city is no longer in need of his services." It was effective as of the following day. There was no word of commendation or thanks expressed for services rendered. He had served eight months less two days.

If Hickok was less than the largely self-created legendary figure, he has become, as Eugene Cunningham put it, "as gigantic and omnipotent as one of the mythical creatures of Norse sagas, credited with Homeric battles and incredible slaughters," his niche in Western folklore secure.

IV

Ben Thompson—He
Walked Wide of No Man

FOLLOWING the accident he and his wife had suffered as they were making the long drive home from the railhead in Missouri, Ben Thompson spent the winter recuperating in Austin. By spring his funds were exhausted. The Bull's Head in Abilene had been sold, but it had netted him very little. Gambling was his business. From friends he raised enough cash to give him a stake and set out for Kansas, where the money was, leaving his wife in Austin.

If we take Ben's word for it, he was born in Yorkshire, England, in 1843. His brother Billy was several years his junior. Of all the crosses Ben had to bear, Billy was the heaviest. He was always in trouble and depended on Ben to bail him out of one scrape after another.[1]

Numerous photographs of Ben have survived the passing years. They show him as he was, but they do not bring him to life, as does Gene Cunningham's capsule description. "That square-jawed, thickset Wizard of the Pistol," wrote Cunningham, "that black-haired, blue-eyed Typical Gunman of the great inky mustache—Ben Thompson, who was variously printer, Confederate soldier, professional gambler, peace officer, and a gunman second to none that Texas ever produced." [2]

The cattle market had shifted from Abilene to Ellsworth when Ben came north for the second time in the spring of 1873. He was thirty years old. The town was overflowing with Texans, hundreds of young trail hands who were bringing thousands of Longhorns up the new Chisholm-Cox Trail, and noted gamblers such as Cad Pierce, George Peshaur, and Neil Cain. The Drovers' Cottage had been moved across the prairies and, like the Grand Central Hotel, was thronged with famous Texas cattlemen, such as Shanghai Pierce, Colonel John Myers, Print Olive, and Seth Mabry.

Unlike Abilene, Ellsworth was a going town with a population of over twelve hundred. It had the trade of nearby Fort Harker, the Army supply post for the Southwest, to aid its economy. Although it welcomed the Texas cattle trade, it had enacted ordinances to prevent being overrun by it. Saloons and gambling parlors had been put under heavy license fees, and a tax had been levied on prostitution that, by midsummer, was bringing in money enough to pay the town's municipal expenses. Furthermore, an ordinance had been enacted restricting public prostitution to the river bottom (promptly nicknamed Nauchville), half a mile from uptown Ellsworth. To maintain the peace, there was a city marshal, a police force of three men, the sheriff of Ellsworth County, and a deputy sheriff.

Anticipating the coming need for a centrally located city police court, the town board leased space on the second floor of the Arthur Larkin Dry Goods Company Building. As early as mid-June, the Ellsworth *Reporter* had occasion to refer to it as "one of the busiest spots in town." With the shipping season only a few weeks old, it was already apparent that the measures taken to maintain law and order were inadequate. This was largely because the police —the so-called four Jacks—Brocky Jack Norton, Long Jack De-Long, Jack Morco, and Jack Branham—were corrupt. They shared in the fines Judge Osborne levied. They made wholesale arrests and conspired among themselves to present evidence to convict.

All of Ellsworth's twelve saloons were provided with gunracks on which a visitor could hang his weapon, get a ticket for it, and reclaim the gun when he was ready to leave town. But the Texans asserted that they couldn't get down from the saddle before they were "jumped by one of these pimp marshals" and yanked off to the judge.

Along South Main Street—the Kansas Pacific Railroad cut Ellsworth in two, giving it two Main Streets, North Main and South Main, with an open space of approximately one hundred yards between them—popular sentiment was strongly Texan. It came from the gamblers and the saloon crowd, mostly Texans themselves, from storekeepers, and from a considerable number of ordinary citizens who felt the trail drivers were the cause of their current prosperity. As the summer wore on and tension increased, there were rumors that the cowboys, several hundred strong, were planning to charge into Ellsworth, take over the town and string up Brocky Jack and his detested associates. Nothing came of it, and the wonder is that it didn't. Lacking a leader, the pro-Texan crowd found one in Ben Thompson, of all men. Choosing him could be compared to attempting to put out a fire by pouring kerosene on it.

Ben, prosperous again, was living with his brother Billy at the Grand Central Hotel, but he had made Joe Brennan's saloon on South Main Street his headquarters. He was in Brennan's place on the afternoon of August 15, 1873, watching Neil Cain dealing monte and Cad Pierce betting against him. Pierce was winning. Other games were being played, but Ben continued to watch the monte game, with the bets becoming higher. Cain asked him to find someone to take his overbets. At the bar, Ben spoke to John Sterling, a Texas gambler disliked by most men. "Sure, I'll take Cad on for what Neil doesn't want. And, Ben, if I win, consider yourself in for half." When Sterling had won over a thousand dollars, he stuffed the money into his pocket and walked out.

"Ben, that tinhorn made you a deal. You going to let him walk out on you?" Brennan asked.

Ben shook his head. "I'll see him later this afternoon."

It was the beginning of an afternoon that Ellsworth was to remember.

Ben went looking for Sterling and found him in Nick Lentz's saloon. He was standing at the bar with Happy Jack Morco, drunk and noisy, and became violently abusive when a settlement was demanded. Reaching out, he slapped Thompson's face. Had Ben been armed, the incident would undoubtedly have ended in a blaze of gunfire. Shocked by what he had done, Sterling stepped back. Morco got him out of the saloon and escorted him up the street to Jake New's saloon on the corner.

After Ben had cooled down, he returned to Brennan's and was telling his story to Cad Pierce and other friends when Morco and Sterling appeared at the front door. "If you Texas sons-a-bitches want to fight, get your guns and come out!" Morco challenged defiantly. He and Sterling then returned to New's corner. Sterling was armed with a shotgun and policeman Morco with his pistols.

Billy Thompson was standing at the bar. Ben called to him and they ran up behind the buildings to New's saloon, where they had checked their guns. Hurrying through the barroom, they came out on the South Main Street sidewalk, Ben armed with a rifle and Billy with a shotgun. Neither Morco nor Sterling were in sight. Ben and Billy then cut diagonally across the open ground to the combination freight-and-passenger depot. There they elected to make their stand.

Where Deputy Sheriff Hogue and policemen Branham and De-Long were while this was happening has escaped the record. But word that a shoot-out was about to occur had spread, and a small crowd was gathered on South Main Street. Marshal Norton had reached the scene and was in Lentz's saloon with Morco and Sterling. When he saw Sheriff Cap Whitney come running around the corner of Seitz's drugstore, he hurried out to meet him.

Allegedly he told the sheriff that he was going over to the

freight platform and arrest the Thompsons, to which Whitney said, "No, they'll shoot you. I'll go; they won't harm me."

The Thompsons recognized Cap as he crossed the street, and put down their guns. Whitney and Ben spoke for a few minutes.

"I haven't any more use for Jack Morco than you have," said Cap. "If we can let this trouble blow over without any shooting, I promise you I'll get him off your back, Ben."

"Okay, Cap. We ain't looking for trouble and we ain't walking away from it. I know we can trust you. Suppose the three of us go over to Brennan's place, have a drink, and forget this business."

Billy was the first to step into the saloon. Cap was just behind him; Ben brought up the rear. He was stepping through the open doors when Bill Langford, a young Texan, cried. "Ben, here comes Morco!"

Ben whipped around and saw Morco, still a hundred yards away, running toward him, pistols drawn, pushing men out of his way. There was a narrow space between Brennan's saloon and Jerome Beebe's general store next door. Ben darted into it, and peering around the corner of Beebe's store, leveled his rifle on Morco. Although recognized as a dead shot with a Winchester, he fired and missed. Beebe's door was open. Morco leaped into the store. Concealing his gun in the open bag of dried beans that stood on the floor, he ran through the store out the back door.[3]

There were many witnesses to what followed, and mostly they agree that Sheriff Whitney hurried out of Brennan's saloon, closely followed by Billy Thompson; that the latter stumbled in his drunken uncertainty; that his shotgun was discharged and Cap fell, mortally wounded.

As Whitney was picked up and carried home, Ben and several of his friends got Billy into Brennan's. They agreed that the only way he could save his neck was to get out of Kansas as quickly as possible. "He'll need money," said Ben. He stripped some bills off his roll, and the others did likewise. Neil Cain brought Billy's horse to the front of the saloon. Cain and George Peshaur helped him into the saddle and he raced out of town.

Mayor Jim Miller reached the scene of the shooting a few moments later. He became so enraged when he learned that his friend Whitney had been killed (actually it was not until five o'clock the following Monday afternoon that Cap was pronounced dead) that he fired the entire police force. Deputy Sheriff Hogue was a county official, and Miller could not fire him. For the next few hours Hogue was the only man in Ellsworth empowered to make an arrest.

The mayor swore in a posse to capture Billy Thompson. It returned to town that evening without having caught sight of him. The general opinion was that they hadn't looked too hard. Ben was relieved. He had been fined twenty-five dollars for violating the gun ordinance. To his dismay, the shake-up of the police force resulted in Jack Morco's being rehired. "He [Ben] knew it was time for him to get out of Ellsworth," said Major Bill Walton, Ben's lawyer-biographer. "If he didn't, Happy Jack Morco would invent an excuse for killing him."

By train and steamboat, Ben got back to Texas. Home in Austin once more, he learned that his brother Billy was living on the old Cain ranch with Neil's father. For the first time Billy learned that he had been indicted for murder and was a fugitive from justice with a reward of one thousand dollars on his head. The news did not disturb him. With several other young men he was mavericking cattle and disposing of the unbranded steers to trail outfits that were shaping up a herd for the long journey north. Ben returned to gambling to support himself.

The panic that swept the United States in 1873 finished Ellsworth as a cattle market. Wichita got the trade and kept it for the next four years. Unable to resist the urge to be where the action was, Ben Thompson came up the Chisholm Trail and established himself at the Douglas Avenue Hotel, the town's finest, his fashionable broadcloth reflecting his current prosperity. He played for big stakes and won oftener than he lost. Men who knew him well expected him to break out momentarily and stand Wichita on its ear. But that didn't happen.

He was back in Austin for the winter when Captain J. C. Sparks of the Texas Rangers, Company C, Frontier Battalion, in rummaging through his desk came across the old reward notice published on Billy Thompson by the state of Kansas. Sparks wired the sheriff of Ellsworth County, inquiring if the old notice was still alive. Back came the answer that it was. Ben knew nothing about it until extradition proceedings began. Again Major Walton, his friend and lawyer, did his best to prevent Billy's being taken back to Kansas to face trial, but to no avail. On August 15, his hands shackled, and in the custody of two Travis County deputy sheriffs, the prisoner began the long journey north. Ben and Major Walton accompanied him.

The size of the crowd that met the train at Ellsworth seemed to unnerve recently elected Sheriff Hamilton. Fearing that the prisoner would be removed from the jail either by his friends or his enemies, Hamilton asked for and got permission to lodge Billy in the state penitentiary at Leavenworth.[4]

Witnesses had scattered, and the trial had to be postponed until September 5. It lasted nine days, largely due to the long-windedness of the prosecutor and the local counsel Ben had engaged to aid Major Walton. When the jury finally got the case, it deliberated for only an hour and returned a unanimous verdict of not guilty.

There is very little hard evidence to confirm Bat Masterson's story that following Billy's acquittal the Thompsons settled in Dodge City. According to Bat, Billy Thompson soon got into trouble again and to repay an old favor he (Bat) owed Ben, he went up the trail to Ogallah, Kansas, and smuggled Billy out of the hotel, where a mob had him treed. I believe this is more or less fiction, comparable to Bat's account of how Ben and a number of Texans, employed to guard the Santa Fe roundhouse at Pueblo,

Colorado, in the brief war with the Denver and Rio Grande Rail-road, for control of the right-of-way up the Royal Gorge, had sold out to the enemy.

Bat, however, was there, heading the small contingent of Dodge City gunslicks he had recruited. Ignoring the fact that he was on the Santa Fe payroll while collecting also his salary as sheriff of Ford County, Kansas, does not appear to have disturbed him.

Ben Thompson was never a wealthy man. But if he was often broke, it was never for long. He was meticulous about repaying a loan, which was one reason why he always had friends when he didn't have much of anything else. Although aware of his hair-trigger temperament and his tendency to end his arguments in gun-fire, many men of good standing admired him. He was fearless and when sober was a good companion; drunk, he was impossible and they avoided him.

"How," asks Cunningham, "could a town the size of Austin, the capital of Texas, consider Ben Thompson for city marshal?" It did, and Ben was narrowly defeated.

He blamed the activity of Mark Wilson, owner of the Senate Saloon and Variety Theatre and an old enemy, for his failure to win. On Christmas Eve he walked into the Senate to break up the performance and square accounts with Wilson. The latter rushed out, armed with a shotgun, and fired blindly. Thompson whipped up a pistol and put three slugs into the man. As Wilson went down, the bartender dropped behind the bar. Ben fired through the thin panel that separated them, the bullet striking the man and inflicting a wound from which he died several weeks later.

In the case of Mark Wilson, it was premeditated murder. But Buck Walton won a verdict of self-defense, and Ben was acquitted. In 1883, he ran a second time and was elected. He began to bear down at once. He got the prostitutes off the streets and ran Billy Sims and his Keno Bank out of town. Austin had a two o'clock closing ordinance. Ben set about enforcing it. George Givens re-fused to toe the line and foolishly drew a gun on the marshal. It was his last mistake. The *Statesman* said: "Marshal Thompson is enforcing the ordinances. That is what he was elected to do."

For relaxation one day Ben took a train to San Antonio. Imbibing freely as he wandered about town, he learned that Jack Harris, the one-armed proprietor of the Vaudeville Variety Theatre, who operated a saloon and gambling parlor in addition to providing the town's theatrical entertainment, was "looking" for him. Former friends, they had fallen out over a disputed gambling debt. Ben marched down to the plaza and walked into the Variety. By chance, Harris walked in a few steps behind him, carrying a shotgun, his favorite weapon. Through the venetian blinds Ben saw him starting up the stairs to his office. "What are you going to do with that gun?" Ben demanded.

Harris swung around, the shotgun raised. Ben let him have it—three slugs that killed him.

For this killing Ben was indicted and subsequently acquitted, the jury finding that both men had made threats against each other; that both were armed. The case was dismissed. No other honest verdict was possible. Following the dismissal, Ben was induced to resign his post of city marshal.

Billy Sims and Joe Foster, partners of Jack Harris in the Variety Theatre, continued to operate the resort. Sims had never forgiven Ben Thompson for running him out of Austin. Foster, whose honesty as a dealer Ben had once questioned, now had additional reason for hating him.

Ben was drinking heavier than usual and making himself obnoxious. Some sources say threats made against him in San Antonio were worrying him. There is no reason to believe it. A more likely explanation is that his brother Billy was in trouble again, this time in Refugio County, where he was being tried on a murder indictment. As usual, Ben had to dip into his pocket to save him.

On a cold, blustery day in early March, 1884—the eleventh, to be exact—Ben encountered an old and notorious acquaintance, sometimes his friend and sometimes his enemy, who cast a shadow

43

as long as his own: King Fisher, border outlaw, bandit, rustler, and now wearing the badge of a Uvalde County deputy sheriff. They spent the morning cutting up some old touches as they grew mellow with whiskey. Whether at King Fisher's suggestion or Thompson's, they caught the late afternoon train for San Antonio. They had supper in a Mexican restaurant on the plaza. About eight-thirty they walked across to the Variety Theatre where, many months past, Ben had killed Jack Harris.

They walked up to the bar, where city policeman Coy, a giant Mexican, was standing. Ignoring him, they were waiting to be served when Ben saw Billy Sims crossing the room and called him over. They were having a drink together when Joe Foster passed them. Ben invited Foster to join them. Foster refused. Coy testified at the inquest that Thompson slapped Foster in the face with his left hand and drew his pistol with his right; that he (Coy) grabbed the gun and tried to prevent Ben from firing it, only to have him wrench it free.

Suddenly hell broke loose. There was a vicious outburst of shooting. When the smoke cleared away, Ben Thompson and King Fisher lay huddled together on the floor, both dead. Coy acknowledged that he, Sims, and Foster were armed. No more.

That is one version of what happened; it is not the story told by the Thompson supporters. They insisted that it was an ambush slaying; that Sims and Foster had half a dozen men armed with rifles posted in the balcony; that Ben was dead before he could fire a shot.

There is no escaping the fact that an autopsy performed on Ben Thompson in Austin revealed that he had been struck eight times, five bullets striking him in the head and ranging downward, their trajectory proving that they had been fired from above. This contradicts the report of the coroner's jury stating that only three bullets had struck Thompson.

It cannot be denied, however, that when Ben and King Fisher walked into the Variety Theatre, they were looking for trouble.

When you went looking for trouble in the Texas of those days, you were very likely to find it.

Ben Thompson was buried in Austin on March 13, 1884. "The funeral attracted a vast concourse of people to witness the burial of our late City Marshal, who died a victim of assassination," reported the *Daily Standard*. "His faults were many, as he was first to acknowledge. He will be remembered as a true Texan."

The *Statesman*'s account struck a similar note, referring to the killing of Ben Thompson and King Fisher as a prearranged ambush slaying.

During the fray Joe Foster had been struck by a slug that passed through his right leg. It was not considered a serious matter, but the wound became infected, and six weeks later he was dead of blood poisoning.

V

Mike Meagher,
Marshal of Wichita

A RECENTLY published book, largely devoted to unraveling the local politics of what we have become accustomed to referring to as the "Kansas cow towns," informs us that, more properly speaking, they were "cattle towns." This is only professorial nit-picking; the old-time cowboy is in no danger of becoming a cattleboy.

In the beginning the Kansas Pacific Railroad had done nothing to further the Texas cattle trade. It was only when it realized what a rich plum it had almost let slip through its fingers that it bestirred itself and built a commodious stockyard, with ten loading chutes, at Ellsworth, to which the market had shifted after being forced to leave Abilene. Furthermore, it had established a shortcut trail from the Salt Fork of the Arkansas, running north through Kingman and Ellinwood direct to Ellsworth, a saving of two days' driving.

Far to the south, however, the Atchison, Topeka and Santa Fe was feverishly pushing its rails across Kansas in a frantic hurry to reach the New Mexican line in time to claim title to the generous land grants offered by the federal government. Located so favorably for capturing the Texas cattle trade that, even as its construction crews began laying track across the Newton Prairies, in July, 1871, it was predicted that the Santa Fe would soon declare its intentions. It came quickly. A sign post was put up, naming the spot Newton—"Bloody Newton," Kansas newspapers were soon calling it. There was no town there, not a building, not even a saloon. Three months later Newton had a population of over five hundred. Stockyards were under construction, Joe McCoy having been brought down from Abilene to build them.

Although it was the end of the season before facilities were completed, Santa Fe agents succeeded in diverting several herds bound for Ellsworth to the new market. While no more than three thousand head were shipped from Newton that year, it was accepted not only as an augury of prosperity to come but of the demise of Ellsworth as the capital of the Texas cattle trade as well.

Before Newton became an organized town of the third class, with a city government, the only semblance of law there was supplied by a policeman hired in self-defense by the saloonkeepers and a Sedgwick County deputy sheriff. In the one year of its importance as a "cow town," more killings occurred within the town limits than were recorded in Abilene, Ellsworth, and Dodge City combined. In the volume in the American Guide Series devoted to Kansas, it is stated that "fifty persons are estimated to have met sudden death in its saloons and dance-halls." Twenty-five would be nearer the truth. Judge R. W. Muse, in his *History of Harvey County*, put the number at twelve. One August night, five men were killed in Perry Tuttle's dance hall in "Hide Park," Newton's notorious red-light district, and several others were seriously wounded. The town was ready to explode. Tom Carson, Wild Bill's deputy at Abilene, was hastily sworn in as deputy marshal. "It looked as though things had got completely out of hand," he said later. "There were several hundred Texans in town and they were blowing off steam. Half a dozen responsible citizens armed themselves and walked the streets with me until daylight."

In 1872, at the height of its prosperity, the end of Newton's days as a cattle market became a certainty when it assumed a $70,000 share of the bond issue voted for the construction of the twenty-four-mile Wichita and Southwestern Railroad, running from Newton to Wichita, in return for which Sedgwick County was divided, the northern half being organized as Harvey County, with Newton the county seat.

It was a victory for shrewd, dynamic Bill Greiffenstein and Jim Meade, the founders of Wichita, who had made it known that they intended to make the new town on the Arkansas River the wheat and cattle capital of Kansas. As former Indian traders associated with the late Jesse Chisholm, they had demonstrated their acumen and become modestly wealthy men.

Most prairie towns began as a collection of shacks, located by chance, and they grew without planning. That was not the case with Wichita. When it was incorporated as a city of the second class in 1872, a municipal code was enacted that guaranteed the town's permanence, the law even specifying the type of building that could be erected on Douglas Avenue, its principal thoroughfare.

Greiffenstein and Meade were named as the incorporators of the Wichita and Southwestern Railroad. That they were acting in collusion with the Santa Fe—that they were, in fact, its agents—cannot be doubted. Practically all cattle coming up the Chisholm Trail had to pass Wichita on the way to market. Establishing shipping facilities there would enable the railroad to capture the Texas cattle trade in its entirety.

With its numerous creeks and sheltered valleys, the surrounding range was better suited for holding cattle than the open prairies. The sixty miles south to the border of Indian Territory had good grass and few settlements.

The infant Wichita and Southwestern was the key to the situation. In its corporate greed the Santa Fe was prepared to sacrifice Newton for the much richer plum to be harvested at Wichita.

On May 16, 1872, the rails of the little road reached their objective. The next day the first herd was driven across town to the sprawling, still unfinished stockyards in the southeastern section of town. That evening the first stock train chuffed out of Wichita in a swirl of smoke and disappeared to the north.[1]

Although the shallow Arkansas was usually a tractable stream as it flowed past Wichita, at times, crossing it was dangerous. Realizing that it presented both a problem and an opportunity for profit, the promoters of the town built a wooden toll bridge extending from the foot of Douglas Avenue across the river to the western bank, where the tough, lawless district called Delano had come into existence.

Trail drivers coming up to the west of the river were so incensed at having to pay toll to get their cattle to market that they threatened to bypass Wichita. So many aroused citizens joined in the protest that the city commission purchased the bridge and made it toll-free. It gave further proof of how important the cattle trade was to Wichita by designating Douglas Avenue as the route by which a herd coming off the bridge must be driven to the stockyards.

It meant that daily twenty-five hundred bellowing Longhorns would be passing the town's principal hotels, business establishments, and saloons, knocking down posts that supported the wooden awnings, raising clouds of dust, and littering the avenue with their dung. But no one complained.

By design Wichita was a wide-open town, its chief concern being to keep it prosperous and growing. At its four main entrances, signboards informed the stranger that:

> Everything Goes in Wichita.
> Leave your revolvers at police
> headquarters, and get a check.
> Carrying concealed weapons
> strictly forbidden.

Booming, bustling Wichita grew like Topsy, attracting men of every stripe. During the four years of its supremacy as a cattle market there was scarcely a gunman or outlaw of note who didn't surface there. Besides Shanghai Pierce and the noted trail drivers who exchanged their cattle for Yankee dollars at Wichita, there were other Texans, such as Wes Hardin, the Clements boys, and Ben Thompson. The Earp brothers, as yet unknowns, were also there.

There was violence, an occasional killing. On the lighter side, there were the bawdy revue to be enjoyed at Saunders' Variety Theatre and the music of the band that Whitey Rupp, the gambler, had imported from Kansas City and installed on the second-floor balcony of his Keno House, on the northwest corner of Douglas Avenue and Main Street, where it played throughout the afternoon and evening—"just to liven things up a bit," said Whitey.

Trail crews, after finishing the day's work at the shipping pens, invariably recrossed the river to their camps on the Cowskin and the other creeks, and with the coming of nightfall headed for the dance halls and girls at nearby Delano, which was outside the town limits. Undoubtedly this lessened the chances of an explosion in Wichita. Another, and greater, factor in maintaining the peace— such as it was—was little brown-haired Mike Meagher (pronounced May-gar), the city marshal. A native of County Cavan, Ireland, he never took a backward step for any man. Appointed Wichita's first marshal in 1871 and elected in 1872 and again in 1873 and 1875, he was the man who "tamed Wichita," not Wyatt Earp, as the movies and television shows would have it.

I don't know why writers have had so little to say about Mike Meagher. Nowhere did any other man serve a town that length of time as marshal. Only once did he serve by appointment; on three other occasions he was elected to office by popular vote, even though the city commission, which ran the police department, invariably supported the opposing candidate—the commission being more concerned about the town's continued prosperity than about bearing down on violators of the law.

When Mike Meagher was named town marshal in 1871, his twin

brother John was made deputy marshal. In 1873 John was elected sheriff of Sedgwick County. That the brothers exchanged information and sometimes rode together was a well-known fact. Sedgwick County was overrun by gangs of horse thieves. When the sheriff learned that the Talbot Gang was in the habit of riding into Delano in the evening and whooping it up in Rowdy Joe Lowe's dive, he went after them, accompanied by his brother and a deputy. The raid resulted in a running fight in which Mike killed Bill Talbot, the half-brother of Jim Sherman, the well-known Texas desperado, the other members of the gang making their escape.

Five years later the slaying of Bill Talbot was to have fatal repercussions.[2]

In the violent, gunsmoke years that he served as city marshal of Wichita, Mike Meagher made hundreds of arrests but killed only two men (including Bill Talbot) which is the best evidence of the nerveless restraint he exercised in taking armed violators of the law into custody. They were not fooled by his mild manner, for they knew that behind it was an iron will that would not let the marshal back down.

By a narrow margin, in 1874, Mike was defeated for reelection by Bill Smith, the handpicked candidate of the city commission. It was quickly apparent that Smith was not another Mike Meagher. The lawless element welcomed the change. Hurricane Bill Martin and his gang of undesirables defied him to his face.

The political junta that had elected Smith had also returned Jim Hope, a wholesale liquor dealer, to office as mayor. His principal concern was to keep Wichita booming. The atmosphere was not what it had been in the past; no longer was there strict enforcement of the city ordinances. Fewer arrests were being made. Fewer arrests meant fewer convictions and fewer fines. By mid-June, with the season a third gone, funds from that source had shrunk to less than $600.

It was too much for Mayor Hope. He demanded the resignation of Marshal Smith forthwith. Although the commission tabled his motion to remove Smith, he succeeded in getting it to raise license fees on saloons, gambling houses, and bordellos, and to add four men to the police force. On June 17, Officers Sam Burris, Sam Botts, John Behrens and Wyatt Earp were sworn in. It marked the beginning of the latter's ridiculously glamorized career as a lawman.

Wyatt had been living in Wichita for some time without any regular means of support. His elder brother Jim was tending bar in Pryor's saloon, next door to the Keno House. Bessie Earp, Jim's wife, was conducting a sporting house at 30 Water Street. In an obvious attempt to build up Earps stature, Stuart N. Lake, Earp's most important biographer, refers to him as deputy marshal. The truth is that he was not then nor at any other time deputy marshal of Wichita. Lake also exaggerates in saying that Earp was being paid a salary of $125 per month. The official record reveals that his salary was $60. Instead of patrolling the streets, Policeman Earp and Officer John Behrens were given the routine duty of collecting the license fees of the saloons, gambling joints, and bordellos.

One evening in mid-August a trail crew, finished at the shipping pens for the day, stopped at a Main Street saloon for drinks on the way back to camp on the Cowskin. The men had tethered their broncs and were crossing the sidewalk when Earp came along. "They were blocking the sidewalk," he says. "To get through, I had to push one of them out of the way." Maybe he did; he was armed and they weren't. That evening a score of Texans, led by Manning Clements, came across the bridge looking for Earp. He was warned in time and hid out in his sister-in-law's establishment until they were gone.[3]

The outfit with which the Clements boys had come north pulled out for home the following morning, which must have relieved Officer Earp. The town had gotten so completely out of hand that outbreaks of violence had become a common occurrence. Fearful of what might happen, a group of responsible citizens organized themselves into a vigilante group and elected lawyer Sim Tucker captain. A large iron triangle was suspended in front of the police station. When it was struck, sounding an alarm, they would gather as quickly as possible, armed for action.

Marshal Smith screamed that they were "a lawless band, without a shred of legal authority; banded together to denounce and destroy me and my department." That was more or less true. What he didn't say was that he had failed in his sworn duty to the city.

The pealing of the triangle could be heard all over town. A warning had been struck three or four times, bringing the group together on the double. They had proceeded to the scene of the disturbance but had not taken any action.

It was nearing suppertime on an August evening when the alarm sounded again. Tucker was in his office, a hundred yards from the police station, talking with District Court Judge Campbell. He kept a loaded shotgun and rifle in his office to be prepared for such emergencies. Seizing the shotgun, he burst out of the office, with the judge following, armed with the rifle. Marshal Smith had already reached the police station, along with Officers Botts, Burris, and Earp. He requested Tucker to order the group to disperse, insisting that this was a matter the police could handle.

The trouble had begun when Botts attempted to disarm a supposed drunk as he emerged from Pryor's saloon. The man refused to hand over his gun. The next moment Hurricane Bill Martin and ten or a dozen members of his gang stepped out of Pryor's, pistols drawn. The odds against him were too much for Botts, and he hurried back to headquarters to report the incident, which Hurricane Bill very likely expected him to do, for the confrontation had undoubtedly been arranged to embarrass the marshal. Judge Campbell told what happened:

"When we got to Horsethief Corner, with Smith and his policemen tagging along behind, Martin and his gang had moved up the street and were standing at a vacant lot. We came up Douglas Avenue and stopped across from them. Smith was still pleading with Tucker to disband. Tucker said no. 'This is the fourth time we have been called out and you haven't made a single arrest. You walk over there and arrest Hurricane Bill, or we will.' 'All right, Tucker,' Smith answered, 'you arrest him.'

"Tucker cocked one barrel of his shotgun, the sound of the hammer coming back so loud it must have been heard across Douglas Avenue. Stepping out into the dusty street, Tucker levelled his weapon. 'Bill, you're under arrest,' he called out. 'Drop those guns.'

"Martin's guns began an upward swing and then stopped. After a moment's hesitation, he said, 'You can take me.' Saying this, he tossed his guns into a patch of weeds. His stunned followers stood frozen for a second, then dropped their pistols."

Brought before Judge Jewett, they were found guilty of disturbing the peace and violating the No Gun law. Fines totaling $600 were levied against them. Fear of vigilante vengeance convinced Hurricane Bill and his followers that it was time to seek greener pastures. "Good riddance," exulted the Wichita *Eagle*.

Following a drought of a month's duration, Kansas was struck by a calamity of a different nature, known ever afterward as "the year of the hoppers." The state had been invaded by grasshoppers before, but never had there been anything to compare with the hordes that now filled the sky. They marched across Kansas devouring every living green thing. Their greasy dead carcasses covered the rails, making it impossible for trains to operate. The Santa Fe sent out gangs of men, armed with brooms and sand, but the rails were no sooner swept clean than they were befouled again. Crops were destroyed. Famine threatened the farmers of central and southern Kansas. The governor appealed to the federal authorities and to Ohio and other eastern states for aid. It was quickly forthcoming.

In Wichita, the *Eagle* collected money and food for the distressed. As usual in such circumstances, the saloonkeepers and the gamblers were the first to respond. "Mr. Whitey Rupp, the popular proprietor of the Keno House, started the ball rolling this morning with a contribution of $250," the *Eagle* reported.

The calamity ended with the coming of winter. It was an unusually cold one, which was welcomed in the hope that it would destroy the pests. Whether or not the cold weather was responsible, Kansas was spared a second invasion the following spring.

Looking back, it cannot be doubted that the *Eagle* was the most powerful molder of public opinion in Kansas. In Marsh Murdock it had a fighting editor. With the elections of 1875 at hand, he began beating the drum for Mike Meagher's return to the office of city marshal. Bill Smith had already declared for reelection. His weak, vacillating performance of the past year and the contempt in which he was held by so many must have warned him that he would not have a chance. Obviously the clique he served believed they could buy enough votes to keep him in office. They almost did.

Back in harness again, Mike set about putting his house in order. Officers Botts, Dibb, Hooker, and Deputy Marshal Dan Parks (Smith's cronies) were removed from the city payroll and Jimmy Cairns, the best man on the force, was made deputy marshal. The men who had been set adrift were replaced by others Mike could trust. The law began to be enforced. The town's undesirables were given the choice of toeing the line or moving on.

Meagher was no saint. Undoubtedly he was squaring some old grudges. In the minutes of the city commission for May 22, the following appears: "The Police Commission [City Marshal Meagher and Police Court Judge Atwood] recommended that the Scrip [wages] of W. Earp and John Behrens be withheld until all moneys collected by them for the city be turned over to the City Treasurer. It was sanctioned and accepted."

The two men did not wait to be brought up on charges; John Behrens was headed for Texas and Wyatt Earp, accompanied by his brother Jim, hurriedly put Wichita behind him and struck off on the long, one-hundred-and-fifty-mile ride across the prairies to Dodge.

This shatters the once widely believed myth that it was in response to the fabled telegram from Dodge City's Mayor Hoover

—YOU HAVE CLEANED UP WICHITA. COME OVER AND CLEAN UP DODGE
—that Wyatt headed for the Cowboy Capital. There is no evidence
that Mayor George Hoover, the prosperous wholesale wine and
liquor dealer, had ever heard of Wyatt Earp. As for the alleged
telegram, it was one of many fictions that were invented in Stuart
Lake's exciting typewriter.

If you were to examine the editorial columns of the *Eagle* for
the years when Wichita's principal concern was the Texas cattle
trade, you would find Marsh Murdock saying repeatedly that one
day southern Kansas would be hailed as the heartland of "the
golden granary of America." The rich, dark loam to be found on
the almost treeless and rock-free prairie seemed to beckon the
plow. The colonization department of the Santa Fe had placed
a colony of three hundred Mennonite families from Russia on land
in Harvey County in 1873.[4] Each had arrived with a bushel of
drought-resistant Turkey Red wheat in the family baggage. The
success the immigrants were having provided the land speculators,
a score of whom had opened offices in Wichita, with their most per-
suasive argument. Every day brought prospective clients to town,
mostly from the Midwest, as well as Germans and Scandinavians
just arrived from continental Europe.

Not all land agents were swindlers, but many were. Settlers
who had been bilked came to the marshal with their problems. He
had no authority in such matters and could do little more than
advise them to consult the county prosecutor.

With the season winding down, the city commission enacted an
ordinance banning women from appearing in the saloons and im-
posing a fine of $25 if prostitutes were found guilty of soliciting on
the street. The action was uncalled for; the girls from the red-light
district had been behaving themselves. Mike had had nothing to do
with it.

One September evening as Mike walked across Emil Warner's
beer garden (which the German ran in conjunction with his brew-
ery), Jim Fisher, a Water Street pimp, floundered to his feet and

gave him a tongue-lashing. Without replying, the marshal continued on, back to Warner's office. Fisher drew a gun and fired, the bullet tearing into Mike's right hip and laming him for the rest of his life. Whipping around, he killed Fisher.

A week or more later he hobbled down to the police station using a cane. Deputy Marshal Cairns was there. Sim Tucker had seen him pass and followed him.

"Mike, why did you give that punk the first shot?" the lawyer asked. "He was liquored up. You might have known he'd shoot as soon as your back was turned."

"Drunk or sober, I didn't think Fisher had the guts to level a gun on me," Mike replied. "That was my mistake. But it taught me something," he added wryly. "When that sort of trash can screw up courage enough to put a slug into me, I know it's time to turn in my shield."

VI

The Border Queen— Wildest of the Wild

CALDWELL, KANSAS, is quiet enough today. But if in 1880 the notorious "Border Queen" was not the liveliest, bawdiest, most lawless town in Kansas, it did not miss that distinction by much. For years it had been just an unimportant trail town wallowing in the dust kicked up by the passing herds of Longhorns being driven north to the Kansas cow towns.[1]

Concealing the fact that they were acting for the Atchison, Topeka and Santa Fe, a group of men incorporated the Cowley, Sumner and Fort Smith Railroad in 1876, and received a charter granting it the right to construct a railroad running from Wichita, via Wellington, the county seat of Sumner County, 26 miles south of Wichita, and southeasterly through Arkansas City for Fort Smith, Arkansas. It was a paper railroad conceived by the Santa Fe to protect its eastern flank. No work was done. However, when, for the second year in a row, cattle shipments from Wichita fell off by as many as forty thousand head, construction of the Cowley, Sumner and Fort Smith began in 1878. Whether it was because of the aftereffects of the panic that had swept the country or for some other reason, work stopped when the rails reached Wellington.

Ten months passed, then suddenly it was resumed. But instead of heading for Arkansas City, the Santa Fe was in a lather to reach Caldwell and the border.

As soon as it became obvious that Caldwell was going to boom, the rush south from Wichita began. Mike Meagher and his wife were among the thousand boomers who headed for the Border Queen.

On level ground, several hundred yards up the slope from the shacks that lined the original Chisholm Trail, Caldwell took shape, with Main Street its principal business thoroughfare. Day and night it was a tangle of trucks and other vehicles delivering lumber, bricks, and stone to the various sites where construction was under way. Unlike the flimsy wooden buildings that were run up in most boom towns, the construction that was going on in Caldwell had a promise of permanency. Major Oatman was personally supervising the building of his three-story fireproof Hotel Leland. [When I was last there in 1959 the Leland was still Caldwell's leading hotel.] Meagher announced that he would conduct a saloon business at 54 Main Street when the building under construction at that address was finished.

Some weeks before the first train could be expected in Caldwell, a party of Santa Fe surveyors arrived and staked out the location of the shipping pens. It placed the yards hard up against the invisible line that separated Indian Territory from Kansas.

The company never offered an explanation. But looking back from this distance, its thinking is readily apparent. No corporation was in a better position to weigh the trend of public opinion in Kansas. There were four major groups in the state that were opposed to the Texas cattle trade. First and foremost was the Grange, the Patrons of Husbandry, who were in constant conflict with the trail drivers. Next there were the "reformers," who called the cow towns "a blot on the good name of the state." They were closely associated with a third group, consisting of the Temperance Party and the Temperance Union. Lastly, and most vocal of all, were the breeders of shorthorn cattle, who were campaigning for a state-wide quarantine law that would ban the entry of all Texas cattle.[2]

It was predictable that sooner or later these groups would join ranks, which would give them the votes needed to jam through the Legislature the reforms for which they were campaigning. However, the banning of Texas cattle could be circumvented by loading the Longhorns at the state line. Once aboard the cars, they could be transported across Kansas without hindrance.

The first train steamed into Caldwell at noon on June 13, 1880. The whole town had turned out to welcome it. Aboard were livestock dealers from the Midwest and buyers for the Kansas City packing plants. On hand to greet them were the owners of the herds being held across the line in the Strip. Loaded stock trains were rolling out of town a few days later. Caldwell was a town gone wild—tough, lawless. Its unique position acted as a powerful lodestone on men on the scout, wanted somewhere for robbery, murder, or other major crimes. When a deputy United States marshal caught up with them, they could slip across the line into the Strip and safety, where few lawmen cared to follow.

In a period of nine months, eleven men were lynched in Sumner County. Three were taken out of the jail at Wellington. Next morning they were found dangling from the railroad bridge. Of the eleven, only one could be classified as a working cowboy. One was a lawyer and another a Caldwell businessman. The rest were saloon characters.

In the afternoon of July 18, 1879, George Wood and Jake Adams, cowboys with one of Ike Pryor's herds, which was being held in the Strip, rode into town. Leaving their broncs at the hitchrack in front of Jim Moreland's saloon they went inside and began drinking. An hour later, crazy-drunk, they mounted their horses and rode up and down Main Street, firing their guns and screeching the Rebel yell. Wearying of their fun, they returned to Moreland's Saloon and continued drinking.

Caldwell's police force was limited to one man, Constable

Henry Mears. Storekeepers urged him to arrest the pair. Being reluctant to go into Moreland's alone, he enlisted the support of three or four men, among them George Flat and John Wilson, both of whom were saloon brawlers and troublemakers. Flat, a coward at heart, often bragged about the number of men he had put under. Urged on by the gathering crowd, he and Wilson crossed the street to Moreland's. Through the window they saw the two Texans standing at the bar talking to the saloonkeeper. Wilson then walked around to the back door and took up his position there; Flat walked into the saloon and bought a drink. As he waited for Moreland to serve it, he placed his pistol on the bar. Taking this as a declaration of war, Adams whipped up his gun and, holding it within a few inches of Flat's face, ordered him to back out of the saloon.

Flat backed all the way to the door, with the cowboy crowding him. As they reached the sidewalk, Flat's six-gun barked twice. It sent Adams rolling into the street, clutching his stomach. A moment later his partner rushed out, trying to reach his horse. Flat killed him as he crossed the sidewalk.

Flat then ran out into the middle of the street and for several minutes refused to allow anyone to come near him. Friends finally got him into Moreland's. After several drinks, he seemed to get his nerve back, especially when he was told that he had nothing to fear from the law; that Constable Mears had deputized him.

The town was full of cowboys that evening and the air was ugly. But Flat's friends had dosed him with whiskey and put him to bed.

There were no repercussions, but against Mike Meagher's advice, George Flat was appointed marshal of Caldwell a few weeks later.

Invariably the character of a saloon reflects the character of its proprietor, running the gamut from respectability to depravity. They struck bottom in Caldwell when Mag and George Woods came down from fading Delano and opened a two-story saloon,

61

dance hall, and brothel on Chisholm Street. To remove any doubt about the nature of the entertainment to be found there, Mag named the resort the Red Light. She and her husband had their living quarters on the ground floor to the rear of the saloon and ballroom; the second floor was cut up into small rooms in which the resident whores plied their ancient trade.

From the night it opened until it was destroyed by fire two years later, the Red Light was the nightly scene of violence. A killing occurred every few weeks. Repeated attempts were made to close it, but Mag fought them off and refused to surrender.

Caldwell was becoming notorious for its violence. There was little effort made at law enforcement. Numerous cases were reported of cowboys being picked up on the street by prostitutes and lured into alleys, where they were slugged and robbed by the women's confederates.

Realizing that a strong man was needed to head the city government, responsible citizens turned to Meagher and elected him mayor. Mike's first act was to dismiss Flat and appoint Deputy Marshal Frank Hunt to succeed him. Two policemen were added to the force.

Flat accused Mike and Hunt of being out to "get" him. Drunk most of the time, he was gunned down as he turned the corner of First and Main streets. It was after one o'clock in the morning. He and his friend George Spears had spent the evening in the Red Light, and Spears was guiding him home. Out of the shadows of a building across the way came a sudden blast of gunfire—seven or eight shots in all, Spears later testified. Miraculously, he wasn't struck.

An investigation led by Marshal Hunt followed. But no evidence was uncovered leading to the indictment of anyone. Flat's cronies contended that George Spears had been hired to lead Flat into a death trap. How else could he have come through all that shooting without being injured? Pointing out that Marshal Hunt had long borne a grudge against Flat, they concluded that it was he who had arranged the ambush.

On the night of October 11, with the shipping season about over for the year, Hunt was standing at an open window of the Red Light, listening to the music and watching the dancers, when a shot was fired outside. He tumbled to the ground, mortally wounded. It was at once regarded as a revenge slaying for the killing of George Flat. Eventually, however, it became just another in Caldwell's list of unsolved crimes. Of its first five marshals, one was booted out of his job and four died from gunfire. Briefly William Horseman took Hunt's place.

The police had to remove one of Mag's girls and her cowboy escort from the barroom of the Leland one evening, which had a strict rule against serving women. The girl was abusive and was lodged in the town jail for the night, charged with being drunk and disorderly. Mag was on hand in the morning to pay the fine. Meagher was in the courtroom. He, rather than Judge Reilly, drew her ire.

Being anxious to devote all of his time to his saloon, which in the short time it had been open had become one of the most popular resorts in town, Mike announced that he would not be a candidate for reelection. Charley Siringo, the famous cowboy and range detective, had located in Caldwell and started a wholesale cigar business. Mike had rented him space in the saloon, from which he was conducting his business, Siringo's presence no doubt adding to the popularity of the place.

A cowboy answering to the name of Charlie Davis rode into town on the afternoon of August 18, 1881, and quarreled with one of the girls in the Red Light. George Woods, Mag's inoffensive husband, interfered on behalf of the woman. Davis leveled his pistol at Woods and fired, killing him instantly. Hurrying to his horse, Davis left Caldwell on the gallop, and although Mag offered a reward of five hundred dollars for his capture, dead or alive, he was never apprehended.

Tough as she was, Mag responded to her husband's death with profound emotion. Over his grave she erected an expensive monu-

63

ment. The Red Light, violent, obscene and godless, continued to flourish.

Early in December, 1881, Jim Talbot (his honest name was Jim Sherman), the Texas outlaw and horse thief, appeared in Caldwell. He was joined several days later by six members of his gang. They rented a vacant house near the railroad depot and spent most of their time drinking in the Red Light and generally making themselves obnoxious.

"I was only a lad at the time but I remember the circumstances well enough," the late Judge John Ryland told me many years ago. "The town was alarmed, the feeling being that the Talbot Gang was waiting for a favorable moment to rob the bank. Mayor Hubbell swore in six special officers to assist the police and instructed Marshal Wilson to keep the bank under twenty-four hours' surveillance. Whether it made Talbot change his plans, I do not know. But he let it be known a day or so later that he was in Caldwell to square accounts with Mike Meagher, who had killed his half-brother Jim near Delano in 1873."

Early on the morning of December 17, after an all-night carouse, the Talbot Gang walked out to the center of Main Street and began firing their pistols. Half a hundred shots had been fired when Talbot ordered his men to run down to the house and get their Winchesters and meet him at Keilflesch's Livery, across the street from the Red Light.

George Spears, who had been with George Flat on the night he was slain, was in the barn, hurriedly saddling a horse, evidently intending to flee Caldwell with the gang. He was struck by a stray bullet and killed.

All accounts agree that no less than a hundred shots were fired in the fifteen minutes that followed, shattering windows, plowing into wooden doors, and pinging off brick walls.

Mike Meagher rushed out of his saloon, armed with a .45, and ran up the street in the direction of the Opera House, accompanied by Marshal Wilson. Wilson saw a man aiming a rifle at Mike from the corner of the Chinese laundry. He cried a warning, but it was too late. Mike crumpled to the sidewalk. "Tell my wife they got me at last," he muttered. They were his final words.

A few minutes after the killing of Meagher, the Talbot Gang charged out of the barn and down the slope to Chisholm Street, crossed the railroad tracks, and disappeared to the east without losing a man. In the weeks that followed, several were picked up by the law and returned to Sumner County and placed on trial. They received short prison sentences. Talbot was apprehended months later in California. Charged with the murder of Meagher, he was placed on trial at Wellington. The trial resulted in a hung jury. Tried a second time, he was acquitted. He returned to California, where he was killed at Ukiah in August, 1926.[3]

It was widely believed in Caldwell that John Meagher had followed him home and avenged his brother's murder. The accumulated evidence says otherwise.

No one knows for certain what Jim Talbot's purpose was in settling down with his bandit gang in Caldwell in December of 1881, renting a house and hiring a woman to do the cooking. It seemed to indicate that they expected to be there a long time. It is unlikely that they would have engaged in such preliminaries if they were there simply to crack the Stockman's Exchange Bank or square accounts with Mike Meagher. Winter, with the likelihood of snow to leave a trail a posse could follow, always curtailed the activities of horseback outlaws. Was it to find a safe refuge until spring, not harassed by Texas sheriffs and Rangers, that brought Talbot to Caldwell?

Spearheaded by the *Messenger*, the slaying of Mike Meagher touched off a vigorous campaign for law and order. The police department was given a shake-up, and Marshal John Wilson was replaced by young George Brown. He was a popular, respected young man but almost totally unfitted for his job by lack of experience.

On June 22, 1882, two cowboys rode up from the stockyards,

stabled their horses, and proceeded to make the rounds of the saloons. Heading for the Red Light, they amused themselves by shooting out a street light and scattering pedestrians. Several businessmen caught up with the marshal as he was passing the Leland and advised him to arrest the two men before they killed some innocent citizen. Without asking the assistant marshal or a policeman to accompany him, Brown proceeded to the Red Light. Mag was at the bar. She told him the two men were upstairs.

One of the girls had seen Brown approaching the resort and, surmising why he was coming, had warned the Texans. They were waiting at the head of the stairs as Brown came up. They shot him dead and got out of town before they could be apprehended.

On July 5, big Bat Carr, another incompetent, succeeded the slain marshal. Carr had been around Caldwell a long time. He was a tough barroom bully, merciless when he was getting the better of a fight.

Several days later Mayor A. M. Colson had a visitor, a stranger, Hendry (not Henry) Brown, no relation of George Brown. He was a lean, colorless six-footer, with a pair of searching gray eyes.

Colson was impressed by the man's appearance and demeanor. The stranger told the mayor a bit about himself. He had served a term as marshal of Tascosa, in the Texas Panhandle, and no town was ever tougher. Before that he had been deputy sheriff of Oldham County, Texas. What he did not reveal was that he had ridden with Billy the Kid in the Lincoln County war. Learning that Caldwell had lost its marshal, he had come up from Texas to apply for the job.

Colson had to tell him it had been filled, but that the town was in need of a deputy marshal. The stranger nodded and said he'd give it a whirl.

Hendry Brown wasn't long taking the measure of Bat Carr. He wanted Bat's job, and he got it. The shipping season was nearing its peak and the town was overflowing with stock buyers, wealthy cattlemen, and gamblers. Brown accused Carr of selling protection to the operators of crooked games. Although Bat hotly denied it, the evidence against him left him no choice but to resign. Hendry Brown was named to take his place.

For the first time in its turbulent history, Caldwell had a marshal who could make it toe the line. Less than two weeks after Brown took over, a man calling himself Ben Wheeler rode into Caldwell.[4] Around Tascosa he had answered to the name of Ben Burton. Whether his appearance in Caldwell was in response to a letter from Brown has never been determined. Certainly they were well acquainted. The two of them were cut from the same pattern. With Brown vouching for him, Wheeler was appointed assistant marshal.

The "good" people of Caldwell wanted law and order, and they began to get it. At Marshal Brown's urging, the city council passed several new ordinances giving him the authority to remove lewd women from the streets and crack down on the bawdy entertainment being presented in the low-grade saloons. The ordinance covering the punishment of undesirables was amended to read that they could be deported as well as fined at the discretion of the court.

Believing that the amended ordinance was aimed at her, Mag Woods screamed her defiance. She was in constant conflict with Marshal Brown. When he posted policemen at the door of the Red Light, she hired a lawyer and went to court to have them removed. She was fighting a losing battle. "The Red Light must go" became a standing headline in the *Standard*, Caldwell's first daily newspaper.

Mag was to have the last laugh, however. Convinced that if she tried to continue she would be deported, she sold her fixtures and liquors, boarded up the windows, and prepared to leave Caldwell. On an August morning she marched her girls and bartenders down the slope to the depot. Ignoring the jeers and taunts of the assembled crowd, they took their seats in the northbound train for Wichita. Mag's attention was fixed on the Red Light. A grunt of satisfaction escaped her when she saw flames breaking through the roof. As a parting gesture of defiance she had set the place afire before leaving.

Caldwell lost some of its excitement. Cowboys no longer raced their broncs up and down Main Street, firing their guns to express their exuberance. There were no more killings. However, two robberies were reported, both of wealthy Texans who had just been paid for their cattle, one occurring at the Southwestern Hotel and the other at the Leland. In neither case was the money recovered or an arrest made, although Brown and his friend Wheeler made a seemingly determined effort to do so. Their position in the community was so secure that no one could have been further removed from suspicion than they. And yet, judging by future events, they were undoubtedly guilty of both robberies.

That Hendry Brown was a villain at heart, trying desperately but unsuccessfully to divorce himself from his past outlawry, is the kindest judgment that can be passed on him. His courage cannot be questioned. He was well educated and had the instincts of a gentleman. I know of no other peace officer who was accepted as their social equal by the leading families of the town that employed him. He attended services at the First Methodist Church regularly and always found time to be present at its social affairs.[5]

On New Year's Day, 1883, he was called into the York, Parker and Draper store and found the mayor and a committee of leading citizens present. Colson made a short speech and presented him with the latest-model Winchester, bearing a silver plate on the stock, inscribed as follows:

PRESENTED TO CITY MARSHAL H. N. BROWN
FOR VALUABLE SERVICES
RENDERED THE CITIZENS OF CALDWELL, KANSAS.

A. M. COLSON, MAYOR, JAN. I, 1883.

The first killing of the year occurred on May 13. Spotted Horse, a Pawnee Indian, and his squaw drove into town in their wagon and camped in back of the Opera House. In the morning they entered several houses and demanded food. On being refused, the Indian drew a pistol and threatened a man and his wife. The husband seized a shotgun and the Indians left. Walking down the alley, they entered the kitchen of a restaurant and helped themselves. The police were called. Marshal Brown responded, and when the Indian leveled his gun at him, Brown killed him.

A coroner's jury found that Marshal Brown had fired the fatal shot in self-defense, and the matter was forgotten. Of far greater moment was the fact that instead of crossing Red River at Red River Crossing, many herds were crossing at Doan's Store and going up the new Western Trail to Dodge.

In March, 1884, after a long courtship, Hendry Brown married Maude Levagood, the beautiful daughter of one of Caldwell's prominent families. Shortly after returning from their honeymoon, he was tempted to engage in an adventure that was to heap shame and misery on his wife and cost him his life.

Nothing is known of what transpired prior to the morning when Brown asked the mayor for a brief leave of absence for Wheeler and himself. According to Colson, the marshal's story was that he had learned where two horse thieves were holed up in the Strip; that he and Wheeler wanted to bring them in and collect the reward money on them. Since it was the slowest time of the year, the mayor had granted the request.

Obviously by prearrangement Brown and Wheeler met the two "horse thieves," John Wesley and Bill Smith, who had enjoyed some success robbing country banks. Hendry Brown had ridden with better men. Looking the pair over, he must have realized that they were second-raters.

But the four struck west together, their destination the little town of Medicine Lodge, county seat of Barber County. It was a prosperous farming community and the home of the Medicine Valley Bank—the bank on which their attention was focused.

In a driving rainstorm they rode into Medicine Lodge two days later, shortly after the bank had opened for business. Tethering

69

their horses in the rear, behind the shed in which the bank stored its coal, they walked along the side of the building and reached the main street. Wesley and Smith stationed themselves at the bank door, guns drawn; Brown and Wheeler hurried inside.

Suddenly the stillness of the rain-lashed morning was shattered by the sound of gunfire in the bank. Across the street, startled passersby, sensing that the bank was being robbed, darted into the stores for cover. Through the windows they saw two of the bandits emerge from the bank. All four then ran back alongside the building to their horses and raced out of town.

Half a dozen men, led by Barney O'Connor, a cattle buyer, hurried into the bank. They found George Geppert, the cashier, dead on the floor, and Wiley Payne, the bank president, lying mortally wounded in front of the locked door of the vault. Obviously he had been struck down as he closed it, thus saving the bank's funds.

Without awaiting the arrival of Sheriff Rigg, who was at his farm north of town, O'Connor and a large group of riders took up the trail of the fleeing bank robbers, who were cut off in the Gyp Hills, two and a half miles southwest of Medicine Lodge. They refused to surrender. Sheriff Rigg reached the scene with the posse he had deputized and took charge. There was some shooting, but it was noon before Brown threw away his gun and walked out, hands raised, and the others followed. It was not until then that Riggs realized that one of the bank robbers was Hendry Brown, the popular marshal of Caldwell, and another was Ben Wheeler, the assistant marshal.

The prisoners were lodged in the one-room log cabin that was the town jail. When word spread late that afternoon that Wylie Payne had died, a mob descended on the jail, demanding that the prisoners be lynched. The sheriff and his deputies forced it to disperse. But that evening, shortly after nine o'clock, a hundred armed men stormed the jail and brought out Brown and the other three. Although it was suicide, and he knew it, Hendry Brown broke away and started to run, preferring death by a bullet to meeting it at the end of a rope.

He had taken only a step or two when half a dozen slugs crashed into him and he pitched face downward into the mud. The other prisoners were marched down into the bottoms at the eastern edge of town and left dangling from a convenient elm.

The mayor and leading citizens of Caldwell hung their heads in shame.

VII

The Mastersons and the Earps

No OTHER city has so successfully exploited its raunchy cow-town past as Dodge—not its real past but the mythical, heavily fictionized past of the Earps, the Mastersons, and Marshal Dillon. It has its Earp Boulevard and its Masterson Street, and annually a quarter of a million tourists visit the replica of old Front Street and the Long Branch Saloon. Few of those who take time to visit Wright Park, Dodge City's beautiful recreation area, know that it was named for Robert M. Wright, the town's leading citizen in the days when it was famous as the Cowboy Capital.

Formerly sutler at Fort Dodge, Bob Wright was one of the founders of Dodge City, five miles west of the Army post. As a member of the firm of Wright and Rath, general outfitters in the days of the buffalo hunters, and later as the head of Wright and Beverley, Bob had become recognized as the foremost trader and merchandiser in western Kansas and Colorado.[1] He served the Sixteenth District in both houses of the Kansas Legislature at various times and left for posterity what many authorities regard as the basic book on Dodge: *Dodge City: The Cowboy Capital and the Great Southwest*. Its most often quoted passage is this hilarious castigation of the old cow town:

72

Beautiful, Bibulous Babylon of the Frontier. Her principal business is polygamy . . . her code of morals is the honor of thieves, and decency she knows not. Her virtue is prostitution and her beverage is whiskey. She is a merry town and the only visible support of a great many of her citizens is jocularity. The town is full of prostitutes and every other place is a brothel.

The Atchison, Topeka and Santa Fe tracks cut Dodge in two from north to south. Front Street paralleled the tracks fifty yards to the north. There, in the space of several blocks, the business houses, the principal saloons and gambling rooms were crowded together. It was policed and the carrying of guns prohibited by city ordinances. In the opposite direction, fifty yards south of the tracks, was the South Side, where the theaters and dance halls and cribs were located. On the South Side you were more or less on your own.

The hundred-yard-wide stretch of sand and sagebrush that separated Front Street from the South Side was referred to facetiously as "the plaza." It was crisscrossed with paths, for there was a continuous back-and-forth traffic after dark.

About ten o'clock on the night of April 9, 1878, City Marshal Ed Masterson, Bat's elder brother, and Assistant Marshal Nat Haywood were walking along Front Street when a flurry of shooting in the Lady Gay Theatre sent them running across the plaza to investigate.

Although it would be another five to six weeks before the 1878 shipping season hit full stride, several small herds from the Panhandle had arrived and were being held on the river bottoms. Being that close to the flesh pots of the South Side, the cowboys who had brought the herds up the trail were riding across the toll bridge over the Arkansas River after nightfall, seeking entertainment.

Masterson and Haywood rushed into the Lady Gay and found Jack Wagner, a cowboy with whom both were acquainted, waving his gun in drunken hilarity. Ed disarmed him, and seeing A. M.

Walker, Wagner's employer in the crowd, turned the gun over to him, telling the Texan to keep it in his possession until Wagner had sobered up.

The incident seemingly settled, Marshal Masterson and his assistant stepped out of the Lady Gay. Wagner and Walker followed them to the sidewalk. Glancing back, Ed saw that Wagner had regained possession of his pistol. For the second time he tried to disarm the cowboy. As they scuffled, Haywood attempted to come to Ed's aid. Walker whipped up his gun and threatened to kill him if he interfered.

Bat came bounding across the plaza, having been informed that his brother was in trouble. As he reached the scene of the struggle, a muffled shot sounded, fired at such close range that Ed's shirt was set afire. He staggered back, mortally wounded. Haywood led him away and got him across the tracks to Hoover's wine and liquor store, where he collapsed.

Bat asked no questions as he reached the scene of the struggle. His pearl-handled .45's spurted flame. He put three slugs into Wagner and two into Walker. Wagner stumbled into Peacock's dance hall next door, where he died a few minutes later. Walker lived to stand trial for his part in the slaying of Ed Masterson, and was acquitted. Bat appeared as a witness for the prosecution, but he was never indicted and brought to trial for the killing of Jack Wagner, nor for that of anyone else. Fiction and pseudohistory may picture him as a skilled gunman, but court records do not bear that out. In self-defense he shot and killed Sergeant King, known as the "Army's bad boy," at Fort Elliot in Texas. King and Wagner were the only men he ever downed.

The Dodge city council appointed popular Charley Bassett marshal to succeed Ed Masterson. It was a temporary appointment, the council wanting time to look the field over before making a permanent choice. Former Assistant Marshal Earp had returned to Dodge City on May 12, after a long absence in Texas. The circumstances would appear to have been peculiarly fortuitous both for him and Dodge: he needed a job, and Dodge needed a marshal. Had Wyatt Earp's record as assistant marshal been as outstanding as his admirers say it was, the city council hardly would have passed him over now. But it did; it confirmed Bassett as marshal and took Earp on in his old slot of assistant marshal.

Authorized to add a policeman to the force, Marshal Bassett evidenced his low regard for the Earp clan by passing over Virgil and Morgan Earp and awarding the job to Jim Masterson, another of the four Masterson brothers.

The pro- and anti-Earp factions have distorted the real Wyatt beyond recognition when measured against the provable facts. There is little in his record as a lawman in Dodge City to suggest that he was better than the average run-of-the-mill Western peace officer. Thumb through the files of the *Dodge City Times* and the *Ford County Globe* of those days and you will find him seldom mentioned, for aside from his connection with the so-called Dodge City Peace Commission, he was never a controversial figure (that is, prior to his days in Tombstone). Fiction did for him what it had done for Wild Bill; it made him famous.

On the night of July 26, 1878, the heart of the shipping season, when the town was overflowing with cattlemen and cowboys, Assistant Marshal Earp crossed the railroad tracks to the South Side to look things over. He stopped outside the open doors of the Comique Theatre, for the night was warm. Eddie Foy, who would become famous as one of our great comedians, and his company had been playing at the Comique for several weeks. He was at the footlights reciting one of his comic songs when a whiskey-reckless cowboy named Ed Hoyt leaped up and began shooting holes through the theater's flimsy walls. The Comique's private policeman rushed up to stop him. Hoyt broke away, and bolting through the open doors, brushed past Wyatt and reached his bronc. Riding away, he turned in the saddle as he neared the toll bridge and fired a wild shot, to which Wyatt replied, seemingly without effect.

A moment later, however, Earp heard the clatter of hooves slow, then stop.

They found Hoyt on the bridge, mortally wounded. He died six days later without regaining consciousness. His friends buried him on Boot Hill.[2] He was the last man to be interred here. More remarkable, official records disclose that Ed Hoyt was the only man killed by Wyatt Earp in his capacity of assistant marshal of Dodge City. Many killings occurred in Dodge, but not by its heavily publicized peace officers. Perhaps most vividly remembered is the slaying of beautiful Dora Hand.

For the past thirty years and more I have had occasion to tell the story of this young woman, who really was not so young—she was thirty-four when she came to Dodge City. It is only after separating fact from the mountain of romantic trash that has been written about her that the real Dora Hand emerges.[3] No evidence has been uncovered to support the story that she was from New England, a graduate of the Boston Conservatory of Music, and had come west in the hope that the bracing air of the plains would arrest the tuberculosis from which she was suffering. Equally fanciful is the tale that an unhappy love affair was responsible for her wandering. Born Fannie Keenan, in St. Louis, she left home to marry Theodore Hand, a vaudevillian and honky-tonk musician, with whom, as Dora Hand, she appeared in the variety shows of New Orleans and the Mississippi river towns.

Although they were divorced in 1876, Fannie continued to use the name of Dora Hand. She had a trained voice of operatic range, which undoubtedly accounts for the stories of her having been a graduate of the Boston Conservatory. It was a time when the sentimental song was a popular feature of the entertainment offered in variety shows. When an opening occurred at Esher's Varieties Theatre in St. Louis, she was engaged as "house singer," besides doubling in the chorus.

Fannie Garrettson, Dora's best friend, had been a member of Sam Esher's company of "artists" for some time. When she received an offer from the Lady Gay Theatre in Dodge, undoubtedly at better money, she left St. Louis for the Cowboy Capital. Several weeks later Dora Hand and Fannie Garrettson were living together in a one-room cabin on the South Side and performing at the Lady Gay, where the entertainment was tailored to appeal to the nightly audiences of whiskey-charged cowboys bent on living it up for a day or two before setting out on the long homeward-bound trip to Texas.

For all their wildness, these men had a keen appreciation of feminine virtue and seldom mistook a lady for a whore. When Dora Hand approached the footlights to render a ballad, they became putty in her hands. Although they might have just come from indulging in the animalistic pleasures of the cribs, they were filled with temporary remorse as she sang about home and mother.

Even before she became an established favorite at the Lady Gay, Dora Hand attracted the attention of popular Jim Kelley, three-times mayor of Dodge and proprietor of the fashionable Alhambra Saloon and gambling parlor, second to none in the city. A bachelor, he lived in a comfortable three-room cottage on the South Side. It was his habit to leave the Alhambra in the early hours of the morning, cross the tracks, and drop into the Lady Gay for a few minutes before continuing on home. Not long thereafter Dora was often seen riding with him on the prairie as he exercised his pack of hounds.

Kelley had never employed a singer in the Alhambra, but he did so now, arranging with the management of the Lady Gay to permit Dora to sing in his saloon for an hour, five nights a week. The town had never done much to succor its very poor, mostly Mexican families living in hovels along the river. Dora's increased income permitted her to set out in the morning with a market basket filled with food for these unfortunates.

That is the picture of Dora Hand Dodge City treasures—a honky-tonk singer by night and an angel of mercy by day. Another equally cherished story concerns Dora's appearance as soloist at the Sunday evening services of the First Methodist Church. Instead of the usual handful of the devout, the church was crowded to overflowing by an assemblage of sinners from Front Street, most of whom couldn't remember when they had been in a church last. Kelley had passed the word and they had responded en masse.

On the evening of August 17, a heated altercation occurred in the Alhambra that was to end in bizarre tragedy. Young Spike (James W.) Kenedy, the son of Captain Miflin Kenedy, the former partner of Captain Richard King of King Ranch fame, and the second-wealthiest cattleman in Texas, had been playing blackjack for the better part of an hour and losing steadily. Suddenly he leaped to his feet, knocked the cardcase to the floor, and accused the dealer of manipulating the cards.

Impugning the honesty of the games a saloon conducted was a serious charge and often the prelude to gunsmoke. Charlie Trask, employed by the Alhambra to keep things under control, tried to quiet Spike, but because of the young Texan's prominence, Kelley pushed Trask out of the way and confronted him personally. They were soon swinging their fists. Spike was no match for the heavier and older Kelley, who put him on the floor and then literally dragged him to the door and pitched him into the street.

The young man spent the rest of the night drinking and threatening to kill Jim Kelley. Instead of returning to Texas with the Kenedy crew, he remained in Dodge, watching his man. It didn't take him long to learn that Kelley always left the Alhambra a few minutes after two in the morning, crossed the tracks to the South Side, stepped into the Lady Gay for a few minutes, and then continued on down the road to his cottage, a hundred yards beyond the Western Hotel. He also found out that he slept in the front bedroom. A man on horseback had only to pump three or four shots through the window to be sure of killing him.

This was premeditated murder, but Kenedy had the stomach for it. There was a streak of fierce pride and savage cruelty in him.

He left Dodge one morning by train for Kansas City to buy

the fastest horse he could find; price was no object. In addition to speed, he wanted a sturdy, grain-fed animal from which he could get forty miles a day. When he found the horse he wanted, he began the long westward ride across Kansas, conditioning the animal for the run that would enable him to outdistance any pursuit that might be organized against him.

Rain was falling when he rode into the South Side at 4 A.M. on October 4. He passed the Western Hotel unnoticed and pulled up in front of Jim Kelley's cottage. A few moments later the pre-dawn stillness was broken by a flurry of shots fired in quick succession.

As Kenedy was fleeing up the river, a man ran out of the Western Hotel and recognized him as he passed. Murder had been done, but it was not Jim Kelley's life that had been snuffed out; Kelley was five miles away in the hospital ward at Fort Dodge, recovering from an abdominal operation that had been performed several days after Spike Kenedy had left Dodge for Kansas City.

Knowing he would be away for three or four weeks, Kelley had invited Dora and Fannie to move into his place while he was gone. Since the cottage was far more comfortable than their own tiny quarters, the women had accepted his offer. When Kenedy fired the fatal shot, Fannie Garrettson was asleep in the front bedroom, Dora in the rear; the two rooms were separated by a thin partition.

The slugs from Spike Kenedy's gun had not struck Fannie, but one had pierced the partition and killed Dora Hand.

Not waiting for daylight, Bat Masterson, Ford County Sheriff, assembled a posse consisting of himself, Deputy Sheriff Tilghman, Marshal Charley Bassett, and Assistant Marshal Earp. Agreeing that fleeing up the Arkansas was a maneuver employed by Kenedy to confuse pursuit and that he would swing around town and head for Wagon Springs Crossing on the Cimarron, they set out on the long ride to the crossing, hoping to cut him off there.

The weather turned foul in the afternoon, and they were pelted by hail for an hour, which slowed them. However, when they reached the soddy at the crossing, the farmer who lived there informed them that no one had passed. The light was beginning to fail when they saw a horseman approaching. It was Spike Kenedy. He was within a few yards of the soddy when he caught sight of the posse's tethered broncs in the rear. He swung around instantly and was galloping away when a bullet from Earp's rifle struck his horse. Kenedy leaped free and started to run as the animal went down. Bat stopped him with a bullet that struck him in the right shoulder and bowled him over.

Spike Kenedy was astounded when he was informed that he was being taken into custody for the killing of a woman, not Jim Kelley. He was brought back to Dodge and lodged in the Ford County jail, in a room with barred windows in the rear of the sheriff's office, where Dr. McCarty performed the required surgery.

Word of his son's predicament had been flashed to Captain Miflin Kenedy at Laguna Madre, his great ranch south of Corpus Christi. This was not the first time Spike had been in trouble. But the old Quaker did not hesitate. By stagecoach and rail he sped north. On October 21, he was in Dodge, where he found Tobe Driskill, the Dewees brothers, and several other wealthy Texans waiting to support him with their presence and their money.

Although Spike Kenedy had been held prisoner for weeks, on suspicion of having killed Dora Hand, no formal indictment had been secured against him. As the days continued to pass without any action being taken, it was predicted that he would never be brought to trial. That proved to be the case. On the morning of October 28, Dr. McCarty informed Judge R. S. Cook that Kenedy was physically able to face a "preliminary" arraignment.

Apparently the details had been arranged. The judge and the doctor repaired to Sheriff Masterson's office. The prisoner was brought out from his cell. No spectators or newsmen were permitted. The proceedings required only a few minutes. No record was made of them other than the notation in the court record:

"State of Kansas vs. James W. Kenedy in re killing of Dora Hand. Case dismissed for lack of evidence."

The verdict may have been purchased—as many have contended. If so, it was no gross miscarriage of justice, for the killing of Dora had certainly been accidental.

No one has satisfactorily explained the sudden affluence of several of Dodge City's most famous badge wearers. When Wyatt Earp arrived from Wichita, his funds were so low that he had to ask the mayor for an advance against his wages. A year later, when he and his brother Morgan joined the gold rush to the Black Hills, they were so hard pressed for money that they survived the winter by cutting wood. The following year, back in Dodge again and serving as assistant marshal, there is no record of Wyatt having received an unexpected windfall in addition to his wages. And yet, ten months later, when he arrived in Tombstone, he was wealthy enough to buy an interest in the immensely profitable Oriental Saloon.

As for Bat, he was a gambler, and depending on how the cards ran, was alternately flush or broke. Shortly after the Spike Kenedy incident, he bought a half interest in the Lone Star Saloon and Dance Hall. It was a sizable investment, but he did not bother to explain how the necessary funds had been acquired. He was running for reelection as sheriff of Ford County. Obviously many voters felt that he was doing a bit too well for himself, for he was snowed under.

If the thousands of stock cattle and mustangs that were trailed north that season are coupled with the known car loadings, 1879 was Dodge City's biggest year. Railroads were creeping across Texas, heralding the day when trail driving would no longer be necessary. Recurring outbreaks of tick fever were hastening the day when a statewide quarantine law would ban the entry of Texas cattle. It was unthinkable, but the Temperance Movement was advancing westward across Kansas and taking dead aim on "wicked" Dodge.

The Queen of Cow Towns, as Stanley Vestal has christened it, still had several good years left, but before 1880 was over, many familiar faces were missing. The *Ford County Globe* noted that "Mr. Wyatt Earp, who has been on our police force, has left for Las Vegas, New Mexico." Las Vegas was only a temporary destination; Earp was bound for Tombstone. Doc Holliday was with him. Morgan had gone to Butte; Virgil was working a mining claim at Prescott, Arizona, and Jim Earp had gone back to Wichita.⁴ Little Luke Short, the gambler, was in Tombstone. Of the Masterson clan, only Jim was left in Dodge. Bat and Tom Masterson were dividing their time between Leadville, Colorado, and Denver. Before leaving Dodge, Bat had turned over his interest in the Lone Star to Jim, who was acting city marshal, filling out the unexpired term of Charley Bassett, who had resigned and left for Arizona.

Bat returned to Dodge on at least two occasions, the first time in response to an urgent telegram from his brother Jim, who was convinced that Peacock and Updegraff, his partners in the Lone Star, were robbing him blind. On reaching town, Bat saw Peacock and Updegraff standing in the plaza. They sensed why he was in Dodge and began emptying their guns at him at once. Dropping down beside the tracks, Bat began returning their fire. With only Updegraff being slightly injured, the three men continued blazing away until they were out of ammunition.

This engagement went down in local history as the "famous" Battle of the Plaza. Mayor Webster finally appeared, brandishing a loaded shotgun, and took the trio into custody. Where Marshal Jim Masterson was all this time does not appear in the record. Bat was fined eight dollars and ordered to leave town within twenty-four hours. It didn't take him that long to dissolve his partnership in the Lone Star with Peacock and Updegraff on satisfactory terms. Jim handed in his resignation as city marshal, and Bat and he took a westbound train for Trinidad, Colorado, that evening.

Bat's second return to Dodge was even more spectacular. In Denver, to the amazement of all who knew him, Bat became an

Kansas State Historical Society

Abilene, Kansas, in 1875.

Marshal Tom Smith, who brought law and order to Abilene.

Kansas State Historical Society

Joseph G. McCoy, originator of the northern cattle market for Texas Longhorns at Abilene.

Kansas State Historical Society

Wild Bill Hickok's last photograph, made at Deadwood several days before he was killed.

Kansas State Historical Society

John Wesley Hardin — "forty notches" was his boast. Most of the men he gunned down were unarmed blacks and Mexicans.

University of Texas Historical Collection

Kansas State Historical Society

Ellsworth in its cow town days, crowned by the famous Drovers Cottage which had been dragged across the prairies from Abilene.

Wichita in 1875, the Longhorn capital of Kansas.

Kansas State Historical Society

University of Texas Historical Collection

Ben Thompson, when he was city marshal of Austin, Texas.

Kansas State Historical Society

"Bloody Newton" — the toughest town in Kansas, in 1874.

The capture of City Marshal Hendry Brown of Caldwell, Kansas, Assistant Marshal Ben Wheeler, and cowboys Wesley and Smith after their bungling attempt to rob the Medicine Valley Bank. Brown, third from right, was shot down in attempting to escape. The others were lynched by a mob.

C. Q. Chandler of Wichita

Kansas State Historical Society

Front Street, Dodge City, Kansas.

Kansas State Historical Society

William (Bat) Masterson, Sheriff of Ford County, Kansas.

William Bonney, alias Billy the Kid. Although widely copied, the origin of this picture is unknown and its authenticity questionable.

Below: The old Lincoln County (New Mexico) courthouse.

Kansas State Historical Society

American Guide Series

University of New Mexico Collection

Sheriff Pat Garrett and deputies John N. Poe and James Brent.

Pat Garrett, former sheriff of Lincoln County, New Mexico, after his appointment as Collector of United States Customs at El Paso, Texas.

Author's Collection

Jim Courtright, marshal of Fort Worth — "a good man gone wrong."

University of Texas Historical Collection

Arizona Historical Society

Ed Schieffelin (seated at right), discoverer of the Tombstone mines. Al, his younger brother, is seated facing him.

Bisbee National Bank

Allen Street in old Tombstone.

Holiday-makers bound for the big Fourth of July celebration at Bisbee, a booming mining camp twenty-five miles south of Tombstone.

Oklahoma Historical Society

Wyatt Earp — the West's most controversial peace officer — on his eightieth birthday.

Dallas Stoudenmire, the two-gun marshal of El Paso.

Author's Collection

Tom Horn, Apache scout, rodeo champion and range detective. Was he guilty of the crime for which he was hanged?

Western History Research Center, University of Wyoming

University of Texas Historical Collection

Butch Cassidy (lower right) with Harry Longabaugh, Harvey Logan, Will Carver and Ben Kilpatrick, the leading spirits of the Wild Bunch, living it up in Fort Worth following the Wilcox train robbery.

George Denison, vice-president of the Katy railroad, for whom Denison, Texas, was named.

M. K. and T. Railroad

Lee (Red) Hall, former Ranger captain and first sheriff of Denison.

Scribner's Magazine, 1873

Indian Ben Colbert's home on Red River at Colbert's Ferry.

Oklahoma Historical Society

active member of the Prohibition Party, appearing on the platform at Temperance Society and Good Templar rallies.

In the general election of 1880, Kansas had voted an amendment to the state constitution prohibiting the manufacture and sale of intoxicating beverages. For six years the state had been waging a continuing battle for the enforcement of the amendment. When a party of Prohibition officers descended on Dodge City in March, 1886, it was led, of all men, by William Barclay Masterson.

It was incredible! Bat was closing the very saloons in which he had caroused and cavorted for years, smashing kegs and bottles and pouring their unlawful contents into the street!

The curtain was falling on the bibulous Queen of the Cow Towns.

VIII

War in Lincoln County

No OTHER incident in the gunsmoke history of the frontier is better known than what occurred in Pete Maxwell's bedroom at old Fort Sumner on the moonlit night of July 14, 1881, when Sheriff Pat Garrett killed William Bonney, the notorious Billy the Kid.

Since then, innumerable accounts of what transpired that night have found their way into legend, many with added fictional trimmings.[1] But the facts are known and are sufficiently dramatic to require no embellishment.

Prior to the night in Fort Sumner, which ended his career of crime, Henry William McCarty, alias William Antrim, alias William H. Bonney, alias Billy the Kid, had been the object of the greatest manhunt in New Mexican history. Strangely, it was not until after his death that the Territory realized how little it knew about him. It remained for the local grass-roots historians, such as Ash Upson, and the weekly Territorial newspapers to put his story together—not visiting writers.

If the myths and legends that have grown up about him are brushed aside, who was the buck-toothed youngster with the ingenious smile, whom the sun-scorched plazas and mountain trails of New Mexico knew as Billy the Kid? He was born Henry William McCarty, in a Brooklyn, New York, tenement, the son of Henry

McCarty, a longshoreman and water-front sot. There was an older brother named Joseph.

Having the grit of the Irish, Catherine McCarty held the family together, but the senior Henry McCarty was barely in his grave when the Widow McCarty headed west with her boys, determined to find a second husband who would be an improvement on the first.

Old records of the Santa Fe County Clerk's office reveal that on March 1, 1873, Catherine McCarty was married to William H. Antrim. The ceremony took place in the parsonage of the Presbyterian Church, with the Reverend D. F. McFarland officiating. Among the witnesses were the McCarty boys, Henry and Joseph.

We do not know when or where their mother became acquainted with Bill Antrim, or how she chanced to be in Santa Fe. Antrim was a blacksmith by profession. With what appears to have been good judgment, he set out from the Territorial capital with his newly acquired family for the booming mining camp of Silver City in southwestern Grant County, New Mexico, where blacksmiths were in demand.

Antrim is important to this narrative only because fiction, masquerading as history, has pictured him as a family tyrant and wife beater. Allegedly the time came when young Billy—he couldn't have been more than fifteen—put an end to his mother's mistreatment by seizing a shotgun and killing his stepfather, which launched him into his "career of crime."

This is a story that has been hard to put down, although the known facts are proof of its falsity. As recently as fifteen years ago, in the old, neglected cemetery at Silver City, a badly weathered headboard marked the grave of Catherine Antrim. The inscription bore just her name and date of her death: Sept. 13, 1874. Below the inscription someone had carved: "Mother of Billie the Kid."

Cemetery records reveal that Antrim purchased the burial plot and paid for the headboard. Young Billy continued to live with his stepfather for two years or more after his mother's death, which seems to indicate that their relations were amicable. It was not until September 17, 1877, that Billy found himself in difficulty with the law. Near Camp Grant, Arizona, he and Frank Cahill got into an argument. Shots were fired, and Cahill went down mortally wounded. He must have made a statement of what the quarrel was about, for the coroner's jury found that the shooting "was criminal and unjustifiable, and that William Henry Antrim, alias the Kid, is guilty thereof."

Young Billy got out of Arizona as quickly as he could and crossed the Territory back into New Mexico and holed up for a week in Georgetown, twenty miles west of Silver City, a silver camp that was then in bonanza. In Georgetown he teamed up with Jesse Evans, another young desperado of some distinction. Together they headed across New Mexico for Lincoln County, where the pickings were said to be excellent for young men of their persuasion.

The Kid had given himself a new name: William H. Bonney. He had other aliases. It is not known why he preferred to be known as William Bonney. Perhaps it was just because he liked the sound of it. But call himself what he would, the law insisted that he was William Antrim.

For men on the dodge, Lincoln County was a haven second to none. Measured in square miles, it was larger than the state of Pennsylvania and almost completely lawless. Although Billy Bonney and the young desperadoes with whom he was soon running scarcely noticed, it was a beautiful country with its tawny mountains, rushing streams, and rich grasslands stretching away to the horizon. The customs and language of its Spanish-speaking Mexicans had been accepted. But the old prejudices remained. Nowhere was that more evident than among the young cattle thieves and outlaws with whom the Kid rode. Going over the list, one will not find more than one or two Mexicans among them.

Politically, however, because of their number, if for no other reason, the Mexicans exerted a powerful influence on the life of New Mexico. Among them were some competent men. But Washington ignored them and appointed its own catchpoles to administer the local law.

Lincoln, the county seat, was an unimproved one-street town, through which a dirt road curved from east to west. Coming in from the east, it passed Alexander McSween's house on the right and in another hundred yards the John Tunstall store. A bit farther on it wound past the Murphy-Dolan store, a two-story building, the upper floor of which housed the county jail, which was reached by a flight of outside stairs. At the back of the building, and hidden from view by high buckbrush, flowed the little Rio Bonito.

On this short stretch of road, the Lincoln County war was to reach its climax on April 1, 1878.

Let's turn back the clock to the summer of 1877, when William Bonney, soon to be known as Billy the Kid, first appeared in Lincoln and fell in with other young men of his age, some of whom were to be his close associates for the remainder of his brief life. There were Charlie Bowdre and Tom O'Folliard, only a year or two older than he; wild as the broncs they rode and reckless to the point of foolhardiness, their greatest virtue was their loyalty to one another. As the old saying had it, they "cottoned" to the Kid. They liked his style, his engaging smile, and sensed that he could be counted on when the chips were down. Without intending to, they made him their leader.

Many of them were already outside the law—Jesse Evans, Doc Scurlock, and Hendry Brown, to name several. Others were small ranchers, such as Jim Brewer, Frank and George Coe, John Middleton, and Tom Hill. Each nursed a grievance against the Murphy-Dolan-Riley outfit, which had begowked or injured them in one way or another. That was the cement that united them. Nor did it trouble their consciences—when they felt the need for excitement and money—to cut several hundred head of Jingle Bob steers out of John Chisum's immense herds, which were spread out over the grasslands of the Pecos Valley, west and north of the home ranch at the South Spring.

Wherever cattle grazed on the open range, there was rustling, but nowhere else did it reach the proportions that prevailed in Lincoln County in the decade from 1870 to 1880. The Santa Fe *New Mexican* reported in April, 1871, that "thirty thousand head of stolen stock had been driven into New Mexico in the past twelve months." Certainly no fewer than half that number had been taken from New Mexico into the Texas Panhandle, where they were readily sold.

It was not only Chisum's great herds (an estimated hundred thousand) that the cattle thieves were molesting. Across the White Sands plateau, up in the region of San Andres Mountains, Pat Coghlan, the so-called King of Tularosa, was counting his losses in the thousands. But he did little complaining, for he was buying as much rustled stock as he was losing. So was John Chisum. But cow thieves were not welcome at his fortress home at the South Spring. Pat Coghlan, on the other hand, not only offered them his hospitality but drank them under the table and won their money at poker.

The Kid and his companions found this two-way thievery an agreeable and profitable business. The most enjoyable part of it was the two or three days they spent laying over in Tascosa, the lively county seat of Oldham County. Among the Texans with whom they fraternized in Jack Ryan's saloon were three or four who were to become famous lawmen. Sheriff Cape Willingham was among them. Jim East was there. And so were John Poe and lanky, heavy-lidded Pat Garrett, the former buffalo hunter, now taking a turn at cowboying for the old L X outfit, sixty miles down the Canadian.

Poe, a short, quiet man, was no taller than the Kid; affable Pat Garrett, with his soft Texas drawl, at six foot three towered above them. As they drank and gambled and enjoyed the pleasures of Hogtown, down the slope, where the dance halls and the girls were, it could not have occurred to them that in the months ahead they would find themselves cast in the sanguinary role of hunter and hunted in the internecine conflict that, many years later, Frederick R. Bechdolt was to dignify as "the battle between the Warriors of the Canadian and the Warriors of the Pecos." [2]

The first hint that times were changing came that fall, when the Panhandle Stock Association, meeting at Mobeetie, ordered its members "to cease and desist from buying unbranded cattle"— which was only another way of identifying such cattle as New Mexican. They were further instructed not to honor a vented brand, the assumption being that the brand had been changed to conceal the animal's true ownership. This was followed by the organizing of a large party of armed Texans to enter New Mexico and recover, by force, if necessary, any Texas-branded cattle they might find. Jim East was named to head the expedition, numbering twenty men in all, including Pat Garrett and many of the young men with whom the Kid and his companions had wiled away some pleasant hours in Tascosa a few months back.

It was nothing short of a declaration of war. As the invaders began moving down the Pecos Valley, they were watched every mile of the way by Jingle Bob riders. The Texans had not expected to have any difficulty cutting out three or four hundred head of Panhandle stock and getting it started for its home range, but when they had got as far down the Pecos as Bosque Grande without sighting the masses of Longhorns they had expected to find, they could only conclude that Chisum, warned of their coming, had driven his herds off the flatlands into the brakes and canyons on the upper Rio Feliz, where his men-at-arms could protect them.

They were breaking camp the following morning when a horseman was observed jogging toward them. He was still some distance away when Garrett and Jim East recognized him as Frank McNab, the Jingle Bob foreman. They didn't know what his business was, but they admired his guts, riding into them like that with the odds twenty-to-one against him.

89

We don't know what was said or what were the terms of the agreement that was reached, but some sort of an arrangement was worked out between John Chisum and the Panhandle riders, for the latter moved into the South Spring Ranch and joined its defenders.

Alex McSween, Chisum's lawyer-banker, freshly arrived from Santa Fe, was present. He had brought the disquieting news that Jim Dolan had hired as many as forty gunmen, who were then on their way to Lincoln.

That Dolan regarded John Chisum as his most dangerous enemy is not open to question. Murphy had retired from the firm of Murphy and Dolan for reasons of poor health, but Dolan had kept the old firm name and taken John Riley into partnership. To protect himself against lawsuits, he had secretly put his holdings in the name of his lawyer, Thomas B. Catron. In addition to his private practice, Catron was district attorney of the Third Judicial District and on his way to becoming the attorney general of the Territory before he had turned forty.[3]

Jim Dolan's bitter hatred of McSween and Chisum was founded on several factors. McSween was responsible for the presence in Lincoln County of John H. Tunstall, a young Englishman—an innocent, with quaint ideas of honor and honesty—whom he had established on a ranch on the Rio Feliz, fifty miles south of Lincoln. McSween had induced Tunstall to open a rival merchandising business and bank in Lincoln, in partnership with Chisum.

But the hatred went even deeper than that. For years the old firm of Murphy and Dolan had been billing the government for eleven thousand rations delivered monthly to the Mescalero Apache Indian Reservation, ten miles west of town, although an honest count would have revealed that not more than three thousand Indians were quartered there. It was a fraud, running into thousands of dollars, that could have been accomplished only with the active cooperation of F. C. Godfroy, the Mescalero agent. Dolan was haunted by the fear that Chisum and McSween knew the facts and sooner or later would expose him. It would seem to explain why he put his assets in Tom Catron's name.

The attempted showdown with Chisum fizzled when Dolan saw that he was outgunned. A great amount of powder was burned, but it was only fireworks. Like the fabled king who marched his soldiers up the hill and then marched them back down, Dolan stormed back to Lincoln.

Although probably untrue, the story persists that Billy the Kid took part in the siege of South Spring. Actually, he was on the Rio Feliz, working for John Tunstall, of whom he is reported to have said, "He's the only man I ever worked for who treated me square." He may have said it. Certainly he admired the young tenderfoot and perhaps pitied him too, for being a lamb cast among wolves.

Including Tunstall and the Mexican cook and two ranch hands, there were ten men gathered together there on the Feliz. There was the Kid, his pal Charlie Bowdre, Bob Widenmann, John Middleton, Hendry Brown, and Tunstall's neighbor, Dick Brewer. Brewer was an estimable young man; the law had grudges against the others, which did not rest too heavily on them, Lincoln County being what it was.

McSween's troubles began to multiply. He was the administrator of the estate of the late Emil Fritz, consisting largely of the proceeds of a $10,000 insurance policy. McSween refused to turn the money over to the heirs—Mrs. Emilie Fritz Scholand and her brother Charles Fritz—until Dolan made an accounting of what the Dolan firm owed Fritz, who had been a silent partner in that firm. Charged with embezzlement, McSween was freed on bond, but his assets had been attached, including his interest in Tunstall and Company and the Tunstall ranch. There was nothing in legal jurisprudence to justify the action taken by Judge Warren Bristol, but it was to result in tragedy.

On the cold, wind-swept morning of February 18, 1878, a sheriff's posse set out from Lincoln. Commanded by Deputy Sheriff

Jacob B. Matthews, a Dolan-Riley handyman, it numbered no fewer than thirty men, an overly large group to carry out its announced business—to attach the Tunstall ranch. If there were any honorable men among them, who honestly believed that they were setting out on a lawful mission, they were outnumbered by the blacklegs and outlaws with whom they were riding. Seven of them were known killers and outlaws. They were: George Davis, Jesse Evans, Frank Baker, Thomas Hill, George Hindman, William Morton, and Buckshot Roberts.

The previous evening in Lincoln, McSween had learned what the morning would bring, and had dispatched a rider at once for the Feliz to warn Tunstall of what to expect. The rider reached the ranch shortly before midnight. Tunstall took the news calmly, said it was a legal matter, and that he would go to Lincoln in the morning and settle it. Dick Brewer just shook his head pityingly. "I know about these things and you don't. If we start for Lincoln tomorrow and that bunch catches us out in the hills, they'll kill every one of us. They ain't riding this far just to attach a few hundred cows. The thing for us to do is fort up and wait till help comes."

Tunstall wouldn't have it that way.

"He was so green you couldn't talk sense to him," Brewer said later. "The Kid and Bowdre agreed with me that the posse meant to cut him down and every man who stood by him."

Young Tunstall had it his way, and they set out for Lincoln after breakfast, taking a course somewhat to the west to avoid a confrontation.

"Middleton and Widenmann rode with me and Tunstall," Brewer told McSween that evening. "The Kid and Bowdre and Brown followed some distance behind as a rear guard. We were coming through the hills to the Ruidoso about noon, when they stopped us. They pulled up for a minute and then came charging at us hell for leather. I waved to the Kid and the others to come on fast. They did and the Kid said, 'We got to get out of here or they'll kill every man of us.' We turned away from the trail and up the slope into the timber. I thought Tunstall was with us, but I looked back and saw him sitting his horse and waiting. I yelled to him but he did not move. A minute later we heard shooting down there. We saw Tunstall lying in the road. He had been pulled out of his saddle and murdered. We exchanged shots with them before they swung their broncs and disappeared down the trail. I asked the boys who killed him. 'There ain't no doubt about it,' said Middleton. 'It was Tom Hill. He snatched Tunstall's pistol out of the holster and shot him with his own gun.' "

Tunstall's body was brought in the next morning, and after it had been prepared for burial, it was removed to McSween's house for the services that evening. All day long, singly and in groups of two and threes, upward of a hundred men had ridden into Lincoln, among them some prominent Mexican Americans, each with a rifle under his leg. The town was ready to explode, but McSween advised his adherents to hold off, do nothing until Sheriff Brady had been given time to act.

When ten days passed without Brady making a move, Dick Brewer decided that he had waited long enough. He passed the word to Frank Coe, his cousin George Coe, Hendry Brown, John Middleton, and Charlie Bowdre, to meet him at San Patricio, down on the Pecos, on March 4. The Kid and Tom O'Folliard were already at the appointed rendezvous.

When Brewer joined them they looked at him a second time before they could believe what they saw. On his shirt he wore a silver-plated law badge.

"Is that for real?" demanded the Kid.

Brewer nodded. "The law is on our side now."

IX

Years of Violence

CERTAINLY Justice of the Peace John B. Wilson, a long-time anti-Dolan man, knew what he was doing when he deputized Dick Brewer a constable and sent him forth armed with warrants for the arrest of the men named by the coroner's jury as the slayers of John Tunstall. Magically, when he took the oath and Wilson pinned a badge on his vest, he became an arm of the law and his followers a legal posse comitatus.[1]

They had a list of the men they wanted and were heartened by word that came from Chisum that Tom Hill had been killed while attempting to rob a sheep camp in Dona Ana County. In the Pecos bottoms, they surprised Frank Baker and Bill Morton. The pair made a break for it. The Kid got them in his rifle sights and that was all there was to it. That left only Jesse Evans, George Davis and Buckshot Roberts unaccounted for.

From behind the low adobe wall that ran across McSween's front yard to the Tunstall store, Sheriff William Brady and Deputy Sheriff George Hindman were ambushed and killed on the main street of Lincoln on the morning of April 1, 1878. Following the killing of John Tunstall by only a few weeks, it created an even greater excitement. Cash rewards totaling one thousand dollars were posted for the capture, alive or dead, of Billy the Kid, John

Middleton, Charlie Bowdre, Hendry Brown, Frederick Wait, and Jim French, the warrants put out on them charging—on what evidence I cannot say—that they were parties to the slaying of Brady and Hindman.

The various Territorial newspapers reported the killing of the sheriff and his deputy at great length. The Mesilla *Independent* labeled it for what it truly was: "retaliation for the brutal murder of John H. Tunstall."

There is little to applaud in Brady's career as a lawman. The best that can be said for him is that he served his masters, Murphy and Dolan, faithfully. Lawyer Alex McSween, with the backing of John Chisum, the "Cattle King of the Pecos," and others, was challenging the Murphy-Dolan regime, but Brady does not appear to have regarded this challenge seriously, nor realized that he had been marked for extinction. In fact, on the morning he was killed, he was on his way to serve an unimportant attachment on McSween.

Andrew L. (Buckshot) Roberts, a first-class desperado whose gun was always for hire, thought his chances of collecting the reward money were as good as the next man's. He rode into Lincoln on his mule on the morning of April 4, asked some questions, bought a bagful of grub, and headed out of town in the direction of the Ruidoso. A shabby, colorless figure, he appeared to be just another wayfarer drifting through the hills. But it was not by chance that in midafternoon he turned off the trail he had been following for hours and started up the dim trace that led to Blazer's Mill, on the southern edge of the Mescalero Reservation. He was acquainted with the old, long-silent mill and the buildings that had been built there. In town, that morning, he had been tipped off that Constable Brewer and his posse were lying out at Blazer's Mill. What he didn't know was that Dick Brewer had arranged to have that bit of information passed on to him. Hoping that it would fetch him, Brewer and his posse were waiting for him to put in an appearance.

95

It was nearly five o'clock when they saw Roberts coming. Concealing themselves in the row of one-room 'dobes in which the millworkers had been quartered in other days, they waited. Roberts got down from his mule, rifle in hand. Frank Coe confronted him. "We've got a warrant charging you with the murder of John Tunstall," Coe started to say, when a flurry of shooting interrupted him. By accident, a slug shattered Coe's right hand; Middleton was shot in the lungs. Shooting from around the corner of a 'dobe, a bullet from Bowdre's rifle tore through Buckshot Roberts's abdomen, inflicting a mortal wound.

Roberts managed to crawl into the adobe from which Frank Coe had stepped. There was a mattress on the bed. He pulled it to the floor and propped himself up against it. Through the open door he commanded a view of the slope below, strewn with old saw logs. Knowing he was as dangerous as a wounded grizzly as long as he could squeeze a trigger, no one had the temerity to rush him. When an hour and more had passed, Dick Brewer made his way down the slope and attempted to pick him off. Roberts saw him peering over a log and put a bullet squarely between Brewer's eyes.

Whatever authority Dick Brewer enjoyed as a lawman died with him; it was not transferable. No longer could his posse claim legal immunity for their actions. But if they were suddenly only a gang, they had to have a leader. They chose the Kid. After giving Dick Brewer a decent burial, they separated.

Some weeks later the Kid was living at old Fort Sumner. There were four or five warrants out on him, but they did not trouble him. He spoke good cow-pen Spanish and he spent his evenings down in the Mexican quarter, dancing at the *bailes* and playing monte. Once a week or oftener he played poker with Pete Maxwell and Pat Garrett, who was managing Pete's store and cattle.

Several months back Garrett had come up the Pecos from the South Spring Ranch with the Texas crew that had helped John Chisum throw back Dolan and his invading army. They were driving some four hundred head of steers, Chisum's payment for services rendered. Lying over for the night at Fort Sumner, Maxwell had offered Garrett the job of ranch manager, which till that day, neither had found cause to regret.

For twenty-seven days, since the killing of William Brady, Lincoln County had been without a sheriff. In Santa Fe, McSween had been putting pressure on Governor Axtell to appoint someone to fill out Brady's unexpired term. Apparently as much to get McSween off his back as because he felt that ex-judge John N. Copeland had the qualifications for the job, he named him high sheriff. It was a mistake, not only because Copeland was not equal to his task, but also because he was a McSween man and consequently an anathema to the Dolan crowd. It was now Jim Dolan's turn to hasten to Santa Fe and confer with the governor.

Evidence that their relations were friendly is found in the fact that Axtell had recently borrowed $1,500 from Dolan and given his note, payable on demand, as security, which may or may not have tilted their negotiations in Dolan's favor. However, when the governor discovered that Sheriff Copeland, as *ex-officio* tax collector, had not posted bond as required by law, he removed him and replaced him with George W. Peppin, a long-time Dolan-Riley man-at-arms.

George Peppin took office knowing what was expected of him and where he was to get his orders. He tried repeatedly to induce the military at Fort Stanton to take a hand in the Lincoln County war. Colonel Dudley, the new commandant, was similarly disposed, but on several occasions he had been expressly warned by General Hatch, commanding the United States Military District of New Mexico, "not to involve the military in the civilian strife of Lincoln County."

Convinced that the showdown with McSween and his allies was rapidly approaching, Peppin began putting together a contingent of half a hundred gunfighters, among them Jack Long, Marion Turner, Henry, Robert, and John Beckwith, and Bob and

Wallace Olinger. From Dona Ana and Grant counties he imported half a hundred desperados under the leadership of notorious John Kinney. To relieve Dolan of the expense of providing their sustenance and wages, he deputized them, which put the burden on the county.

McSween was not unaware of what was happening. Harassed by lawsuits, his property tied up with attachments, his spirits were at a low ebb. He knew he didn't have the audacity and iron will that he so sorely needed to win the fight in which he was engaged. But he couldn't cut and run without betraying the men who were loyal to him. Depressed, he set out on the long ride to South Spring Ranch, to seek John Chisum's advice and gain strength from him.

Talking to the "King of the Pecos" stiffened McSween. Heading back to Lincoln, ten of Chisum's best warriors rode with him. As they rode along, he was further encouraged when he saw other men joining their ranks—farmers, sheepmen, Mexicans; humble men but armed and resolute, ready to fight McSween's battle because his enemy was their enemy.

Forty-eight hours after he left South Spring Ranch, McSween rode into Lincoln with his followers, half a hundred in all. It was evening. He placed his men as though preparing for a battle; the Mexicans making camp in the high brush along the Bonito and a dozen or more cowboys taking position at the crest of the slope to the rear of his house. Into the house, he crowded a dozen others. Before midnight the Kid, Bowdre, and Tom O'Folliard arrived. They were fighting men and doubly welcome.

Somehow Susan McSween, Mrs. Shields, her sister-in-law, and Ruth Ealy, the wife of a neighbor, got the men fed. Although the house was well supplied for the McSween family, there was not enough to feed half a hundred men. Just before daylight, additional supplies were brought in.

By midnight of July 19, 1878, there were upward of a hundred armed men gathered in Lincoln. Numerically the opposing forces were about evenly divided. However, when measured as fighting men, Peppin's gunslingers had a seemingly overwhelming advantage. Some accounts say there was sporadic shooting throughout the night. If so, it was to no effect.

In the early morning a number of Peppin's deputies rushed the camp on the Bonito where the Mexicans were bivouacked. There was considerable shooting before the Mexicans fled. Peppin's deputies then established their own camp on the Bonito. This made the position of the McSween partisans, who had forted up on the slope above the McSween house, untenable. Any possibility of their charging down the slope without being cut to pieces was gone. After firing a few shots at the unseen enemy on the river, they withdrew. By nine o'clock McSween's forces had been reduced to the score or fewer men who were gathered in his house.

Sheriff Peppin had secured a warrant for the arrest of Alex McSween. In an exhibition of foolhardiness as well as courage, he started up the road, accompanied by John Beckwith, but on reaching the walk that led to the front door of the house he stopped abruptly when he saw half a dozen Winchesters trained on him. After exchanging a word or two, he and Beckwith turned back and retreated to the Dolan-Riley store.

"We had our chance and you let it get away," the Kid is alleged to have stormed at McSween. With his hard practicality it undoubtedly was the way he saw it.

An incident, seemingly unrelated to the battle of Lincoln, occurred half an hour later. Benjamin Robinson, a black trooper belonging to Company E of the 9th U.S. Cavalry, stationed at Fort Stanton, had just tethered his horse at the hitchrail at the Dolan-Riley store, when four shots were fired at him from the general direction of the McSween house, one of which nicked him in the shoulder. It turned the tide of battle in Lincoln Town and Lincoln County. Peppin apparently realized as much at once. He immediately dispatched a letter to Colonel Dudley, informing him that one of his troopers had been shot at and wounded, and imploring him to march into Lincoln with his troops, to "protect innocent women and children."

The only woman or child in Lincoln in need of protection was

Susan McSween, who resolutely refused to leave her husband's side, come what might. Peppin knew it; he also was aware that practically everything consumed at Fort Stanton was being purchased from Dolan-Riley, and that an "arrangement" had been arrived at which the firm and Dudley found mutually profitable. The sheriff was also confident that Colonel Dudley, having been given an excuse for sending his troops into town, would do so at once. His expectations were more than realized. It was not yet eleven o'clock when Dudley, a lieutenant colonel, three captains, half a dozen lieutenants, sixty troopers, one Gatling gun, one howitzer, and a column of ammunition and supply wagons clattered into Lincoln and set up camp in the center of town.

Business came to a standstill as citizens sought shelter. The Gatling gun and howitzer were brought up and trained on McSween's house. There were three women and two children in the building. McSween urged them to leave. Mrs. Shields, McSween's sister, and Mrs. Ealy, the wife of a medical missionary, left; Mrs. McSween refused to go.

Ignoring Sheriff Peppin, Colonel Dudley had taken charge of the situation. He deployed his command and persuaded Justice of the Peace William Wilson to issue John Doe warrants against the men barricaded in McSween's home, charging them with unlawful assembly. Having neither the authority nor the grit to serve them himself, he turned them over to Peppin. The sheriff was as reluctant as he to approach McSween's door and attempt to make an arrest.

Dudley had begun boldly by putting the town under siege, but as the morning advanced, he appears to have had second thoughts about it. His cannon were still trained on McSween's house and presumably could quickly have reduced it to kindling and ended the confrontation. But the big guns remained silent throughout the day. The troopers paraded the street in pairs, their carbines slung over their shoulders. About noon Peppin made an abortive attempt to set fire to the house.

A second try that evening was successful. Dry wood was piled

100

up against the kitchen door and doused with kerosene. In a few minutes, the flames were leaping high. Five men, including Bowdre and O'Folliard, dashed through them and made their escape. After the McSweens had had a few minutes alone together, Mrs. McSween opened the front door and stepped out. A score of rifles leaped to shoulders as she walked across the yard to her sister-in-law's house, resolute, her head held high. Slowly the embarrassed gunmen lowered their rifles, only to snap to attention as McSween walked out, followed by his partisans. He was unarmed. He was killed as he took his first step.

Vicente Romero, Francisco Zamora, and Harvey Morris died with him. Peppin lost only one man, Bob Beckwith. The Kid had leaped out with McSween, and although a volley of shots were directed at him, he reached the 'dobe wall from behind which Sheriff Brady had been killed, leaped over it, reached the Bonito, and escaped unmarked.

The battle of Lincoln was over, but it did not bring peace to Lincoln County, nor to Colonel Dudley, Sheriff Peppin, or Jim Dolan. In an obvious attempt to persuade the people that law and order had been restored, Peppin dismissed all but two of his deputies. Naturally, the men who found themselves cut off from the county payroll objected violently and vented their anger by breaking into the old Tunstall and Company store, which had been padlocked for a month, and made off with boots, blankets, and other wearing apparel to the value of $8,000. They got out of Lincoln with their plunder, and no attempt was made to track them down.

Several weeks after the slaying of her husband, Susan McSween had established residence in Las Vegas, the county seat of San Miguel County, 150 miles north of Lincoln. It caused Jim Dolan some uneasiness when he learned that she had placed her legal business in the hands of Huston J. Chapman, the vigorous stormy petrel of the New Mexico bar.

Chapman had accidentally lost his left arm as a young man, but he boasted that he could accomplish more with one arm than most

101

men could with two. He was both dynamic and fearless. Political hacks feared him because he was addicted to dashing off stinging letters of criticism to the Territorial press. He held Governor Axtell responsible for the troubles in Lincoln County and called for his removal.

Echoes of the storm Huston Chapman was kicking up must have been heard in Washington, for on September 20, 1878, President Rutherford B. Hayes appointed General Lew Wallace to succeed Axtell. Being governor of New Mexico at a miserable salary of $2,400 a year was not the sort of job Wallace felt he was entitled to. His father, David Wallace, had been governor of Indiana. His brother-in-law was former United States Senator Henry Smith Lane. As for himself, he had served with distinction in the Mexican War and again in the Civil War. Many honors had come his way.[2] What he had hoped to receive was an appointment as ambassador or minister to some foreign country, which would give him enough free time to complete the novel on which he was working. (Needless to say, the book was *Ben-Hur*, destined to make him world-famous.)

After cooling his heels in Washington for ten days, hoping for something better to turn up, he entrained for Santa Fe and the West. Three weeks after he became governor of New Mexico, Lawrence Murphy, the ailing former head of L. G. Murphy and Co., and overlord of Lincoln County, was brought to Santa Fe from his Carrizozo Ranch, where he died on October 20, leaving a legacy of violence and lawlessness with which Wallace had to contend. Letters appeared in the *New Mexican* that were sharply critical of him. Lawyer Huston Chapman wrote him personally from Lincoln:

> Loath as I am to criticize you, you are being remiss in your duty, remaining in Santa Fe when you should be here acquainting yourself with the condition of affairs in Lincoln County. The McSween men are willing to stand trial in the proper courts of the

102

Territory, but they will never allow themselves to be arrested by murderers like Col. Dudley and Sheriff Peppin. . . . There is not an honest man in Lincoln who would believe Col. Dudley on oath. He is responsible for the killing of Alexander McSween and should be relieved of his command.

From Judge Warren Bristol (on the other side of the fence for once) came a long letter giving his reasons for not holding the October term of court in Lincoln County:

The Sheriff it seems has either abandoned or been driven from office or duty and taken refuge at Fort Stanton for protection. The prosecuting attorney is absent from the Territory. . . . It is impossible to obtain fair juries whose verdicts will not be tainted with gross partisanship.

The spotlight had shifted away from Jim Dolan and settled on Colonel Dudley. "The Lincoln County War had ruined the Dolan-Riley business," we are told. "Dolan now owned the Carrizozo Ranch and not much else." Sheriff Peppin resigned and went to work at Fort Stanton as post butcher.

On November 15, the governor published his celebrated Amnesty Proclamation. It failed to create any great amount of excitement among the citizens of Lincoln County. However, an ambiguous sentence aroused the ire of Colonel Dudley and his officers. "The foregoing pardon," it stated, "shall not apply except to officers of the United States Army stationed in said County during the said disorders."

In effect it meant that the military was to be pardoned for all alleged offenses against the civilian population. In intemperate letters to the press, Dudley rejected the proffered amnesty as an insult to himself and his staff.

Although Lew Wallace had been governor of New Mexico for well over three months and Colonel Dudley had become his bitter antagonist, the two men had never met face to face. The governor

103

was not familiar with the man's checkered Army career, but his old friend General Edward Hatch, commander of the United States Military District of New Mexico, 1878–1882, was. Dudley had been court-martialed on several occasions before being ordered to Fort Stanton, found guilty, and relieved as post commander at Camp McDowell and again at Fort Union, the charges against him including disobeying the orders of his superiors, insubordination, and drunkenness.

Charging that Dudley was largely responsible for the current unrest in Lincoln County, Wallace, with the prejudiced approval of General Heath, requested Secretary of the Interior Schurz through regular channels to relieve Dudley of his command at Fort Stanton. The request was not only denied but brought a sharp rebuke from Secretary of War W. T. Sherman.

Huston Chapman had been in Lincoln for a week, attending to legal matters in connection with settling the McSween estate and letting it be known that he was preparing an article that would definitely establish Dudley's responsibility in the killing of Alex McSween. At noon on February 18, 1879, as he was standing on the post-office steps, he was shot and killed by two men, identified by eyewitnesses as William Campbell and Jesse Evans, the latter the slayer of John Tunstall. Jake Matthews, a Dolan hanger-on, was in their company when the shots were fired.

Sheriff George Kimball, who had succeeded Peppin, despite the opposition of the Dolan faction, and a deputy were returning to town from White Oaks with a pair of Mexican horse thieves but were forty miles from Lincoln when Chapman was gunned down. However, Chapman's friends dispatched news of his slaying to Wallace at once.

The governor was suddenly in a lather to reach Lincoln as quickly as possible. The following day, with General Hatch riding at his side, he struck out for the south at the head of his little expedition of sixteen cavalrymen, sixty horses and mules, a Gatling gun, and a supply train of ten wagons and three ambulances. Three days later, which was excellent time, considering the miles covered and the conditions of the roads, he established camp on the eastern edge of Lincoln and sent for Kimball at once. The sheriff had been doing his best to take the Kid and Charley Bowdre into custody for the killing of Buckshot Roberts at Blazer's Mill in April, 1878. Wallace was more interested in arresting the killers of lawyer Chapman.

When the three men were reported to be at Dolan's ranch, Wallace requested General Hatch to send a sufficient force to arrest them and remove them to Fort Stanton, where they were to be held under close security until brought to trial. That was done. Simultaneously General Hatch instituted proceedings against Colonel Dudley to remove him from his command. The farce began in March and dragged on until July 5, when Dudley was found innocent of all charges. In the meantime, Evans and Campbell had very conveniently escaped from Fort Stanton. It put a different angle on the secret face-to-face negotiations Governor Wallace had been conducting with William (Billy the Kid) Bonney.

The Amnesty Proclamation had freed the Kid from some of the old indictments against him, but the one charging him with complicity in the killing of Buckshot Roberts was still very much alive. From the several letters that passed between Billy and Wallace and which have been preserved, it is unmistakable that the governor promised the Kid immunity from prosecution if he would testify against the killers of Huston J. Chapman. The Kid took Wallace at his word and surrendered to Sheriff Kimball at San Patricio on March 23. He was taken to Santa Fe.

He testified as agreed, but he did not go free. Judge Bristol ordered the prosecutor to have the Kid bound over to stand trial for the killing of Buckshot Roberts. Bristol further showed his vindictiveness by ordering a change of venue to Mesilla, in Dona Ana County, where he would be more comfortable in his home town and where a pliable jury of Mexicans could be impaneled to guarantee a verdict of guilty.

105

The Kid's lawyer, Ira E. Leonard, fought hard for him and he was tried for the killing of Sheriff Brady, rather than for being party to the killing of Buckshot Roberts. But he was found guilty and sentenced to be hanged on May 13, in the County of Lincoln, "between the hours of 9 A.M. and 3 P.M."

Although the Kid maintained a jaunty air of self-confidence as he was taken back north, he must have realized that his situation was desperate. His old *compadres*, who would have risked their own freedom in his behalf, were beyond helping him. Charlie Bowdre had been killed by Deputy Sheriff Pat Garrett's posse at Stinking Springs, Tom O'Folliard had been cut down in the outskirts of Fort Sumner, and Dave Rudabaugh had fled to Texas. Between Garrett and the range detectives employed by the Panhandle Stock Association, the valley of the Pecos had been sealed off. Garrett had been rewarded by being elected sheriff of Lincoln County.

Lincoln County had bought the old Murphy-Dolan store and, with some slight alterations, had made it the courthouse. The second floor was still used as the county jail. [It was from this room that Frank Coe escaped on the evening preceding the burning of the McSween house.] There the Kid was incarcerated, with Deputy Sheriffs Bob Olinger and J. W. Bell assigned by Garrett to stand guard over him day and night.

If Garrett visited his famous prisoner in the fifty-odd hours he had him in custody, no mention is made of it in the supposedly reliable accounts of what appeared to be the Kid's last hours, even though the two of them had once been friends. Perhaps the sheriff was busy overseeing the building of a scaffold.

We know, however, that about six o'clock on the evening of April 28, Olinger walked across the street to the hotel to eat his supper and to bring back with him the prisoner's supper. This left Bell in charge of the prisoner. Anticipating Olinger's return, Bell foolishly removed the handcuff from the Kid's right hand. It was no sooner done than the prisoner brought the steel cuff crashing down on Bell's head, knocking him unconscious. The Kid got possession of Bell's pistol and killed him. From the closet in which the arms were kept, he secured a rifle and cartridges. Olinger, crossing the road, a tray of food in his hands, heard the shot.

"Bob!" the Kid called to him, and when Olinger looked up, he killed him.

From the landing at the head of the stairs he called down to Godfrey Gauss, the caretaker, and ordered him to get him a steel file and have a saddle horse waiting. Across the road in front of the Wortley Hotel a crowd watched spellbound as Bonney freed himself from his shackles, ran down the stairs, and mounted the horse old man Gauss was holding for him. A moment later, flinging up his hand in a parting salute to the crowd, he raced out of town. It was not until several hours later that Sheriff Garrett and his chief deputies, Tip McKinney and John Poe, returning from San Patricio with two young Mexican horse thieves, learned of Bonney's escape.[3]

There are many photographs of Pat Garrett in existence. Almost without exception they show him as he looked in his early and middle forties, a man with a determined, tenacious face, which makes it difficult to realize that he was scarcely more than ten years older than William Bonney, with whom his name will be forever associated. If he is regarded as one of our great Western peace officers, it is largely because folklore has supplied him with an imperishable antagonist in the person of that super-desperado, Billy the Kid.

Following his dramatic escape from the Lincoln jail, Billy became a hunted man, always on the move, and Garrett and his deputies always somewhere behind him. On July 13, he holed up in Fort Sumner, where he had loyal friends and a girl in whom he was interested.

During the day Garrett was told that Bonney had been seen at Fort Sumner. He couldn't believe it; according to his calculations the Kid was far south in the Poison Springs country. He decided to investigate. Accompanied by Deputies McKinney and Poe, he reached Fort Sumner sometime before midnight. They left their horses in the old peach orchard at the fort and reached Pete Maxwell's house. McKinney and Poe sat down on the porch that ran the length of the building and Garrett walked into the room where Maxwell was sleeping. The two men were talking, according to McKinney, when the Kid came up on the porch. "He was in his stocking feet and carrying a butcher knife. There was a side of beef hanging on the porch. He evidently meant to ask Pete's permission to slice off a piece of it. [This is a supposition but believable.] The shadows on the porch were deep. He spoke to us in Spanish, thinking, I imagine, that we were a couple of Maxwell's hired men."

"I recognized the Kid immediately," Garrett wrote later. "I was sitting on the side of Pete's bed. '*Quién es?*' the Kid demanded anxiously. '*Quién es?*' I half turned and shot him. My second shot was unnecessary." [4]

New Mexico did not realize it at once, but the killing of Billy the Kid marked the end of the era of unbridled lawlessness. The railroads were soon to end New Mexico's remoteness and isolation. As for Billy the Kid, his memory was to remain green, for in all the history of American banditry there are only two others like him —Joaquin Murrieta in California and Jesse James, "our Jesse," in Missouri.

X

The Saga of Jim Courtright

JIM COURTRIGHT was born in eastern Iowa in the early 1840's. Farm-raised, he was skilled in the use of shotgun and rifle, as most young men of his acquaintance were. Adventurous and strongly antislavery, he left home in 1861, crossed the Mississippi River, and made his way to Springfield, where he enlisted in the first regiment of Illinois volunteers being raised by Colonel (later General) John A. Logan. For the duration of the long war, he served on Logan's staff as scout and dispatch carrier. Later they were together in Texas during the Reconstruction period.

Courtright was a tall, lean six-footer. His black hair, which he wore long, and his black eyes and swarthy skin gave him the look of an Indian. Contrary to the experience of most Northerners in Texas, he was well liked. He put in a year cowboying, in the course of which he went up the trail with a herd bound for Wichita. At Red River Crossing, on the homeward journey, a score of men were there, laying over for the night. A foolish, drunken quarrel erupted, in which several trail crews became involved. Two men leveled their guns at Courtright and fired. With a motion so swift that the eye could not follow it, he slapped leather and his single-action Colt coughed twice. That was all that was required. The suddenly sober crowd gazed at the two men

109

sprawled out on the ground and then at Long-haired Jim Court-right. They could appreciate wizardry with a pistol.

A week later in the Lone Star Saloon in Fort Worth, Cal Win-frey, the trail boss of Courtright's outfit, told the group standing at the bar with him, "I've seen some fast draws in my time, but this boy showed me something; he don't have to take second place even for Ben Thompson or young Hardin."

The single-action gun could not be fired until it had been cocked, which was accomplished by thumbing back the hammer. As soon as the hammer was "seated," it was necessary only to squeeze the trigger to fire the weapon. A man's expertise in thumb-ing a gun usually spelled the difference between death and survival.

The Texas Pacific and the Houston and Texas Central railroads had spelled the end of trail driving to the Kansas markets. Fort Worth, always a cattleman's town, was wild and thriving as a major shipping point. Courtright turned back to scouting for the Army in New Mexico and Arizona for a time. After that, he is known to have been employed as a range detective for several stock associations in northern Texas and the Panhandle. Somewhere he had acquired the sobriquet of Hammer-Thumb Courtright, obvi-ously referring to some shooting match from which he had emerged victorious.

He was appointed city marshal of Fort Worth in the spring of 1881. Fort Worth had always been a wide-open town, and the political ring that controlled it wanted it kept that way. Courtright quickly discovered that he had a very narrow path to tread, un-bridled license being only one step removed from lawlessness. But he was bullheaded as well as fearless, and he attempted to run the town without regard to whose toes he stepped on. His popularity with the saloon and gambling element suffered.

"What the politicians want me to do is straddle the fence," he told his friends. "That's not my style."

He proved it by resigning and was at loose ends, when he received a wire from his old friend, Captain Jim Gillette, the famous ex-Ranger, asking him to come to El Paso, where Gillette was city marshal. "I have something lined up for you," read the brief telegram. Two days later, Jim Courtright reached the border town on the Rio Grande across from the sprawling Mexican town that in 1888 was to change its name from El Paso del Norte to Ciudad Juarez, which Americans promptly shortened to plain Juarez.

Both towns were ports of entry, and the value of the merchandise and raw products that passed through customs on both sides of the river was largely responsible for the prosperity of El Paso as well as that of Juarez. The popular conception of El Paso in the 1870's is of a tough, ugly town on the edge of nowhere and separated from the rest of Texas by hundreds of miles of sand, sagebrush, and mesquite.

Its remoteness and the ease with which a man on the scout could slip across the border and find safety in Mexico was exactly what made El Paso attractive to some of its population. However, to the majority of its citizens it represented the true frontier as no other Western community had ever done. El Paso was the commercial and mining capital for most of southern New Mexico and Arizona as well as for a considerable slice of West Texas. As a consequence some bizarre and remarkable characters were to be encountered in its saloons and sun-splashed plazas—none more vocal than fiery Colonel Albert J. Fountain of Mesilla, lawyer, mine owner, and politician.

Before settling in Mesilla, Fountain had been a resident of El Paso County, Texas, and been elected to the Texas state senate. Of him, William Keleher says: "Fountain didn't know much about the law, but was aggressive and never lacked for clients." [1] He attracted wide attention as one of the two court-appointed attorneys to defend Billy the Kid against the charge of murdering Sheriff William Brady, which resulted in the Kid's conviction. It was on Fountain's behalf that Gillette had wired Jim Courtright to come to El Paso. Gold had been discovered in Lake Valley, New Mexico, and Colonel Fountain had joined the rush and struck it rich. Lake Valley had become a wild, booming camp almost overnight, with no semblance of law nearer than Rincon, thirty miles to the east. Ore thieves were making life miserable for mine owners. "It didn't take the Colonel long to get to the point," Captain Gillette recalled later. "I was city marshal and thinking of retiring at the time. I was tired of forever looking down the muzzle of some fellow's gun. But Fountain made me a proposition; he told me if I'd take over at Lake Valley, they'd pay me twice what I was pulling down in El Paso.

" 'No,' " I told him, 'I'm too old to take on the job of bringing law and order to a wild camp like Lake Valley. That's a job for a young man with plenty of starch in his make-up.' He asked me to recommend someone. I thought of Jim Courtright, the ex-army scout. The upshot was that he made me get off a wire to him. Jim arrived in El Paso two days later. They left together for Rincon that evening. It must have been no more than two weeks later that I read in the El Paso *Times* a story from Rincon that Marshal Courtright of Lake Valley had caught two thieves making off with a sack of highgrade ore from the Aztec mine and that in the gun-battle that followed, the thieves were killed."

But like most New Mexican gold camps, Lake Valley's life was brief. The veins pinched out and the inhabitants began to drift away until they were all gone. Courtright had given a good account of himself, but once again he was out of a job.

How and where Courtright spent the last months of 1883 and the first months of 1884 appears to have escaped the written record. It seems likely, however, that he was somewhere in southern New Mexico, presumably employed on a cattle ranch and corresponding with his old friend and military commander, General John Logan. We know that they met in El Paso late in May. This was not a chance meeting; Logan had requested it. He was serving his second term as United States senator from Illinois, and through the nepotism inherent in American politics had become a rich man. Among his investments was his big J L cattle ranch in American Valley, New Mexico.² It was a valuable property, and he was on his way to visit it when he stopped over in El Paso to discuss with Courtright the problem that was facing the range cattle industry everywhere.

From the Canadian border to the Rio Grande, cattlemen were facing the growing menace of the thousands of nesters, who were settling wherever there was living water. Barbed wire had made its appearance, and the nesters, the "sodbusters," were fencing off the streams and water holes without which the vast herds of beef cattle could not exist.

There were two sides to the story. The millions of acres of so-called grasslands were government land, unsurveyed, and to which title could not be had. The cattleman was not interested in owning the land; all he wanted was the use of it. On the other hand, the plowman coveted only a fraction of the grasslands, a choice bit, it is true. By fencing himself in and turning the sod under, he could hope to claim title to it by the right of preemption.

It was the cattleman, not the nester, who had spilled his blood to make the grasslands safe for the white man. But public opinion turned against him, and the epithet "range hog" was invented for him. He struck back and the violence began. Fences were knocked down, cabins burned, and men killed.

"I want you to run the squatters off my range," Logan told Courtright. "There's half a dozen of them. Some will give you some trouble—a couple of Frenchmen named Lalonde. I don't want you to take on this job alone. Can you find a good man in a hurry?"

"Jim McIntire is in town. He worked with me up in the Panhandle a year ago. He'll do."

The three of them took the train north that evening. The following morning they were driven by buckboard to the J L Ranch, west of Rincon. Courtright and McIntire spent a week making

113

themselves familiar with the Logan range and its unwanted inhabitants. By then the squatters were aware that Senator Logan had brought in two gunmen to remove them. As a consequence, when Courtright and McIntire appeared at the Lalonde cabin, there was an immediate argument. There was gunfire. When the smoke cleared away, Giles and Henri Lalonde were dead.

Several days after the burials, there was a mass meeting of farmers, twenty or more, some of whom had ridden a long way to attend. All the talk was of reprisals. Jim Courtright and McIntire heard that warrants charging them with murder had been issued. Had Senator Logan been there, they might not have panicked. But he was on his way back east. Left to themselves, they decided to make a run for it. McIntire evidently went no farther than El Paso; Courtright returned to Fort Worth, where he had friends who would go out of their way to help him.

Jim Courtright walked the streets of Fort Worth without a hand being raised against him. After all, he was the better part of a thousand miles away from the crime with which he was charged. In the past, that much distance meant that you were home free. But it was no longer so; the railroads and the telegraph had bridged the miles. Although Courtright was unaware of it, the law was even then snapping at his heels. Deputy Sheriff Richmond of Dona Ana County had arrived in Austin, armed with warrants for the arrest of Courtright and McIntire and with the necessary papers for their extradition, signed by Governor Sheldon of New Mexico. Texas Governor John Ireland granted extradition and assigned Lieutenant Grimes and Corporal Hayes of the Texas Rangers to assist Deputy Sheriff Richmond in taking into custody the two men named in the warrants.

Undoubtedly the Ranger organization had informed New Mexican officials regarding the whereabouts of Courtright. Richmond, accompanied by Grimes and Hayes, arrived in Fort Worth, and late in the afternoon of Saturday, October 18, put him under arrest.

Word that Courtright had been arrested and lodged in the Tarrant County jail spread quickly, and on the following evening he was to be hustled back to New Mexico to be tried for his life by a prejudiced jury of dirt farmers.

By evening Fort Worth was seething. It was not only Jim Courtright's friends who were threatening to take him out of jail, mount him on a fast horse and get him headed for Mexico; hundreds of others were making war talk, and for no better reason than that they were Texans with a congenital hatred of sodbusters. At suppertime, Richmond and the two Rangers led Jim down Main Street to a restaurant. The crowd, which had followed them from the jail, charged inside. The three officers never had a chance; the shackles were removed from the prisoner's hands; he was given a .45 and a saddle horse.

That he was befriended along the way can be taken for granted. He did not stop running until he was south of the border. The next that is known of him he was in Puerto Barrios, Guatemala, which had a colony of Americans against whom the law had grudges. Life was easy, and he had no difficulty supporting himself with his gambling and taking an occasional turn at tending bar. Some accounts have it that he teamed up with Jim McIntire again. McIntire had been picked up by the Rangers but had managed to escape. He was somewhere in Mexico, but there is little reason to believe that his trail ever crossed Jim Courtright's.

Two or three years passed before Jim Courtright returned to the United States of his own volition and surrendered himself to New Mexican authorities. In any case, during the great railroad strike of 1886, in which a number of the strikers were maimed or killed, he was employed by the Texas Pacific Railroad as a special constable, or strikebreaker, which cost him the goodwill of many of his former friends. As for his participation in the killing of the two Lalonde brothers, he had correctly evaluated his chances of having the old charges against him dismissed; the few witnesses had scattered and the racial climate of New Mexico had changed. The

115

jury could not agree on a verdict and the charge against him was dismissed.

Returning to Fort Worth, he rented a shabby office near the old courthouse and established the T.I.C. Commercial Detective Agency. It didn't take the gamblers long to discover that what Long-haired Jim had for sale was protection rather than detection. For staff, he hired two saloon gladiators who were reputed to be fast with a gun. In response to the campaign of the "reform" element, Fort Worth had recently enacted a stiff new ordinance against gambling. To their great annoyance, professional gamblers were being dragged into court and fined. Courtright offered them protection against such harassment for a weekly fee.

Such well-known saloons as the Maverick, the Lone Star, the Alamo, and the White Elephant either conducted their own games or leased the privilege to a gambler on a concession basis. However that was, they were hard-nosed men, and they resented having to pay tribute to Courtright or being raided if they refused.

A break came when the White Elephant Saloon changed hands and the new owner, a little man of about 150 pounds, a neat dresser, informed big Jim that he didn't propose to pay him or anyone else for the privilege of doing business in Fort Worth.

When Courtright and the new owner of the White Elephant Saloon confronted one another for the first time, it was as strangers. But it has to be believed that Jim Courtright knew that he was dealing with one of the West's celebrated saloonmen and gamblers, a man who had left his mark on Dodge City, riotous Leadville, and Tombstone, where in a street duel witnessed by hundreds he had killed the celebrated gambler Charley Storms. He was none other than Luke Short, friend and associate of the Earp Brothers, the Mastersons, and Doc Holliday.

Courtright realized that unless Short could be made to knuckle under, other gamblers would break away and refuse to continue paying him tribute. That would spell the end of his profitable racket. His hatred of the little man ripened into an obsession with him, and when whiskey loosened his tongue, he told whoever was listening that he was ready for a showdown with Luke.

An air of expectancy hung over Fort Worth. Men who were acquainted with Short by reputation and who knew Courtright from long personal observation were convinced that a shoot-out was inevitable. Although Long-haired Jim Courtright had lost the esteem in which he had once been held, old-timers who remembered his flashing swiftness and accuracy with a six-gun were of the almost unanimous opinion that soft-spoken little Luke, who had often demonstrated that he had ice water in his veins on such occasions, would be no match for him.

So the town waited and held its breath.

About seven-thirty on the evening of February 8, 1887, Courtright walked up to the bar in the Alamo and poured himself a glass of bourbon. He spoke to no one and walked out. On the corner he passed a policeman and exchanged a nod with him. Halfway down the block, he stopped on the sidewalk in front of the White Elephant and spoke to a man who was about to enter the saloon: "Tell the little runt I'm here, and I want him to come out."

The door opened and Short stepped out a few moments later. There was an exchange of angry words. As he stood there, the famous gambler had his thumbs hooked in the armpits of his vest. Almost imperceptibly his hands began dropping to his gun belt. Courtright caught the movement. His right hand flashed to his holster and as he flung it up, his fingers closing about his favorite single-action gun, Short fired. It was a wild shot that would have missed Courtright had it not clipped off the tip of Courtright's thumb as he was cocking his weapon. With catlike swiftness, he tossed his gun from right hand to left. Before he could fire, little Luke had pumped three slugs into him, one of which was fatal.

The crowd that quickly gathered stared in disbelief at Jim Courtright, sprawled in death on the sidewalk. They had not expected the confrontation to end this way. Short appeared to be as surprised as they were.[3]

Jim Courtright is largely forgotten today. The spotlight of publicity never focused on him as it did on Wild Bill, the Earps, and many others. But he deserves his own peculiar niche in the gallery of gunfighters.

XI

Tombstone—
the Legend That Will Not Die

THE Tombstone story has been told countless times, each version usually claiming to be the true story of that boisterous mining camp, high up on the desolate eastern slope of the San Pedro Valley in southeastern Arizona. A few accounts set out bravely to tell an impartial story, only to become mired in the sticky feud that swirled about the Earp brothers—Wyatt, Jim, Morgan, Virgil, and young Warren—abetted always by Doc Holliday, the consumptive little dentist who appointed himself Wyatt's bodyguard.

Whether the Earps were knaves or honorable men is debatable; the important thing is that they were there; if they had not been, the Tombstone story would have very little to distinguish it from the tales of other booming silver camps of Apacheria, that vast region of untimbered desert mountains and scanty rainfall.

On the map of Arizona we find Cochise County in the extreme southeastern corner of the state. The grandfathers of living men knew it as Cochise's Stronghold, for it was from there, in the Chiricahuas Mountains, that Cochise, the great Apache chief, made war on the white man. For ten years no white man entered the

Mules, the Whetstones, the Dragoons, or the Chiricahuas without gambling with his life.

It took a long time for Cochise to realize that he was losing a war that he seemed to be winning: if white men were being killed, so were Indians, and the Apaches could not be replaced. On the other hand, the Army always had fresh troops to throw into the fray.

Cochise sued for peace, and for six years the raiding and butchering ceased. But Cochise, a gaunt old man, died, and two firebrands, Geronimo and young Victorio, took over. The burning and butchering began again. Arizona took on the appearance of an armed camp as the War Department brought in additional regiments of cavalry to put down the uprising. The Apaches fought back doggedly to retain possession of what Eastern newspapers mistakenly referred to as their homeland. Actually, the Apaches had originally hunted buffalo on the Llano Estacado and had been pushed west of the Pecos by their more numerous and powerful neighbors, the Comanches. If they fought to retain their new home in Arizona, it was because they had nowhere else to go.

Cochise was no longer among the living when Ed Schieffelin, the future hero of Tombstone, prospected in the San Pedro Valley in the fall of 1877 and made camp at a place known as Goose Flats, two miles west of where Tombstone was to rise. All he had to show for his summer's work were a few samples of silver float. He wasn't a mining engineer, nor even an assayer, but he was convinced that some of his samples were rich in silver content.

On Goose Flats there was an old adobe that marked the site of the abandoned Brinckow Mine. Schieffelin had once worked as a guard at the Brinckow for William Griffith, its eccentric owner. Ed had been making the old adobe his headquarters. His grubstake was gone and so was his money, and he was packing his burro one morning, preparatory to setting out for Tucson, when Griffith and the two prospectors who had been working for him chanced to pass. They stopped to exchange a word or two. Griffith suggested that the four of them travel together. Schieffelin accepted the invitation.

It was a seventy-mile walk to Tucson, and Ed could not resist showing his ore samples. It was the verdict of Griffith and his party that the samples were of dubious value. However, court records reveal that Griffith, on September 3, 1877, recorded a mining claim known as the Tombstone in his and Schieffelin's name. Griffith appears to have lost interest in the Tombstone immediately thereafter, and his name does not occur in connection with it again.

Ed spent his last thirty cents for tobacco and set out for Globe, where his brother Al was working at the Silver King Mine, bumming handouts along the way. In Globe, further disappointment awaited him; Al had left the Silver King and moved across the Territory to the McCracken Mine at Signal. Half starving, Ed went to work for daily wages in the Silver King. A few weeks later, back in funds again, he left Globe and set out for the booming camp at Signal. It was one of the luckiest moves he ever made.

Al Schieffelin was several years younger than Ed. For seven years the brothers had roamed the mining camps from California to Arizona, prospecting wherever the country appeared to be mineralized. They had nothing to show for those rugged years and the privations that had been their lot. Both were practical hard-rock miners, and when the need arose, they had always been able to find jobs to tide them over. But Al was finished with prospecting, with chasing rainbows. Ed knew it, and the two of them had been working at the McCracken Mine for several months before he mentioned his precious samples to his brother. Al at first waved them aside as worthless, but finally agreed to ask Dick Gird, the McCracken's mining engineer, to run an assay on them.

Gird was still young but already established as a competent, highly paid mining engineer. When he got around to assaying Ed's samples, his boredom vanished as he calculated the results. "The values run as high as two thousand dollars a ton," he told the excited brothers. "Where did you get this stuff?"

121

"I won't tell you where," Ed said. "But I'll take you there."

Without the scratch of a pen to verify their agreement, a deal was made. Gird quit his job, put up the money for a grubstake, and began putting together the expedition that was to take them to the valley of the San Pedro. In February, 1878, they left Signal and disappeared into the wilds. An engineer of Gird's standing could hardly throw up his job and head out of camp for an undisclosed destination, accompanied by two seasoned prospectors, without setting rumors flying. But they were neither spied on nor followed.

The light spring wagon in which they traveled made the long journey fairly comfortable. On the rocky bastions of the Mules and the Dragoons the last of the winter snows had not yet disappeared; down below, the normally sun-scorched world was temporarily green. Soon the Apache would be raiding again, but the Third United States Cavalry was slowly but surely taking the sting out of them. Handling the reins with the unerring instinct of a homing pigeon, Ed Schieffelin piloted the little party back to Goose Flats.

Taking possession of the old adobe, they made it their permanent headquarters and began working up the valley. They opened the Tombstone, Ed's original find, only to discover that the vein of silver was pinching out. Eventually they disposed of the claim for as little as $10,000. But they made other strikes—the Tough Nut and the Contention, and capped it with the fabulously rich Lucky Cuss, which was assayed at $15,000 to the ton. When news that a strike of bonanza proportions had been made went flying across Arizona on the wings of the wind, it brought Anson Safford, financier and former governor of the Territory, hurrying to Goose Flats. For a one-quarter interest in the claim, Safford agreed to furnish the money for building a reduction mill and to raise the capital to develop the mines. The Tombstone Mining and Milling Company came into existence, and the Schieffelins and Gird suddenly found themselves wealthy men.

The rush to the San Pedro had begun. On Goose Flats a tent,

adobe, and wickiup town began to take shape. Some unknown dreamer gave it the name Watervale. But such nonsense was soon cast aside and it was renamed Tombstone, which, considering its bleak appearance, was more fitting. By the end of the year Tombstone had a population of eight hundred. The nearest timber was in the Huachucas. The logs were dragged down to the San Pedro, where a primitive sawmill whipped them into building lumber. Roads that had been trails a few months back were cut into tawny dust by the traffic from Tucson and the west.

The Territory was sparsely populated; no Arizona town or mining camp had yet heard the lonely wail of a steam locomotive. If a man wanted to go to Tombstone, he got there by saddle, wagon, or on foot. But however limited the means of transportation, when the Pied Piper sounded his call of gold or silver, men dropped whatever they were doing and hit the trail. It had always been so, and Tombstone was no exception. Without any choice in the matter, it gathered unto itself an amalgam of honest men, thieves, gamblers, desperadoes, and whores.

Keeping the growing camp supplied with food was no problem. Meat was plentiful, and it was cheap. Mostly it was Mexican beef that had been rustled south of the border and run into Arizona. In addition, local cattle were being marketed. They came from Sulphur Spring Valley in the Mules and from the Dragoons, where grama grass grew stirrup high. But ranching in a country that had no vestige of law and was menaced daily by murderous Apaches was a precarious business. The half a hundred or more engaged in it were hard, desperate men. They had previously done their carousing at such pinpoints of civilization as Galeyville and Charleston, but by the fall of 1879, Tombstone, with its saloons, its gambling, its canvas-roofed theater, and its red-light district had become their fun town.

When Wyatt Earp left Dodge City in the fall of 1879, his announced destination was Las Vegas, New Mexico. It proved to be only a stopover; he was bound for Tombstone. Doc Holliday caught up with him at Las Vegas and accompanied the Earp party to the booming camp at Goose Flats. In addition to Holliday, the group included Jim, the eldest of the Earp brothers, and Warren, the youngest. Wyatt handled the reins and chose a course that followed the future Atlantic and Pacific Railroad right-of-way.[1]

At Holbrook, Wyatt struck off to the southwest and on reaching Prescott found his brother Virgil waiting to accompany them to Tombstone. Obviously this was by prearrangement. Virgil had mining claims east of Prescott and had been doing some work on them. They appeared to be worthless, so it could not have been difficult to persuade him to join the expedition to Tombstone.

The only one of the Earp brothers still missing was Morgan. We have Wyatt's word for it that Morgan was in Butte, Montana, where he was on the police force, and that he (Wyatt) had urged him to throw up his job and join him at Tombstone, which Morgan did. That this gathering of the clan had a purpose seems indisputable. What seems to have been a clue to Wyatt's plans appears in the fact that on leaving Prescott he did not strike out on the much shorter route to Tombstone, via Globe, but drove south to Tucson.

Earp presented himself to Charles Shibell, sheriff of Pima County. Although Shibell was not acquainted personally with his visitor, it can be taken for granted that he knew him by reputation. Although there is no evidence to prove it, I believe that the former assistant town marshal of Dodge and Sheriff Shibell had exchanged letters and that Wyatt knew the job of deputy sheriff of Pima County, with headquarters in Tombstone, would be offered to him when he reached Tucson. In the southeastern third of sprawling Pima County, there was no official empowered to enforce the law, issue licenses, and collect taxes. It was tax collecting in which Shibell was interested. From what he knew of Earp, he believed he was the man for the job.

On December 1, 1878, Deputy Sheriff Earp and his little party drove into booming Tombstone, where hammer and saw were busy from sunrise to sunset. The raw little town was beginning to show promise of eventually amounting to something. The business community had established a town board and charged it with designating property lines and aligning the principal streets. It was already obvious that Allen Street was to be the camp's principal thoroughfare, with the most valuable location being the intersection of Allen and Fifth streets, where the Oriental Saloon occupied the northeast corner and the Crystal Palace Saloon the northwest corner.

Tombstone's spectacular growth continued throughout 1880. It had passed the five-thousand figure and was still growing. As deputy sheriff and tax collector, Wyatt had become well acquainted with the outlaw and rustler element; he didn't bother them, and they did not bother him. Virgil Earp had been appointed chief of police and had named his brothers Morgan and Warren as constables. Jim Earp, a half brother, who was ailing, had left Arizona for Colton, California, then a village near San Bernardino, where his parents and a sister were making their home.

Two competing stage lines had been established, running from Tombstone to Tucson, and transporting passengers and bullion. Holdups occurred less frequently after Wells, Fargo put its fast stages on the run. The company built relay stations and sent its coaches over the road with shotgun guards on the box with the driver. Wells, Fargo offices were opened in Tombstone and Charleston, and experienced men were brought in to manage them and undercover agents to gather information on the road agents. Superintendent Valentine came to Tombstone and hired Wyatt to ride shotgun when a particularly large amount of bullion was going through.

The advance information Earp began to receive from the Wells, Fargo agent not only alerted him to be ready to go out on a run but told him where other stages, proceeding with only one guard aboard, might be stopped and robbed with little chance of running into serious trouble. For years many of Earp's detractors have charged him with being the mastermind responsible for many of the holdups on the Tombstone-Tucson run, which may or may not have been true. Certainly in his lifetime he was a controversial figure, arousing extremes of loyalty in some men and bitter hatred in others.

The Southern Pacific Railroad, building eastward from California, put its first train into Tucson on March 17, 1880. Seven months later the S.P. rails reached Benson, twenty-five miles down the valley from Tombstone.[2] The little village of Benson boomed with the transition from stage station to rail point; Tombstone hailed the event as of monumental importance, its escape from isolation—which it was. Its two newspapers, *The Nugget* and *The Epitaph*, agreed (which they seldom did) "that Tombstone's preeminence as the commercial and financial capital of southeastern Arizona is assured." With newcomers rushing in at the rate of a hundred or more a day, John P. Clum,[3] owner and editor of *The Epitaph*, assured his readers that before the end of the year the population of Tombstone would pass the ten-thousand mark.

For the better part of a year, Tombstone had had what it called a town government, complete with a mayor, councilmen, a chief of police, and other functionaries, including a justice of the peace—all operating without legal credentials, for Tombstone was still without a charter. Pima County finally got around to granting one in November, and Tombstone became an incorporated city of the third class. An election was held in January. The town government continued in office, the only important change being that it was not legally empowered to assess and collect taxes. Virgil Earp was kept on as chief of police.

In January, 1881, half a dozen rich Tombstoners were in Prescott, entertaining legislators and spreading money around where it would do the most good. They evidently spent wisely, for a bill slipped through the legislature creating the new county of Cochise by clipping off the eastern third of Pima County. It created wild rejoicing in Tombstone and dismay in Tucson.

Cochise County, named for the old Apache chief, had to have a government before it could begin to function. Eleven months passed, however, before an election was held. The legislature appointed a set of temporary officials to conduct the county's business. In the meantime, Wyatt Earp wanted to retain his lucrative position as deputy sheriff but was forced to relinquish it to John H. Behan, a professional politician for whom the Democrat-controlled legislature could always find a job.

It marked the beginning of the long, bitter Earp-Behan feud that in its final stages was to be decided in Johnny Behan's favor. As to who was right and who was wrong there are two opinions, and they will never be reconciled. One thing is certain: Behan was not the corrupt weakling, allied with the rustler-outlaw element, that Earp makes him out to be. Nor is there sufficient evidence presented to confirm Behan's repeated charge that the real purpose of the war the Earps were making on known blacklegs was to screen their own outlawry.

Wyatt's prospects brightened when Crawley P. Duke, United States marshal for Arizona, appointed him deputy marshal for southeastern Arizona. It seems rather obvious that the appointment had been engineered by Wells, Fargo to strengthen its hand during the period of transition in Cochise County.

"I supported Behan in the election of '82," says Wyatt. "We had reached an understanding. If he was elected he was to appoint me deputy sheriff. He won, but I didn't get the appointment."

We have to take Earp's unsupported word for this bit of skulduggery. That is almost invariably true of most of his statements. It was never his way to see both sides of the coin. Billy Breakenridge became deputy sheriff, and the consensus is that he was a good one, despite being accused by the Earp faction of being the tool of the outlaw element.

Bat Masterson and Luke Short, who had been dealing faro in the Oriental, decided that they had had enough of Tombstone. Bat went to Denver and little Luke to Fort Worth and his confrontation with Long-haired Jim Courtright. Wyatt must have regretted their leaving. He had bought an interest in the Oriental and made it his headquarters.

Unquestionably Tombstone was the most violent of all Western mining camps. Even the thousands of miners and mineworkers, a large percentage of them stalwart Cornishmen, interested primarily in the good wages they were earning, were drawn into the conflict. Today, almost a hundred years later, it is the violence, the blood-letting and killings that occurred on its streets, reaching its climax in the famous Battle of the OK Corral, that holds the public's attention. It really was not much of a "battle" until motion pictures and television transformed it into a supersaga of the West that has been subject to many repetitions.

It has been estimated that at least three hundred desperadoes were living in Cochise County at that time. George W. Parsons, one of the founders of the Law and Order Party and a friend of the Earps, notes in his diary on April 30, 1882, "In the past ten days fourteen murders have occurred on the streets of Tombstone, Charleston and Contention City." Judging by the newspapers, this figure seems accurate.[4] However, columns of *The Epitaph* and *The Nugget* indicate that very few so-called law-abiding citizens were being killed; it was the outlaws, quarreling among themselves and settling their differences of opinion with gunfire, who were populating Boot Hill.

They were split up into factions, each with its own leader. Only two or three could command the loyalty of all. Among the latter was N. H. (Nick) Clanton, known even in death as Old Man Clanton, to distinguish him from his three sons, Ike, Phin, and Billy. He was an experienced rustler, smuggler, and all-around outlaw. On his ranch in Sulphur Springs Valley, rustled cattle were held and rebranded before being sold. Raiding across the Mexican border and cutting out anywhere from a hundred to three hundred head of cattle and driving them down the San Pedro River was a highly profitable business. An even more lucrative operation was to

128

waylay Mexican bandits running silver coin out of Sonora into Arizona.

On such ventures Old Man Clanton usually had as many as ten men riding with him, including, in addition to his sons, notables such as Johnny Ringold (or Ringo), Curly Bill Broscious, Buckskin Frank Leslie, young Billy Claiborne, and one or both of the Mc-Lowry brothers, Frank and Tom.

He was so uniformly successful in his raiding that he never had any difficulty recruiting men to ride with him. They included, among many others, characters such as Pony Deal, Zwing Hunt, Rattlesnake Bill Johnson, Hank Swilling, Pete Spence, and Florentino Cruz. But success was responsible for their undoing. Not satisfied with capturing a silver train, they killed the smugglers and were celebrating their victory when a large party of Mexicans caught them in Skeleton Canyon.

Most accounts agree that a dozen men, including Mexicans, died that afternoon in Skeleton Canyon. Old Man Clanton was one of them. His sons survived him and with appropriate ceremonies saw him buried in Tombstone's Boot Hill two days later.

Among the cowboy outlaws were three or four individuals—Curly Bill Broscious, Johnny Ringo, Frank Leslie, even Ike Clanton—who might have been expected to bid for leadership of their kind. That did not happen. Why? Because even though they hunted in packs, their overriding loyalty was to themselves, for at heart they were loners.

XII

The Last of the Fighting Earps

In 1931, shortly after publishing his sensationally successful *Wyatt Earp: Frontier Marshal*, which lifted Earp from obscurity to fame, Stuart N. Lake was quoted as saying: "For the last seven months of his life, I was with Wyatt part of every day. He was eighty-three. We began the morning by reading what I had written the previous evening and making the minor changes on which he insisted."

Earp died in January, 1929. The book was not published until two and a half years later. The strongest evidence exists that he never saw the manuscript and that he was not acquainted with its contents. Lake says so himself in a letter threatening legal action against the publishers of *The Colorado* in the popular Rivers of America Series, stating that "Wyatt never dictated a word to me, never saw a word of my writing and died two years before the book was published."

Although Lake destroys the credibility of the book, it remains the yardstick by which the Fighting Earps of Tombstone, real or mythical, must be measured.

On the night of March 15, 1881, a Kinnear and Company stage rolled out of Tombstone, bound for Benson and the railroad. Popular Bud Philpot was handling the reins of the six-horse hitch. Rid-

130

ing shotgun with him was Bob Paul, former deputy sheriff of Pinal
County. The night was cold, and snow covered the ground. In
addition to the eight passengers crammed together inside the coach,
a ninth traveler, Peter Roerig by name, rode up on top in the
dickey seat.

In the steel Wells, Fargo treasure chest, bolted to the floor, was
$8,260 in specie—not the $60,000 in silver bullion that some accounts have it.

On reaching the foot of the long climb at Drew's Station, Philpot pulled up the team momentarily and changed seats with Bob
Paul so Bud could warm his hands. It was to cost him his life, for
as the team reached the crest and slowed to a walk, four masked
men stepped out of the shadows cast by the high mesquite. Rifles
raised, they called on Bob Paul to pull up. Paul, instead of comply-
ing, lashed the horses with the reins, and the frightened animals
topped the rise and were disappearing down the far slope when the
road agents unleashed a blast of gunfire that killed Philpot and
mortally wounded Roerig. As Bud pitched forward, he knocked
the reins out of Paul's hands. The latter stepped on the pole and
recovered them. The team was still running when he rolled into
Benson, from where, by telegraph, he notified Deputy United
States Marshal Earp and Sheriff Behan of the holdup. By daylight
the region around Drew's Station was swarming with deputy marshals and sheriffs.

Reading the various accounts of life in Cochise County in the
early 1880's, one can only conclude that such holdups were com-
monplace; something one had to live with and that could quickly
be forgotten. Not in this instance, however, for the incident resulted in wholesale accusations and charges that were to end in the
political warfare that finally sent the Earps fleeing from Arizona.

Although Sheriff Behan and Marshal Earp were working at
cross purposes, they agreed on one thing—that four Clanton followers, Bill Leonard, Jim Crane, Harry Head, and Luther King,
who had spent the evening of the holdup at a nearby adobe, were

131

involved in the crime. There followed ten days of frantic riding, with one posse spying on the other and getting in the other's way. When the posses returned to Tombstone, apparently having accomplished nothing, the wanted men were safely across the border in Mexico.

An ugly rumor implicating Doc Holliday in the attempted holdup got into circulation, spread unquestionably by the Behan faction. John Slaughter, ex-Confederate soldier, ex-Texas Ranger, trail driver, and the most important cattleman on the San Pedro, was alleged to have said that he had seen Holliday racing across his range shortly after midnight on the night of the attempted robbery. Slaughter denied having said it, but the tale spread. Sheriff Behan began an investigation that turned up the incriminating fact that Holliday had left Tombstone on a rented horse that afternoon and had not returned until sometime after midnight.

Behan placed him under arrest. Judge Wells Spicer heard the case against him. Eventually Doc was acquitted, but looking back, it is obvious that the bloody battle for control of Cochise County had begun. Sheriff Behan surrounded himself with known outlaws and desperadoes and deputized them as undersheriffs; Deputy U.S. Marshal Earp, with the support of the Law and Order League and *The Epitaph*, put together a formidable force, including his brothers Warren and Morgan and City Marshal Virgil Earp.

On the night of March 22, 1881, Earp and his posse bivouacked several miles east of town and at daybreak began a sweeping search of the San Pedro Valley, hoping to make contact with a large party of Behan men, captained by Curly Bill Broscious. They put in thirty-five miles of riding without catching sight of them. It was after dark when Earp and his followers warily approached the water hole at Iron Springs, their intention being to spend the night there if they found they had the place to themselves. Earp had dismounted and was leading the way, his right arm looped over the bridle reins, his shotgun at the ready. He was within thirty yards of the water hole when a man reared up out of the brush and covered him with his double-barreled gun.

"There was light enough left for me to recognize him," says Wyatt. "He was Curly Bill. He fired first, one ball scratching me. I squeezed both triggers and he got the full blast. I knew I had killed him. There was a wild scramble as Pony Deal, Frank Patterson, Frank Stillwell, Rattlesnake Bill Johnson, the Hicks brothers and two or three others leaped into the saddle and got away."

The marshal's losses amounted to one man slightly wounded and one horse killed. Pony Deal took over for Curly Bill, but after a brief skirmish they withdrew. With the coming of daylight, Curly Bill was buried where he fell. In his time he had killed eleven men. "In his loss," says historian John Myers Myers, "outlawry in Cochise County received a blow from which it never fully recovered." [1]

October 26, 1881, began as many others did in Tombstone at that time of the year—with the skies overcast and a cold, raw wind whipping down from the Whetstones. A larger number than usual of known and suspected desperadoes was in town. They had been riding in throughout the morning. In violation of the law, all were armed. City Marshal Virgil Earp made no attempt to disarm them as they roved up and down Allen Street, drinking in the Crystal Palace, the Oriental, and the Grand, but avoiding Hafford's saloon at the corner of Allen and Fourth streets, a popular Earp stronghold.

Ike Clanton, who did most of his fighting with his mouth, had appointed himself leader of the group and, as usual, was making some wild threats to the effect that if the Earps wanted a showdown, they could have it. If he was bidding for reinforcements, his inflammatory talk failed to produce them, even though by noon a dozen or more gunslicks of the caliber of Buckskin Frank Leslie and Johnny Ringo were in town and on the alert. At full strength, Ike's party consisted of himself, his younger brother Billy, Tom McLowry, Frank McLowry, Billy Claiborne, and Wes Fuller, the latter a doubtful addition, for he promptly disappeared when the lead began to fly.

In Spangenberg's gunshop the men bought additional arms and

ammunition, a fact with which the town became quickly acquainted. Using the passageway through the stables of the OK Corral, they rendezvoused in the corral yard that opened on Fremont Street, which paralleled Allen Street. On the left side of the yard there was a one-story building occupied by an assay office and the photographic studio of F. C. Fly.

At this point in time it was the obvious duty of City Marshal Earp to deputize as many men as he thought necessary and proceed to the OK Corral and take the armed men gathered there into custody. Instead, he limited himself to conferring briefly with Sheriff Behan, requesting him to accompany him to the corral and to assist him in arresting the rustlers. Behan refused to go, agreeing, however, to demand that they surrender their arms. This, of course, they refused to do.

Although the pro-Earp faction has always insisted that the showdown that followed was forced on Wyatt and his brothers, the evidence says otherwise. It was about two o'clock in the afternoon when the three of them stepped out of Hafford's saloon and started walking up Fourth Street in the direction of Fremont. They had gone only a few yards when Doc caught up with them. He was indignant at having been left behind. He was wearing a long black overcoat and carrying a cane. Virgil took the cane and handed him a Wells, Fargo shotgun. All four were tall men, dressed in black. They were a sinister-looking group.

On reaching Fremont Street, they left the sidewalk and took to the middle of the street. Wes Fuller saw them coming. He gave the alarm and fled. Behan was in the yard. He took refuge in Fly's studio. Billy Claiborne was only a step or two behind him, having suddenly decided that he wanted no part of Ike Clanton's troubles. With the first shot fired, Ike tossed away his pistol and ran up to Wyatt crying, "I ain't armed! Don't shoot!"

"I told him the fight had begun; either to get into it or get out," Earp declared later.

Ike didn't wait to hear more. Running to the opening that led through the stables, he reached Allen Street and disappeared. It left only Frank McLowry, his brother Tom, and Billy Clanton to do the fighting.

The battle that ensued was brief, but it was deadly. According to witnesses—and there were many—it didn't last more than a minute, which differs radically from the fight at the OK Corral as presented on the screen and on television. There were no screaming, wounded horses tearing about the corral; no dying men futilely trying to work their empty guns. Huddled on the ground were Billy Clanton, Frank and Tom McLowry, as dead as they were ever going to be. As for the aggressors, a slug had scratched the back of Doc's neck; Virgil had a bullet in his right arm; Morgan had been shot through the shoulder.

Their injuries were painful but not serious. If they had been marked for destruction prior to the OK Corral shoot-out, it became doubly certain in its aftermath. Tombstone stood divided, as it had never been before. On the surface, the tension that gripped the town was not apparent, but among the several thousand men who made the nightly rounds of the Allen Street saloons or crowded into the Bird Cage Theatre or attended the performances at Schieffelin Hall, there were few who hadn't taken sides.

City Marshal Earp was back on the job several weeks later. As he was making his rounds on the evening of December 28, he was ambushed in front of the Cosmopolitan Hotel. A blast of buckshot felled him with a shattered left shoulder. He was carried into the hotel and eventually recovered but never regained full use of his left arm. In the election of January 3, 1882, Dave Neagle replaced him.

Wyatt accused Ike Clanton, Frank Stillwell, and Hank Swilling of the attempted slaying of his brother. If he had any evidence to that effect, he never produced it.

Warren Earp decided to leave Tombstone to go to work as a stock detective for the Arizona Cattlemen's Association, with headquarters at Lordsburg. With Virgil still incapacitated, it left Wyatt with only his brother Morgan to turn to. But that was not to be for long.

On the night of March 18, after attending a performance of *Stolen Kisses* at Schieffelin Hall, Wyatt returned to his hotel and Morgan went to Campbell and Hatch's pool hall, where he had arranged to play a match game of billiards with Bob Hatch. The game had just begun when Wyatt walked in and took a chair along the wall to watch the play. In response to a hunch that Morgan might be in trouble, he had changed his mind about turning in for the night.

A door whose upper half was of glass led to an alley at the rear of the pool hall. Anyone standing there could peer into the pool hall with little chance of being seen.

Morgan was chalking his cue and watching Bob Hatch make a difficult billiard when the glass top of the door was shattered. The glass had not stopped falling when two heavy revolver shots were fired, the first slug passing through Morgan and fatally wounding another spectator. Wyatt leaped across the room, but as he struggled to open the door, the sound of running horses told him that the assassins were gone.

Wyatt dispatched two friends to the Cosmopolitan Hotel to fetch Virgil to the pool hall. Morgan was dead when Virgil got there. Wyatt made a hard decision. "Virg, you'll have to leave town. Tell Allie to get ready. We'll take the noon train tomorrow for California. I'll go with you as far as Tucson." [2]

The coroner's jury named Pete Spence, Frank Stillwell, one John Doe Freeze, and a character named Indian Charlie as the probable slayers of Morgan Earp.

For what moral support his presence might supply, Doc Holliday insisted on making the trip westward with Wyatt. They sat in the same coach with Virgil and Allie but, for safety, not together. Adding to the grimness of the occasion was the knowledge that in the baggage car Morgan Earp was making his last journey.

Just before dark the train was stopped a few miles east of

Tucson, and Deputy United States Marshal Joe Evans of Pinal County came aboard. He informed Wyatt that Pete Spence and Frank Stillwell had been in Tucson all day and had been joined within the past hour by Ike Clanton and Hank Swilling.

It being before the introduction of dining cars, the train stopped an hour for supper at Tucson. Wyatt and Doc took up vantage points on the station platform and did not enter the dining room. Through the dining-room windows they watched Virgil and his wife eating supper. Night had fallen when Wyatt put Virgil and Allie aboard the waiting train and said his good-byes. Standing on the car platform before swinging down, he saw, in a reflected beam of light from the locomotive, four men crouching down behind some barrels. Wyatt was armed with a double-barreled shotgun. As he leaped to the platform and ran toward them, they parted and fled. He took after the nearest. It was Frank Stillwell.

When Stillwell found himself cornered, he whirled around to face Wyatt. He was armed, but he did not jerk his guns.

"I let him have both barrels," Earp admitted to Colonel William Herring, his attorney, the following morning. "They almost tore him apart. I have no regrets; I know I got the man who killed Morg."

Herring has left a good account of his meeting with Earp. "That he meant to go after Ike Clanton, Spence and Swilling was uppermost in his mind. 'Wyatt,' I told him, 'you are already in serious trouble. Stillwell was killed in Pinal County. That crowd over there will make something of it. Warrants will be put out and Sheriff Bob Paul will be over here to take you into custody. Once they get you behind bars, they won't let up on you.'"

Johnny Ringo's body was found in a motte of oak trees in Turkey Creek Canyon, in the foothills of the Chiricahuas on the morning of July 14, 1882. He had been on a week-long drunk when he disappeared, which suggested that he might have committed suicide. That theory was abandoned when his Winchester, fully loaded, was found leaning against a tree a few yards away.

His revolver was in the holster and had not been discharged. His horse was not in evidence and the body, in a sitting position, was propped against a tree trunk. Death had resulted from a bullet that had passed through the left side of the head.

Suspicion fell at once on Buckskin Frank Leslie and John O'Rourke, the latter better known as Johnny-behind-the-deuce, a tinhorn, minor-league gambler. The nature of the crime fitted the latter and was a cut below what might have been expected of Buckskin Frank. In any case Johnny Ringo was dead, and outlawry in Cochise County had received another staggering blow.

Ignoring Herring's warning that he might suddenly find himself in difficulties over the killing of Frank Stillwell, Marshal Earp, at the head of a posse of five men, had been scouring the San Pedro Valley and the mountains to the east and west of Tombstone, looking for Ike and Phin Clanton, Frank Spence, and the half-breed Florentino Cruz. Out of grub, their horses saddle weary, they had been forced to return to town without having made contact with the men they were hunting.

Bad news awaited Wyatt. Pinal County had finally got around to issuing warrants charging Doc and him with killing Frank Stillwell. Pinal County, and especially Tucson, had never forgiven Tombstone for dividing the county and relegating Tucson to second place in county affairs.[3]

"I advised Wyatt and Doc to get out of Arizona before Sheriff Bob Paul could serve the warrants he had in his possession," Herring recalled some years later. "They left the Territory in a matter of hours. Warren went with them. Shortly thereafter it became common knowledge that they were living in Gunnison, Colorado."

Papers for their extradition were signed by Governor Tritle, and Sheriff Paul and a deputy were dispatched to Colorado to bring the wanted men back. Most accounts have it that Wyatt's old friend Bat Masterson, who was then operating a gambling saloon in Gunnison, had interceded in their behalf with Colorado Governor Pitkin. Pitkin's statement in refusing to act was curt and to the point. "To return these men to Arizona would be equivalent to condemning them to death. Extradition refused."

As he tarried in Gunnison, Wyatt won over ten thousand dollars at faro. When he was ready to move on, he headed for California and the Pacific Coast. He was never to set foot in Arizona again. In San Francisco he married Josephine Marcus, his Tombstone mistress, who had come to Tombstone with a touring show troupe. Both Sheriff Behan and Earp had wanted her. Wyatt was the winner. She was less than half his age and must have been quite a bundle.

With his fast horses and his stable of boxers, Wyatt Earp became an important figure in the sporting world of the Bay area.[4] When the great gold rush of 1898 to the Yukon and Alaska got under way, nothing could hold him back. His Dexter Saloon in Nome became famous. Returning to California in time to get in on the San Diego real estate boom made him a modestly wealthy man.

Whether he was knave or hero—and he appears to have been alternately both—even his detractors agree that he had one virtue: he never betrayed a friend. He died peacefully in Los Angeles in 1929, at the age of eighty-three. He was the last of the famous brothers; Warren was killed in Lordsburg in 1900 and Virgil passed away in Goldfield, Nevada, in 1906.

XIII

The Mitchell-Truitt Feud

In the thirty-five years following the conclusion of the War Between the States, men who had something to conceal, hiding their true identity under various aliases, lost themselves in the great migration to the West.

While the vast majority of such footloose men, looking for a new start in life, contributed to the settling of the country, it is equally true that between two and three thousand remained "on the scout," as the old saying had it, until they were cut down by gun marshals or lodged in prison. If we accept the dictionary definition of outlaw as "one living in defiance of the law and excluded from its benefits and protection," they were outlaws.

However, crime was not as prevalent as that figure and the wallowing in violence of Western movies and television shows would seem to indicate. Law on the hip, every man for himself, gave way to statutory law and order. It separated the sheep from the goats and promised a man that he could be safe in the possession of his life and his goods—a promise that was not always fulfilled.

If there was more violence in Texas than in any other Western state, it is not difficult to understand. Almost without exception the pioneers who moved out beyond Red River hailed from the Carolinas, Virginia, and Tennessee. They were fighting men, jealous of their rights, and they brought their quarrels and family feuds with them.

At least that is how folklore would have it. Undoubtedly it was often true. But not always. The Mitchell-Truitt feud, one of the most noted in Texas history, is said by some commentators to have originated in North Carolina, from where it was brought to Texas by third- and fourth-generation members of the two families. The only evidence ever presented to that effect is that the two families had been acquainted long before they removed to Texas. There, after a break of fifteen years, during which there had been no contact between them, they became neighbors at Mitchell's Bend (formerly Takersley Bend) on the Brazos, in Hood County.

Both Nelson (nicknamed Cooney) Mitchell and Perminter Truitt (called Mint for short), the respective heads of their clans, were old men when they became neighbors in Mitchell's Bend in 1868.[1] (At that time in sparsely settled Hood County, anyone living within thirty miles could properly be regarded as a neighbor.) Born in Granville County, North Carolina, in 1802, Cooney Mitchell was the older of the two, a lean, vigorous six-footer, white-bearded and the father of a numerous brood of sons and daughters presented to him by his second wife, a mixed-blood Cherokee whose distinguished appearance was reflected in her children.

There were four girls: Lou, Annette, Georgiana, and Armenta. When they married, their husbands automatically became members of the Mitchell clan. As for the boys, of whom there were three—Bill, the eldest, who was to be hunted down by the law for thirty-three years, Dan, who appears to have led an exemplary life, and young Jeff, the baby of the family.

With little justification many commentators have endeavored to liken the clashing of the Mitchells and the Truitts to the bloodletting of those premier feudists of West Virginia and Kentucky, the Hatfields and the McCoys. There is nothing in the evidence to warrant such a conclusion. For four or five years before moving on to Texas, Cooney Mitchell had been farming in Arkansas and had lost all track of the Truitts. It was after he had disposed of his Arkansas property that he settled in Mitchell's Bend on the Brazos and with his sons began clearing land and raising cotton. Although being far from a wealthy man, he was thrifty and in fairly easy financial circumstances.

That could not be said of the Truitts. Old Mint and his sons had been moving around Erath and Bosque counties for years without getting ahead, until—apparently by chance—they settled in Mitchell's Bend. It is at this juncture that most of the published accounts of the so-called Mitchell-Truitt feud begin. With one exception, they are highly prejudiced in favor of one side or the other.

It is a matter of record that Cooney Mitchell sold Truitt fifty acres of fine land on the east bank of the Brazos on the strength of his unsecured note, with no money changing hands. On this land in Mitchell's Bend, Truitt built a log dwelling and a smokehouse. We are told that Cooney Mitchell and his boys helped the Truitts build their new home. It would not be surprising if they did, that being the custom of the country. However, I doubt that Cooney was such a good Samaritan that he took meat from his own smokehouse and hung it in the Truitts'.

From the door of the Truitt place, the Mitchell house could be seen half a mile to the southwest, surrounded by a fringe of live oaks. On a gentle slope to the rear, half hidden by the trees, were the barn, smokehouse, and the corrals. Between the road and the river, a small orchard had been set out, still several years from coming into production. The place had an air of prosperity about it not found elsewhere on the thirty-mile stretch of the Mambrino Road north to Granbury, the county seat. It was the result of hard work and frugality.

Astride his big gray mare, Cooney Mitchell had become a familiar figure on the dirt roads of Hood County. He had had no formal education, but he had the shrewdness of his Scottish ancestors, and it seldom failed him. A lean, tireless old man, his face half hidden by a long white beard, he looked harmless, but he could match wits with men in the full vigor of their youth. He bought and traded land, purchased promissory notes at a discount, and lent money at usurious rates of interest (which made him no friends).

During the winter of 1873, the Truitts and the Mitchells had confronted each other at the country dance and box suppers. On several occasions trouble had been narrowly avoided. Basically it was the ages-old distrust of the "haves" for the "have-nots" that was readying them for violence.

Perminter M. Truitt had fathered ten children, which was about average for a Texas ranch family of that time. James, Sam, and Mary were by his first wife; John, Isaac, Alfred, Perminter, Leander, Lucretia, and Amanda by the second. All of them were seldom together under one roof, the girls being shunted off on unappreciative relatives. The eldest of the Truitt boys, James, had just passed his twenty-fifth birthday when the calamitous year of 1874 was ushered in. Banks were closing, railroads going into receivership, and business was at a standstill as the country wallowed in its first great depression.

Photographs of Jim Truitt show him to have been a tall, lean, handsome young man with an intelligent face. For the past several years, determined to acquire an education and rise above the environment to which he had been born, he had been cutting ties for the Texas and Pacific Railroad, besides devoting himself to advancing the spiritual and financial goals of the Methodist Church, then a powerful voice in Texas. It was his ambition to become an ordained minister of the gospel. He had the presence and voice for it, and several months before the trouble erupted on the Mambrino Road, he had been "admitted to preach on trial by the Northwest Texas Conference."

Truitt and his brother had reached manhood convinced that they were a cut above the more prosperous Mitchells. Perhaps so.

They were better mannered. Their father had given them the rudiments of an education, and although they were churchgoing, there was plenty of fight in them.

The facts relating to the paying of a disputed note, which may have triggered the tragic encounter on the Mambrino Road late in the afternoon of March 28, 1874, are well known. Cooney Mitchell had lent Truitt seven hundred dollars and taken Truitt's note in exchange. When the note became due, Truitt had the money to pay it. He met Cooney in the office of Mitchell's attorney. In addition to them, two men, strangers to Cooney and Truitt, were seated in the old-fashioned office, waiting impatiently for Lawyer McGinnis to put in an appearance. They were land agents from Fort Worth and were not interested in what passed between Cooney and Mint Truitt. But when located months later and put on the witness stand in the lawsuit Cooney had brought against Truitt for the nonpayment of the loan, they testified under oath that they had seen Truitt pay his indebtedness and accept a receipt for the money, instead of the canceled note, which Cooney Mitchell stated he had mislaid and would turn over as soon as he found it.

If the lawsuit old Cooney had filed against Mint Truitt had any other purpose than the further harassment of an old enemy, I cannot put my finger on it. Certainly he could not have expected to collect the same debt twice by resorting to legal skulduggery.

Saturday, March 28, 1874, was a gloomy, overcast day, typical of that time of the year in east Texas, when winter drags on and spring seems reluctant to take over. But it was Court Day in Granbury, and the sleepy little town was crowded with litigants and their lawyers. If the onlookers failed to drift away, it was because the suit between Truitt and Mitchell was on the docket. It promised to set off some fireworks. And it did, but not of the nature the courtroom crowd had anticipated.

Mint Truitt was not present, being home sick in bed with

pneumonia. His sons were on hand; so were the Mitchell boys and old Cooney.

But late that afternoon, when the judge banged his gavel for adjournment, the case had not been reached. As the contending parties were filing out of the courtroom, old Cooney exchanged some hot words with Jim Truitt, accusing him of collecting a month's wages from the Mambrino School District to which he was not entitled.

"You were off preaching more time than you were teaching school."

"Anytime I took off was with the board's permission," Jim retorted hotly as he brushed past.

With D. A. Shaw, his neighbor and trusted friend at his side, Cooney walked up the street to the hotel, where early that morning he and his "boys," as he referred to them, had stabled their horses in the hotel barn. Besides Cooney, there were four in the Mitchell party: Bill Mitchell; Mit Graves, a tawny-skinned young man who lived with the Mitchells; Bill Owens, a son-in-law; and D. A. Shaw. When they reached the hotel, Owens continued on a few yards to the home of N. L. Cooper, the Mitchell lawyer, and picked up two loaded shotguns. By the time he returned, the others were mounted. Owens handed one gun to Bill Mitchell and the other to Mit Graves.

None of the published accounts of what was to transpire on the Mambrino Road in the course of the following hour fail to mention the two loaded shotguns that Owens had obtained at lawyer Cooper's house. Had the Mitchell party arrived in Granbury that morning armed for trouble? Or had Cooper supplied the shotguns from his own collection of arms? There were not many men in Hood County who didn't own a shotgun or two. It would be interesting to know the answer, and it would shed some light on who was responsible for the bloodletting.

When the Mitchell party jogged out of Granbury in the early evening, openly displaying that they were armed, at least to the extent of a pair of shotguns, was it a warning to the Truitts that if they ran into trouble before reaching home they meant to be ready for it?

The Mitchells were the first to leave town. The Truitts, James (already being given the honorary title of Reverend although he was not ordained until a year later), Isaac, and Sam, soon galloped past them, "hurling insulting remarks at my boys," Cooney charged. All accounts favorable to the Truitt side insist that James, Sam, and Ike were not armed. Suffice it to say that a derringer, two chambers of which had been exploded, was found in the dust beside young Ike Truitt's body when he was picked up.

Once they were ahead after leaving town, the Truitts remained in the lead for the three miles or more to where Contrary Creek crossed the Mambrino Road. Contrary Creek was a favorite watering place, and the Truitts pulled up when they reached it. Bill Mitchell and Mit Graves had stopped a hundred yards back, waiting for them to finish. Old Cooney, his son-in-law Owens, and Shaw were another three hundred yards back at the moment, walking their horses.

A short distance above the crossing, the Truitts pulled up sharply, and as Bill Mitchell and Graves passed them, they hurled insulting language at them and "waved their pistols in threatening fashion," according to the sworn testimony of Cooney Mitchell.

At that point the road struck off downhill to the right in the direction of the Brazos, cutting through a tangled jungle of scrub timber. A hurrying horseman named Ray swept around the bend in the road and passed the Truitts a moment or two later. He raised a hand in salute. He testified later that he heard no shooting. If he can be believed, he was the last man to see all three Truitt brothers alive. He passed the Mitchells a few moments later but again swore that he heard no shooting.

Bill Mitchell and Mit Graves took the road into the woods. The three Truitts, James, Ike and Sam, rode in behind them, which, local legend says, "gave Mitchell and Graves reason to believe that they were about to be attacked. Knowing that the Truitts were armed, no other conclusion was possible."

Guns roared in the close confines of the woods, and it was all over in a matter of several minutes. Dan Randall, a cedar cutter working some distance away, heard the shots. Dropping his ax, he ran to the scene of the shooting. He found Ike Truitt lying in the road, mortally wounded. He then ran to Sam Truitt and found him lying dead. Jim Truitt, who had apparently been trying to get away, was found kneeling in the road, fifty yards from his brother Ike, blood gushing from the ugly shotgun blast he had received in his right shoulder.

Remembering that Hood County was sparsely populated, that little Granbury was the only organized town in half a hundred miles, it taxes credulity to report that within a few minutes of the shoot-out on the Mambrino Road, four men, unrelated to the principals and scarcely acquainted with them, were on the scene.

James Maxwell got there a few minutes after Dan Randall, the cedar cutter. Between them they got Jim Truitt on a horse and took him to the house of Fletcher Ford, west of Mambrino. Maxwell told what he knew several different ways and was not called as a witness in the criminal investigation that followed. Doc Barker, his cousin Jim Barker, and Cool Jackson took the bodies of Sam and Ike Truitt to Ford's place. Ford and Maxwell were still ministering to Jim Truitt, but without much success. Doc Barker, a George's Creek rancher, who was no doctor, but a handy man when it came to buckshot surgery, took charge and succeeded in patching up the wounded Truitt.

It is only speculation, but it has often occurred to me that if Jim Truitt had died along with his brothers, the Mitchell-Truitt Feud would have been over. As it was, it ushered in a period of fresh hatreds and demands for vengeance that were still alive half a century later, and which were to twist and punish the lives of the innocent as well as the guilty.

Sam and Isaac Truitt were not yet in their graves when newspapers across Texas began their crucifixion of Cooney Mitchell, charging him with being responsible for the killing of the two Truitt boys and demanding that he be brought to justice for the crime. Even the little Granbury *News* devoted its front-page to describing the crime, calling it a "cowardly and cruel murder."

All this unfavorable publicity caused feelings to run high against Cooney. While it was admitted that he had had no hand in gunning down the two Truitts, he had whipped up hatred against them by shouting "Give 'em hell, boys! Give 'em hell!"

No one else had heard the old man screaming that—soon to become a famous battle cry—only the Reverend James M. Truitt. I doubt that he ever heard it. But as it became evident that he was going to survive, he fed reporters what the public wanted to hear. Throughout the state, the Methodist Church took up the cudgels against the Mitchells, demanding that in accordance with the old biblical law of an eye for an eye they be brought to trial and made to pay "for their heinous crime."

On Friday, April 4, warrants were issued on the persons of Nelson Mitchell, William Mitchell, Mit Graves, Bill Owens, Jeff Mitchell, a boy of seventeen, and D. A. Shaw, a neighbor. With a large posse, Deputy Sheriff Joe Walton left Granbury for Mitchell's Bend. During the night they watched the Mitchell house from the cedar brakes up the slope, in the rear. With the coming of daylight they moved in and arrested old Cooney, D. A. Shaw, Bill Owens, and young Jeff Mitchell. In irons, the prisoners were taken to Granbury and lodged in the Hood County jail by a Major Kingsbery and two possemen. Sheriff Walton and the rest of his force combed the country as far south and west as the Bosque, searching for Bill Mitchell and Mit Graves. They failed to find any trace of them.

Perhaps it should be interjected here that thirty-three years were to come and go before the law caught up with Bill Mitchell, which is a record for a man continually on the dodge. By then his father was largely forgotten.

Old man Cooney, Owens, Shaw, and young Jeff Mitchell had been lodged in the Hood County jail early in April, 1874. Jeff was released almost immediately, but the court refused to free the others on bail. In fact, attorneys for the defense were thwarted at every turn. Further delay was encountered when the Hood County courthouse burned to the ground in the spring of 1875. Finally, Owens and Shaw went on trial. Both were found guilty "for abetting the killing of Sam and Isaac Truitt" and sentenced to life imprisonment.[2]

When Cooney was led to the witness stand, he realized that he was fighting for his life; that he was facing a hostile jury. Sixteen months had passed since the slaying of Sam and Isaac Truitt and the near-fatal wounding of their brother James. In that long interval nothing had occurred in the bucolic life of Hood County to divert attention from the prosecution of Cooney Mitchell.

Few people believed that he had fired the fatal shots, but it was almost unanimously agreed that he had abetted and encouraged the shooting. If that was so, then under Texas law he was guilty of murder in the first degree.

In Texas of the 1870's, the public expected histrionics from its prosecutors. It got them from young Samuel Lanham, not yet thirty, ambitious and the possessor of a voice that shook the rafters when he turned it on. Time after time he paraded back and forth in front of the jury box, arms raised and giving voice to the cry that more than anything else convicted Cooney Mitchell: "Give 'em hell, boys! Give 'em hell!"[3]

Cooney was returned to his cell in the Hood County jail a crushed man, stunned by the knowledge that only a few weeks of life remained to him, that he was to die a disgraceful death at the end of a rope. His lawyers tried in vain to save him. His kin visited him and so did a young minister.

Instead of the few weeks of life Cooney believed were all he had left, a month passed, and another and another without the state exacting the penalty he owed it. The only excuse given for the

149

delay was that certain papers had been destroyed in the courthouse fire and that Austin was slow in providing necessary copies. Even allowing for the ineptness of political bureaucracy, it left the skeptical wondering. Was it possible that someone in authority was trying to manipulate the cards in Cooney Mitchell's favor? When a prison guard found a loaded pistol in the old man's cell, it became evident that he had friends on the outside who still hoped to save him from the ignominy of death by the hangman's noose.

We don't know who smuggled the gun in to him or how long he had had it in his possession. Certainly long enough for him to exercise the option of attempting to shoot his way out or being blasted into eternity. If he did nothing, it may well have been because he had been instructed to wait until an attempt was made to rush the jail from the outside.

If a conspiracy had been afoot to free Cooney, it died aborning with the discovery of the loaded pistol in his second-floor cell, the window of which looked down on the tangled slope of scrub oaks and cedars that fell away to the river. Understandably, Sheriff George Wright, feeling that another attempt might be made to free the old man, posted two deputies to guard the slope by night.

After months of cruel and unnecessary delay, the court announced that the execution of Nelson A. Mitchell would occur on the morning of "Friday, October 9, 1875, in the town of Granbury, Hood County, Texas."

Young Jeff Mitchell, not yet nineteen, spent an hour with his father on Wednesday. Although Cooney had been informed that he was to die in another forty-eight hours, he was not unduly distraught. Undetected by the guard, Jeff passed a length of twine to his father.

"Tomorrow morning when it's darkest just before dawn, I'll be down there beneath your window," he told old Cooney. "You drop one end of the string to me. In the package I tie on to it, there'll be a pistol and a bottle of laudanum. You'll have to decide whether to use the gun or swallow the poison. Understand?"

Cooney nodded. Either alternative would be preferable to being hanged.

With the coming of night, Sheriff Wright, understandably nervous, bedded down on a cot outside the door of the old man's cell. All afternoon he had heard stories that a jail break would be attempted. To make sure not to be taken by surprise if the threat materialized, he had four of his deputies guarding the approaches to the building. George Wright, Jr., the sheriff's son, and George Randall were stationed at the head of the scrub-covered slope on the north side that ran down to the Brazos.

In the predawn darkness they saw something moving uphill. They fired several shots at it. It stopped and after a brief threshing in the brush all was still. Some accounts say that they tossed a burning newspaper down the slope to see what they had killed. More likely they waited until daylight before investigating. The dead man was young Jeff.

When his father was informed that his son had been killed, his courage deserted him and he could not be consoled. Left to him were twenty-four hours of life, hours of such agony as few men are ever called on to endure. But there was iron in the withered, white-haired old man, and he was ready when Sheriff Wright came for him on Friday morning.

A flatbed farm wagon had been driven up to the jail door. On it rested the plain pine box that was to be Cooney's temporary coffin. The sheriff assisted the old man in climbing aboard, then got in with him, and the two settled down on the box. Wright nodded to the driver, who jerked the reins, and the wagon moved down the road to the northern outskirts of town, where a scaffold of sorts had been erected. A number of Wright's deputies were on hand to control the morbid crowd of four hundred men and women who had gathered to watch the proceedings.

Sheriff Wright stepped to the ground and spent some minutes moving the wagon back and forth until it was in the right position for the fall. Climbing back to Cooney, he adjusted the noose

151

around the old man's wrinkled neck and asked him if he had anything to say. "I have," was the spunky answer.

Cooney's roving eyes had located Jim Truitt standing at the rear of the crowd. He called on him to step forward. According to local historians, the Reverend James ignored the challenge and disappeared among the other spectators. However, in the accepted folklore of Hood County, he listened with head unbowed to Cooney's bitter denunciation of himself. The old man called on his missing son Bill to right the wrong that was being done him.

"Bill, if you are still alive, no matter where you are, no matter how long it takes, I'm looking to you to even the score with my murderers!"

Sheriff Wright had heard enough. He gave the signal to the driver and the team bolted away, jerking the old man into the air and leaving him swinging back and forth until he strangled to death.

A postscript should be added: Bill Mitchell was very much alive—an embittered, dangerous man, dodging the law and at long intervals tempted to risk capture for news from home. Always on the dodge, condemned to follow the dim trails or losing himself in wild country where there were no trails at all and men were few, thirteen years were to pass before he learned where to find James Truitt, the man responsible for the hanging of his father.

XIV

Bill Mitchell, Alias Baldy Russell

FOLLOWING the brief but fatal encounter on the Mambrino Road, Bill Mitchell and Mit Graves lost no time getting out of Hood County. Dan Mitchell, Bill's brother, was ranching near Stephenville, in Erath County. They headed for it and loped into the yard sometime before daylight. Dan supplied them with fresh horses and grub enough to last them several days.

We don't know how long Bill and Graves remained together after leaving Stephenville. It couldn't have been for more than a day or two. Months later it was rumored that Graves had been seen in California. It has always seemed that folklore and the grass-roots historians, in telling their story of the Mitchell-Truitt Feud, have had as little as possible to say about Mit Graves. They have not succeeded in concealing the fact that he was a deadly little man.

Was he related by marriage, if not by blood, to old Cooney's family? And what about his nickname of Mit? Was it a contraction of Mitchell? That information must be available somewhere, but I have not found it. If he *was* guilty of murder for his part in what happened on the Mambrino Road, he was just as guilty as Bill Mitchell.

That was not the way the law saw it; Bill Mitchell was the man it wanted, and it went after him and forgot about Mit Graves.

153

With the true instinct of the hunted, Bill kept on the move until he had put two hundred and fifty harsh, thinly populated miles of mesquite and catclaw between himself and Hood County.

A look at the map shows us where the West Fork of the Nueces cuts southeastward across the Edwards Plateau and begins its long journey to Corpus Christi and the Gulf. Somewhere in that big, parched land where there were no improved roads and only two or three tiny settlements, Bill supported himself as a hunter of wild animals on which there was a bounty and by working for wages as a water mason. He called himself Bill Russell when identification was necessary—an alias he used for the rest of his life.

In the course of the ten years that he lived in Kinney County, Bill Russell appears to have won the respect of the men and women with whom he came in contact, and that included the numerous Beckett family. Old Calamese Beckett, the octogenarian head of the clan, was as careful about offering the hand of friendship to a stranger as he was about taking care of his money. Calamese and old Cooney had been poured from the same mold, which may explain why Bill and the head of the Beckett clan got on so well together.

The Becketts had been among the pioneer settlers of Kinney County. For years they had been clearing their land, a few miles north of Brackettville, the county seat, burning off mesquite and hoarding the scanty rainfall in earthen tanks. With five grown sons and three daughters living at home, it took a large house to accommodate the family. Even so, they welcomed Mary Jane, the second-eldest of the Beckett girls, and her children when they came up from Brackettville to make their home with the family.

Bill Russell was in his mid-thirties and prematurely bald when he met Mary Beckett. She was a tall, willowy, attractive young woman. At a time when divorce was not common in Texas, the courts had freed her from a worthless husband. The scars both had suffered were forgotten when they met.

Relying on fact rather than fancy, we know that when Bill

asked Mary to marry him she didn't have to search her heart for her answer. But that's about all we do know. Whether Mary left Kinney County by herself on the long, seven-hundred-mile journey to New Mexico, by train and stagecoach, or whether she and Bill left together, is questionable.

However it was, we have the sworn statement of Arrie Therrell, Mary's elder sister, to the effect that "Bill and Mary were married in my home in Seven Rivers, New Mexico, on April 28, 1884."

There is no reason to doubt it. In 1884, Seven Rivers was the busiest and toughest town on the Pecos Trail. Bill had no difficulty finding employment as a freighter, driving bull trains to the forts and reservations. He also acquired the moniker of Baldy Russell. Several times he saw Texans whom he recognized. He couldn't be sure if they had not recognized him.

Since the next man he met might be the one who would lead to his undoing, it must have occurred to Bill once again that all men were dangerous and that he was safest where they were fewest.

Setting out from Seven Rivers to lose their identity in the Datils or on the Plains of Abraham, Bill Russell and Mary were as colorless as their outfit—an old flatbed wagon, with wooden bows over which a tilt could be stretched when it rained (which it sometimes did in New Mexico)—and drawn by a pair of wiry little mustangs. They didn't have the vast, silent country that had been the background for the Lincoln County War strictly to themselves; other wayfarers were moving over the dim trails looking for land that promised a better living than the rocky acres they had left behind them.

It was the custom among the heads of the migrant families to lay over for a day or two on reaching a back-country store. It gave the womenfolk an opportunity to break the monotony of their humdrum lives and visit back and forth. Had it been left to Bill, he would have made the necessary purchases and driven on without stopping. But he could not deny Mary the obvious pleasure it gave

155

her to be able to exchange pleasantries with members of her own sex.

He knew well enough that among the hard-eyed men he met on the trail were others who, like himself, were on the scout. One May evening in 1886, as Mary and he were camped at Tularosa Springs, south of Tularosa, a wagon that Bill had been watching turned off the trail and drew up a few yards away. The driver, an old man, hailed him. "You got any objection to the missus and me spending the night on the flat with you?"

"None at all," Bill called back. "We'll have supper cooked and be finished with the fire by the time you've watered your horses and turned 'em out to grass."

The couple were on their way to Carrizozo to visit their son, who was superintendent of the old Murphy-Dolan ranch. The man startled Baldy when he informed him that evening that he had lived in Hood County, Texas, most of his life. "Nothing much has happened since the hanging of Cooney Mitchell, back in seventy-five," he said.[1]

It needed only a question or two to supply Baldy Russell with the news he had been waiting so long to hear. Returning to Seven Rivers, he left Mary with her sister Arrie Therrell and disappeared without taking her into his confidence, it being his conviction that the less she knew, the better off she would be.

How he crossed Texas on horseback we do not know. There is no doubt about the purpose of his errand, however; he meant to find James Truitt, wherever he might be, and kill him to avenge the hanging of his father. Since he could not read, he wasted no time thumbing over country newspapers. Talk was his only weapon, and in cow camps and crossroads saloons and stores he listened to what was being said and asked discreet questions. Somewhere—we can't be sure where or how—he learned that Jim Truitt had quit the ministry and established himself as the publisher and editor of the Timpson *Times*, in Shelby County, east Texas.

Timpson was a new town, hacked out of the corn fields with

the arrival of the railroad. It is in the northwest corner of Shelby County, approximately a hundred and eighty miles slightly southeast of Fort Worth. Its population could not have exceeded five hundred in 1886, promising no better than lean pickings for a country weekly. But Jim Truitt and his wife Julia were apparently content with their prospects. When they moved into their new home at Timpson, they were the parents of two boys and a girl.

Dan Mitchell had prospered in the years that had passed since he had last seen his brother Bill. The Texas sun had bleached the color out of his hair and stained his face a walnut brown. If he ever gave any thought to it, he doubtlessly took it for granted that Bill was changing too. And yet, early one July morning, when he saw a tall, rawboned horseman jogging up to the kitchen door, he knew at once that it was Bill. They walked down to the corral together and talked.

"When he told me he was on his way to Timpson to kill Jim Truitt, I did my best to dissuade him," Dan declared some time later in a statement made to Sheriff A. J. Spradley.[2]

"He wouldn't listen. He asked me for directions. There wasn't too much I could tell him, not being acquainted with the country east of Corsicana. 'No matter,' he said, 'I'll find it. Fix me up a bag of grub and let me have your best horse.' I had a big blaze-faced sorrel, not much on speed but he could take a lope and hold it all day. While Bill was putting his saddle on the sorrel, I went to the house and put enough grub together to last him several days. I haven't seen him since." That was undoubtedly true.

But as soon as word spread that the law was interested in the tall stranger in the white Stetson, astride the big sorrel, a dozen men claimed to have encountered him. Strangely, they all remembered that he carried a small tin coffeepot tied to a ring in the cantle of his saddle. One or two said they had observed him bivouacking at the roadside, brewing coffee.

A week or more back, Baldy had struck the branch of the Texas and New Orleans Railroad that ran through Timpson on its way to Shreveport. Knowing it would take him to where he wanted to go, he followed it. On the morning of July 20, 1886, he stopped at a blacksmith shop some five miles west of Timpson and had his horse fitted out with a set of new shoes.[3] Soon after he came in sight of town, he watered his horse at a roadside spring, and, leaving the highway, pushed through the brush that bordered it and bivouacked in the shade of an ancient live oak.

As the long, hot July day merged into evening, he fried some bacon and boiled a pot of coffee. Lamps had been lighted and darkness was falling when he rode into Timpson. He stopped a young black boy and told him he'd give him a dime if he would show him where Mr. James Truitt lived.

"That's where," the youngster told him, pointing to an unpainted frame house on the corner. He pocketed his dime and scurried off. Baldy tethered his horse and walked to the door. Through the uncurtained window he saw Truitt dictating an article to his wife. With his gun raised, he pushed inside. He fired only once but the shot was deadly, the bullet striking Truitt behind the left ear and killing him instantly. Julia screamed and her parents rushed in from a rear room. Baldy swung up into the saddle and was gone before anyone could attempt to stop him.

Word was flashed to Sheriff Sims at Center, the county seat of Shelby County, only twenty miles away, but it was morning before Sims reached Timpson. A number of people had seen the killer, but they could not identify him. Nor could Julia Truitt. "I don't know who he is, but I'll never forget that face and those eyes."

Sims demonstrated his unfitness for the position he held by calling in A. J. Spradley, for thirty years sheriff of Nacogdoches County, and turning the investigation over to him.

Although twelve years and more had passed since the hanging of Cooney Mitchell, Spradley was convinced that the killing of Jim Truitt was connected with that tragic event. He took Dan Mitchell into custody, charging him with being an accessory both before and after the fact. After days of grilling, Dan acknowledged that "Bill showed up at my ranch one morning this month and borrowed a horse, which he returned a week or so later."

"Did he say anything about Timpson?"

"No . . ."

"Did he say where he was headed?"

"South Texas," Dan answered, hoping to throw dust in Spradley's eyes. "He mentioned Fort Clark. He spoke as though he was acquainted with that country."

If Dan knew anything, it was that Bill was not pointing back to his old haunts on the Nueces. But Spradley took the bait. He entrained for Spofford Junction, and aided by a detail of Texas Rangers, spent a fruitless month searching the country north of Brackettville. Dan Mitchell had to be given his freedom.

Interest in the whereabouts of Bill Mitchell waned. So quietly that even members of his family disagree as to the date, he returned to Seven Rivers, New Mexico, sometime in February, 1888.

Leaner, balder, and grimmer, he didn't know how to show Mary and her sister that he was happy to be back with them. Mary didn't belabor him with questions, knowing that when he was ready he would tell her what he wanted her to know.

As the snow went off in the weeks that followed and the trails became passable again, Baldy purchased a pair of big black mules and the best outfit he had ever owned. Stowing the family and what little they owned into the wagon, he took off without any particular destination in mind. Spring came early to the desert that year, and they found the Tularosa Valley aflame with flowers. The mines at Lake Valley were in bonanza. Confident of finding employment at good wages, Baldy headed that way.

Three months of Lake Valley were enough for him. Recrossing the Rio Grande, he pointed north through the San Andres Mountains and out across the dreaded Jornada del Muerto, the Mexicans' "Journey of Death." The Santa Fe Railroad had taken the bite out of the Jornada when it built down from Albuquerque in the eighties, crossing it from end to end, drilling for water at its stations and finding it. Engle, Estey City, and several other pinpoints of civilization sprang into existence. Baldy squatted on land three miles north of Lava Gap and dug several wells. When he struck water, the Jornada became his permanent home—at least as permanent as any he was ever to know.

H. M. Denny, sheriff of Otero County, New Mexico, was undoubtedly a brave and efficient peace officer. It is equally true that he had become convinced that Baldy Russell was a wanted man living under an alias. But he did nothing until he received a communication from the sheriff of Hood County, Texas, informing him that the man calling himself Baldy Russell was Bill Mitchell, wanted for murder, and offering to pay Denny a fee of fifty dollars and expenses "on delivery of Mitchell to me in El Paso." [4]

Denny and Deputy Sheriff Ben Wooton took Baldy into custody at his ranch near Estey City on March 23, 1907. It rubs off some of the glamour with which we have traditionally surrounded our Western peace officers to be told that such a niggardly sum as fifty dollars was enough to stir Denny to action.

When Bill Mitchell, alias Baldy Russell, found himself a prisoner in the Granbury jail, thirty-three years had passed since he disappeared from Hood County. When he was brought to trial, it was for complicity in the shooting of Sam and Ike Truitt on the Mambrino Road.

After the lapse of a third of a century, the prosecution could produce no witnesses to aid it in making a case. It left the court no choice but to declare a mistrial. Baldy was immediately rearrested by Shelby County officials and charged with the killing of James Morgan Truitt. He was hurried off to Timpson.

A surprising chain of events now occurred in the case of the State of Texas vs. William Mitchell. Although he had no money, Bill suddenly found himself represented by a battery of young and able attorneys.

The feeling in Timpson was so hostile against the prisoner, including the threat that he would be taken out of jail and lynched by a mob, that a change of venue was granted—the first of several. As the legal maneuvering continued, it became evident that public sentiment had swung over to the defendant. Even Julia's positive identification of Bill was disregarded by the jury and he was given his freedom under bond of $20,000, a sum which his friends must have been hard put to post, in addition to lawyers' fees and court costs. But they did, and Bill returned to New Mexico, temporarily a free man.

It was a respite that lasted almost two years. In October, 1910, he surrendered himself to the sheriff of Cherokee County at Rusk and went on trial again. His second trial was largely a rehash of the first. The verdict was Guilty. His attorneys exhausted the means left at their disposal, but the Court of Appeals denied their request for a new trial, and on March 16, 1912, Bill was sentenced to "life imprisonment at hard labor."

When the iron doors of the Texas State Penitentiary at Huntsville clanged shut behind him, Bill Mitchell was sixty years old, still straight as an arrow and still able to do a day's work. But the "hard labor" to which he was assigned proved to be nothing more strenuous than keeping down the weeds in the prison garden.

On July 14, 1914, Bill "escaped" (if that is the correct word for it, which I doubt) from Huntsville. The story heard most often has it that "he just walked out and kept on going." Bill himself is reputed to have said as much. The stories told about his years behind the walls leave little doubt that he had been given special treatment by prison officials. The fact that no effort was made to return him to Huntsville is evidence enough that the authorities were not interested in bringing him back.

Whether as Baldy Russell, John W. Davis, or whatever name he gave himself, most accounts agree that Bill Mitchell was back on the Jornada with Mary approximately three months after he "walked out" of Huntsville. He settled in his old stamping ground around Estey City and Oscura Peak and endeavored to put the scattered pieces of his life together. But no one has explained how he got there. Obviously the long journey across Texas could not have been accomplished without the help of friends and relatives.

As the years piled up on Baldy, he became more cantankerous and irascible. His friends made allowances for him. He continued to make a living, finding jobs that he had the skill and experience to perform. In the early summer of 1925, Mary and he left the Jornada and struck off to the southwest, hoping to find some place where a better living might be found. Eventually they landed in San Simon, Arizona, where artesian water was being brought to the surface and a minor land boom was taking place. There they found themselves among old friends they had known around Estey City. Baldy bought some land and prospered in a small way. It was to mark the end of the trail for him.

For half a century and more Baldy had packed a gun. But the old order of things had changed. Reluctantly, he bowed his head to the changes that had taken place and hung up his .45. That he was over the hill and didn't have long to go became apparent to him when he suffered a series of heart attacks. On April 5, 1928, friends made him comfortable on the back seat of a Model T and took him to the hospital at Douglas. Several days later, as Mary and an intern were taking him to the bathroom (he would not submit to bed care), he was fatally stricken, which must have been a source of satisfaction to him: he died on his feet; not in bed.

XV

El Paso: Toughest of the Tough

In 1882, the slumbering little town of El Paso on the banks of the wide and shallow Rio Grande served notice that it was going to amount to something. It was not foreseen, however, that as the "Gate City" of the future it was to dominate the commerce of the American Southwest.

The arrival of a single railroad was usually enough to guarantee the future growth and prosperity of a town; El Paso had—or soon was to have—four. Three of them—the Santa Fe, Southern Pacific, and Texas & Pacific—were among the most important freight and passenger carriers west of the Mississippi. An influx of two hundred persons a day began. El Paso had made no preparations to house them. Hotels began to rent their rooms by the hour rather than by the night. Many of the stores and eating places remained open twenty-four hours a day. Prices soared. El Paso and San Antonio streets, the principal thoroughfares, were as busy after midnight as before. Saloons and the town's two variety theaters were jammed, as was the flourishing red-light district. Every night lines of men, among them soldiers from nearby Fort Bliss, cued up in front of the bawdy houses waiting to be admitted.

For a stretch of two blocks on El Paso Street, every other building housed a saloon. Without exception they depended on gambling for a major share of their income. Women were permitted. In Uncle Ben Dowell's place one had to fight to get up to the tables. Dowell, a veteran of the Mexican War as well as of the War Between the States, had been elected mayor of "The Pass," a responsibility that rested lightly on him, and this attitude was shared by the town council, by Marshal George Campbell, and by inefficient Deputy Marshal Bill Johnson, a notorious drunk.

The Mexicans, who formed a considerable percentage of the population, settled their differences among themselves with knife or gun. When justifiable cause could be presented, a nice clean killing was not regarded as a major crime. Of course it was an easy matter to dump a body into the river and have it carried downstream. But as the holdups and robberies uptown became more frequent, the day came when newly elected Mayor Magoffin and the city council were forced to acknowledge that what El Paso needed was a strong dose of law and order.

Marshal Campbell had served as deputy sheriff of Young County in north Texas before coming to El Paso. As a peace officer, his record was good, but in his ten months in El Paso he had become too closely associated with the saloon and the underworld to give a good account of himself. His closest friends were the three Manning brothers, Jim, Frank, and Dr. George F., who, in addition to their saloon, operated the Coliseum Variety Theatre, both on El Paso Street, and both immensely profitable. They were recognized leaders of what, for lack of a better term, can be put down as "the sporting crowd."

Campbell did not take kindly to the criticism he was receiving. "One man can't police this town," he informed the mayor. "I'm doing the work of two men and not being paid for it." This was an obvious reference to Assistant Marshal Johnson. "Either pay me what I'm worth or fire me and get yourselves another man."

"All right, you're finished," the testy Magoffin informed him.

Bill Johnson was brought in and named city marshal pro tem. Temporarily, El Paso was a floundering ship with a sot at the helm.

The two newspapers came off the press that afternoon carrying an identical ad, signed "Vigilance Committee." It charged that Mayor Magoffin and his cronies had removed Marshal George Campbell from office and turned the town over to the thugs and criminals: "Make your voice heard. Demand that Marshal Campbell be rehired before it is too late."

It was learned later that the Manning brothers, Uncle Ben Dowell, and other prominent "sports" had paid for the ad. They were now rising to Campbell's defense because as peace officer he had given them the sort of town that was profitable to them. What they feared was that some two-fisted, two-gun stranger would drift into El Paso, be hired to succeed Campbell, and enforce the town ordinances that they were openly violating.

That midnight, the shank of the evening in El Paso, as the crowds were pouring out of the theaters and heading for the saloons and gaming tables, a bomb exploded at the intersection of El Paso and San Antonio streets. As startled men and women looked about for an explanation, rifles began to crack. Windows were shattered and doors splintered.

Before the firing ceased, several hundred shots had been fired. The miracle was that no one was struck by a bullet. It was not intended that they should be; this was a mock battle staged by the Vigilance Committee to convince city hall that El Paso was tottering on the brink of disaster.

By daylight the town presented a battered appearance. Mayor Magoffin took one look at it and promptly sent a messenger post haste down the valley to Ysleta, where Captain Baylor was camped with C Company of the Texas Rangers. A police detail of six Rangers was dispatched to El Paso at once, with Corporal Jim Fitch in charge. To Fitch and his bronzed companions, who had spent the summer fighting Apaches, policing El Paso for a week or two was nothing short of a vacation. As they walked the streets, the town became monotonously quiet.

Special assignments like this were limited to a week, ten days

165

at most. The Rangers were mindful of that. One morning they saw the stage from the Southern Pacific's end of track, twenty miles west of town, pull up in front of the new El Paso Hotel and recognized the blond, six-foot-three giant with the rocky jaw who stepped down. He was an old ex-Ranger acquaintance, Dallas Stoudenmire by name.

"Where you from, Dallas?" Corporal Fitch inquired.

"Deming. I been doing some police work there. When I heard that El Paso was likely to be in the market for a marshal, I didn't lose any time getting here." He looked around. "This town doesn't look as tough as I heard it was."

Fitch and his men exchanged a laugh. "That's because we've been here a week. Under the skin she's plenty tough."

The big man with the Dutch name was a Southerner, a native of Mason County, Alabama, and a veteran of the War Between the States, one of the starving, ragged thousands who had laid down their arms with the surrender of General Joe Johnston at Greensboro, North Carolina, in February 1865. Moving on to Texas, he had served an enlistment in B Company of the Rangers. He was now in his mid-thirties, which, as ages were reckoned on the frontier, was not regarded as young.

Stoudenmire was sworn in as marshal of the Pass City that afternoon, and Bill Johnson was dismissed. But Johnson still carried the keys to the calaboose. "I'll get 'em," Stoudenmire assured the mayor.

Late in the afternoon of his first day as marshal, Stoudenmire made the rounds of the El Paso Street saloons, looking for Johnson. He found him in Neal Nuland's Acme Saloon, at the corner of Mesa Avenue and El Paso Street. As usual at that time of day, Johnson was afloat on a cloud of alcohol.

Although the big man's nickel-plated badge of office was prominently displayed on his coat, Stoudenmire introduced himself and asked Johnson for the keys to the jail. The latter refused to hand them over, growling that he hadn't been informed that a new

166

marshal had taken over. Stoudenmire reached out and, wrapping his fist around the collar of Johnson's shirt, shook him until his teeth rattled. Taking the keys from the helpless wretch's pocket, he strolled out as though nothing had happened, even disdaining to glance back to see if Johnson was drawing a gun on him.

The sporting crowd saw enough of the moustached blond giant with the rocky jaw in the next few days to realize that the law had suddenly found some muscle. Naturally, they didn't like it.

A report was brought into El Paso that the bodies of two young Mexicans had been found in the high brush, six miles upstream near Canutillo. Two Rangers went up the Rio Grande to investigate. The bodies of the dead men were brought to El Paso and an inquest was ordered by the sheriff of El Paso County. If it is surprising to learn that the slaying of two unknown young Mexicans could attract so much official attention, it is only because the writers of Western shockers have been dinning it into our ears for half a century or more that "killing Mexicans don't count."

The inquest was held in a vacant adobe store on El Paso Street. The town's big Mexican population turned out by the hundreds to witness the proceedings. Whether the two youths were wetbacks, illegally in the United States, or cowboys who had followed straying cattle across the Rio Grande and lost their way in the *tornillo* brush, and been gunned down by overzealous cowboys, was the principal question that the coroner's jury had to decide.

The sheriff summoned witnesses, among them Johnnie Hale, the manager of a small ranch owned by the Manning brothers, and a puncher named Len Peterson, who worked on the spread. Suspicion pointed to these two as the killers. Bringing the Mannings into the investigation heightened the building tension. Stoudenmire was present—alert and apprehensive. So were ex-marshal Campbell, Bill Johnson, and the Rangers. Doc Manning pushed his way into the crowded room and exchanged a glance with Johnnie Hale. Gus Krempkau, a former Ranger, had been named interpreter.

Noon came, and Sheriff Walters declared a recess. Most of the crowd drifted away. Johnnie Hale accosted the interpreter, accusing him of twisting the Mexican testimony he was receiving. Krempkau angrily denied the accusation. Hale's hand flashed to his gun. It roared, and Krempkau fell dead.

Stoudenmire sprang forward as Hale stood staring down at the man he had just killed. Drawing both pistols, the marshal accidentally killed a Mexican spectator. His second shot rubbed out Johnnie Hale. Campbell drew his gun. Before he could fire, Stoudenmire had dropped him. Four men killed in as many seconds! It was a record even for El Paso.

The jury rendered its verdict early in the afternoon. It was the old, familiar one that had sufficed in a hundred similar cases: "The deceased came to their death as the result of gunshots fired by parties unknown." Fewer than a dozen people were present to hear it read; of far greater concern now was what Jim Manning and his brothers were going to do about the killing of their friends George Campbell and Johnnie Hale.

Instead of resorting to their guns to get what was loosely termed "justice," as was expected, they launched a campaign of vilification against Stoudenmire, employing Deputy United States Marshal William M. Mills to oust him from his job as city marshal. El Paso, both town and county, was preponderantly Democratic, which the federal government was not. Mills was a professional politician and had wangled his appointment strictly on party lines. He was unpopular and distrusted.

When Mills failed to unseat Stoudenmire, the Mannings turned to another pliable tool, bibulous Bill Johnson. Becoming a freeloader at their bar, they had no difficulty in convincing him that Dallas Stoudenmire was his mortal enemy; that he had shamed him and made him the laughingstock of the town.

The Mannings did not suggest to Boozy Bill that the only way he could square accounts with the big man was to kill him; they left it to Johnson to arrive at that decision by himself. They did

168

supply him with the shotgun he carried as he waited behind the pile of bricks that had been dumped at the corner of El Paso and San Antonio streets, where a building was under construction. It was no later than ten o'clock in the evening when Johnson saw the marshal step out of the Acme Saloon on his nightly rounds and head in his direction. When Stoudenmire was within thirty feet of him, Johnson raised his shotgun and fired both barrels. To the consternation of a number of ambushed conspirators, he missed his target. Stoudenmire leaped toward him, and drawing both guns from his hip pockets, blasted the life out of his would-be slayer. The half dozen or more conspirators beat a hasty retreat.

Although the underworld howled that he was a wanton killer, the marshal had the substantial citizens with him. In fact, he had never been so popular. The town council had given him James B. Gillette, an ex-Ranger sergeant, for deputy marshal. No two men were ever more unalike, but they got along well, and a better choice could not have been made. Beneath his friendly surface suavity, soft-spoken Gillette was a steel-hard man.

Stoudenmire was suspicious of most men, feeling that they were trying to get ahead by climbing over him. He never entertained that feeling about Jim Gillette. They were old acquaintances of Ranger days, and until the big man began "going to the bottle oftener and staying longer," as Eugene Cunningham once said of Ben Thompson, they made El Paso a reasonably safe town. Stoudenmire chose the moment to marry and leave the town in Gillette's capable hands.

There seems to be only one photograph of Stoudenmire that has been preserved. It has been reprinted countless times. It shows him wearing a double-breasted frock coat (a Prince Albert), a white shirt and bow tie. For ornament, his law badge is pinned on his left lapel. A heavy watch chain dangles from a vest pocket. He is fingering a cigar and looking solemn.

If this seems to be rather dudish attire for the marshal of a tough frontier town, the explanation is that it was donned for a special occasion: his wedding and honeymoon trip to his bride's home in east Texas. His working garb was more traditional: vest, cotton shirt, and gray woolen breeches, with leather-lined vertical hip pockets in which he carried a brace of silver-mounted .45's.[1]

Along with a bride, Dallas had acquired a brother-in-law in the person of Doc Cummings, whose Globe Restaurant was the finest in town. Cummings was an outspoken admirer of the big man, and a staunch friendship had developed between them. In Stoudenmire's absence, a tale was spread that the marshal was shaking down certain red-light resorts. Doc traced the tale back to Jim Manning. He was not a fighting man, but with Acting Marshal Gillette bedded with "the ague," he took it on himself to protect the family's good name. Arming himself with a .45, Doc announced that he was going to get a retraction from Manning or kill him.

To bolster his courage, he stopped in at Bill Coffin's Old Boss Saloon, across the street from the Mannings' Coliseum Theatre. After he had downed three or four drinks he was sufficiently whiskey-brave to announce to anyone who cared to listen that he was going over to the Coliseum and blow Jim Manning's head off.

But he had lingered so long at the Old Boss bar that word of the threats he was making preceded him across the street. Jim Manning was waiting when Doc stepped into the Coliseum and cut him down before he could raise his gun.

Manning accepted responsibility on the grounds of self-defense, and the charge was written off as a justifiable homicide. But that settled nothing; Stoudenmire had yet to be heard from. He returned to El Paso at once, and Gillette was at the depot to meet him. The big man was steaming. "If the Mannings want a showdown with me, they sure can have it," he told Gillette.

Influential citizens, friends of both parties, drew up a document pledging that there would be no further hostilities and got both sides to sign it. It was another of those meaningless peace treaties that only postponed the inevitable showdown.

Obviously Stoudenmire knew what the score was. He sought

to relieve the strain he was under by going to the bottle oftener. When he was in his cups, he became surly and difficult to get along with. By the middle of that summer, even his friends tried to avoid him when they saw him coming. Gillette tried to cover up for him, but the situation got out of hand when the *El Paso Times*, long Stoudenmire's staunch supporter, demanded his removal from office.

When Stoudenmire was summoned to the council chambers two days later, he knew what it meant. Stalking into the room, he glared about him like an enraged bull and, ripping off his shield, flung it on the table.

"There's your badge!" he growled. "And you're welcome to it!" He glared the mayor and councilmen to silence and stamped out angrily.

On his record, Jim Gillette was his logical replacement, but when the post was offered him he hesitated to accept, having no desire to become involved in a feud with an embittered and wrathful Dallas. The ex-marshal met him halfway and advised him to go ahead. "Don't worry about me. I'll find something to do."

Very likely he was counting on the political deal that Mills, the Republican boss, was making, and which resulted in Mills' being named United States Collector of Customs at El Paso and Stoudenmire's being appointed to replace him as Deputy United States Marshal for the western district of Texas.

Strangely enough, the arrangement brought a sort of surface peace to the town. It was not to last for long. Returning to El Paso from Las Cruces, New Mexico, in the early morning hours of September 22, Stoudenmire, needing a drink and finding the Manning brothers' saloon open, stepped in. He was still there at eight o'clock. When Gillette came on duty he caught sight of Stoudenmire staggering up the middle of El Paso Street. He offered to help him, but Dallas would not have it.

"I don't need your help! I'll go home by myself or I won't go home at all!"

171

Realizing it was useless to argue with the man, Gillette trailed him at a distance until he saw him turn into Mesa Street and home.

The ex-city marshal was back downtown in the middle of the afternoon, stone sober as he headed for the Acme Saloon, his favorite hangout. The Acme was owned by Neal Nuland, Walt Jones, and Cliff Brooks, three old friends from his days as a Ranger in Colorado County. They gave him hell for barging into the Manning brothers' saloon looking for trouble.

"I was doing nothing of the sort!" the big man protested. "It was four o'clock in the morning when I got back to town from Las Cruces. I needed a drink, and their place was the only one open. I'll go down there and explain things to them."

"I'll go with you," Walt Jones volunteered, pocketing a .45.

They found Jim Manning at the bar. Dr. George Manning was at the pool table, knocking the balls around.

"I understand there's some misunderstanding about what I was doing in your place last night," said Stoudenmire. "If Frank's around, I wish you'd call him; I want to explain to the three of you."

Jim nodded. "I'll get him."

Will Bridgers, former prosecuting attorney of El Paso County, was not only personally acquainted with the participants in what followed, but was an eyewitness. "When Jim Manning left the bar to find his brother Frank, Dr. G.F. dropped his cue on the table and came up to Stoudenmire and angrily accused him of breaking their agreement. 'Whoever says that tells a damned lie!' Dallas retorted angrily."

Walt Jones got in between them and tried to push them apart. The doctor was a small man compared to Stoudenmire, not more than five foot eight and weighing perhaps a hundred and sixty pounds, but he was a fighting gamecock with a hair-trigger temper. He and Stoudenmire drew their guns and hurled Jones out of the way. Manning fired twice before Dallas could jerk his twin Colts.

Struck in the right arm and right breast, he shot the pistol out of the doctor's hand.

Although a second bullet staggered him, George dropped his gun and flung his arms around Dallas and clung on in a desperate effort to avoid being killed. Locked together in an embrace of death, covered with blood, they struggled through the open door to the sidewalk.

Marshal Gillette and Ranger Joe Deaver were standing in front of Kerskie's stationery store conversing when the sound of gunfire up the street reached them. They started running in that direction but were fifty yards away when Jim Manning burst out of the Manning Saloon, gun in hand, and started firing. His second shot struck Stoudenmire in the left temple, killing him instantly.

Frank Manning ran out and joined his brothers as Gillette and Ranger Deaver reached the scene. The marshal placed the brothers under arrest and they handed him their guns.

"All right, Gillette," Jim Manning told him. "But for God's sake help me get my brother inside; I don't want him to die in the street."

When that had been done, Gillette recovered Stoudenmire's silver-plated .45's and had the body of the slain man covered with a blanket until the undertaker's wagon arrived. Deputy Sheriff Gonzales had reached the scene of the slayings. He claimed custody of the prisoners.

"Which was his right," says Bridgers, "a killing being a state offense. The charges against Frank Manning were dropped. Jim Manning was brought to trial and promptly acquitted, the evidence presented establishing that he had acted to save the life of his unarmed brother."

The Manning-Stoudenmire feud had snuffed out the lives of seven men. There was a lesson in all this, but El Paso refused to heed it. The town was tough and gloried in it. We read about how tough Dodge City was, and Tombstone. El Paso was tougher than any of them. Beginning with Dallas Stoudenmire and running through characters such as John Selman, Jeff Milton, and George Scarborough is testimony enough that El Paso's marshals and chiefs of police ranked with the best. When on the evening of August 19, 1895, years after the West was said to have become "civilized," Wes Hardin, the desperado with forty notches on his guns, was shot down by Constable John Selman in the Acme Saloon, El Paso still refused to write "finis" to its gunsmoke past.[2]

XVI

Butch Cassidy and
the Wild Bunch

In THE glittering yellow dust of the corrals and branding pens, they were shabby figures in their faded overalls, sweat-stained Stetsons, and faded cotton shirts. In the saddle, being expert horsemen, they were impressively picturesque—rough, tough young men who could ride anything on four feet.

Their home range was that wide, lonely land of little rain in central Utah, where the weird, wind-carved sandstone buttes march westward to lose themselves in the blue haze that hangs over the San Rafael Swell. Somewhere in that region of dim trails not pinpointed on the maps was that half-mythical outlaw rendezvous which they called the Robbers' Roost.

There were times when some of them had business there; when they had other things on their minds, they pointed their broncs either north or south to enjoy the pleasures to be found in the little towns of Vernal or Moab. There they gambled, drank the throat-parching red wheat whiskey, and frittered away their money on girls.

In the saloons, they cemented their acquaintance with the snake-eyed young men, usually no older than they themselves, who rode the owlhoot trails and made a business of selling Wyoming horses in Utah and running Utah horses across state lines into Wyoming and Colorado. Judging by the money they squandered, they led an easy life, sparked with danger.

It was the kind of life that appealed to George Leroy Parker. In 1889, when he first appeared in the Wind River country of Wyoming, he was twenty-one years old, a laughing, tow-headed young rowdy with a pair of puckered, inquiring blue eyes. He apparently had already done a bit of rustling when he appeared in Lander. He had dropped his honest name of George Parker, very likely to protect his family, who were respected people, and called himself Butch Cassidy. Why Cassidy, no one knows. Whatever the reason, he stuck with it and was to make it one of the most colorful names in American outlawry.

When he arrived in Lander he had some money and a partner by the name of Al Hainer, a typical small-time gambler and rustler. The two bought the Peterson ranch on Horse Creek and brought in a band of horses, very likely stolen, for they soon seemed to have more money than they could have come by honestly.

Old-timers liked to recall how Christmas came to upper Wind River for the first time in 1889, when Annie Simpson invited every man living within forty miles of her home to have Christmas dinner with her and her son Jim, who had just turned twenty and was soon to be elected district attorney of Fremont County. "Eighteen of us put our feet under her table that day," one man recalled. "Cassidy was there and he kept us in stitches with his nonsense."

Butch and his partner sold their place in the spring and drifted away. They were not seen again in Lander until eight months later, when Deputy Sheriff Bob Calverly and his possemen rode into town with forty stolen ponies they had recovered and two prisoners: Butch Cassidy and Al Hainer. Hainer had not resisted arrest and was unmarked; Butch's scalp had been laid open and his nose broken. They stood trial a few weeks later; Hainer was acquitted and Cassidy sentenced to two years in the state penitentiary at

Laramie City. He had served all but two months of his sentence when his historic meeting with the governor of Wyoming occurred.[1]

When Governor William A. Richards, former president of the Wyoming Stock Growers' Association and himself an ex-cowpuncher, sat down with Cassidy in the warden's office, it was a case of like meeting like. Richards was not only governor of the young state but the representative of the unofficial government that controlled it, the Wyoming Stock Growers' Association. He knew why Cassidy had sought this interview. For the past several months a petition asking him to grant the young prisoner a pardon had been circulated. Even Judge Jesse Knight, who had sentenced Cassidy, had signed it.

"Why are you asking me to grant you a pardon?" the governor asked.

"I've served most of my time. I've got only a couple months to go. It can't make much difference to the state if I go now, but it makes a heap of difference to me. I've some property down in Colorado that I'm going to lose if I can't get down there to take care of it."

Richards knew exactly how far he was prepared to go, but he pretended to think it over. "If you'll give me your word that you'll go straight, perhaps—"

Butch shook his head.

"No, Governor, I've gone too far to promise that I'll change my ways, and I won't lie about it. But I'll tell you what I'll do. If you give me a pardon, I'll promise that I'll never molest the state of Wyoming again."

So the deal was made, and Cassidy respected it. He may have helped plan the depredations of the Wild Bunch that followed, but there is no evidence that he took part in them.

He returned to Lander to what some writers have described as a hero's welcome. He was penniless, and in the Green River jail two of his friends were awaiting trial for rustling and in need of

177

money for lawyers' fees. Cassidy had never robbed a bank, but he had often thought about it in the months he had been behind the walls at Laramie City. Now, accompanied by two men whose names have escaped written history, he crossed the state line to Montpelier, Idaho, and, as the old expression has it, "cashed his six-shooters" for $8,000.

In Rock Springs, Wyoming, Cassidy arranged with a lawyer for the defense of his friends in the Green River jail, after which he disappeared in the Brown's Hole country of northwestern Colorado. A glance at a map of the region shows us that Colorado, Utah, and Wyoming have a common boundary. There, where the Green River fights its way through the eastern flank of the Uinta Range, Brown's Hole, later dignified as Brown's Park, offered sanctuary to riders of the Owlhoot Trail, which began as far north as the Musselshell in Montana and ran south to the Spanish-speaking settlements in southern New Mexico. The desperadoes who rode it always knew where they could find a meal, a fresh horse, and information.

The marshals, the sheriffs, and the Pinkertons gave Brown's Hole a wide berth. They reported that as many as a hundred wanted men were making the Hole their headquarters. But such tales were born of hearsay, not personal observation. Across the river, two days' riding to the west, was a mesa on the Uinta Plateau to which Cassidy and his men resorted after a strike until the heat was off. He labeled it Robbers' Roost, and the name stuck. The nearest settlement was tiny Green River, where Matt Warner operated a ferry and saloon. When flush, Butch and his longriders pushed enough money across the bar to buy the place.

We read today of how bank robbers "cased" an institution before striking. The word was not in use in Butch Cassidy's time, but that was exactly what he was doing when he rode into the coal-mining town of Castle Gate, Utah, one summer evening in 1894. It is located in a deep, high-walled canyon in the Wasatch Mountains, with the Denver and Rio Grande tracks only a hop, skip, and jump from the two-story stone building that housed the offices of the Castle Gate Coal Company. It was the evening before the monthly arrival of the paymaster with the company payroll, the big day of the month in Castle Gate. Professional gamblers from Denver and Salt Lake had arrived and set up their tables for the expected "killing," when Cassidy rode into town and was invited to sit in on the game they were playing just to pass the time.

Presumably he was no slouch at poker, but by ten o'clock his chips were all gone. "You've cleaned me, boys."

Walking over to the bar, he told the proprietor his story. His outfit, he said, was camped just outside of town and he had promised to bring back three bottles of whiskey.

"I'm in a fix now, out of money. I hate to disappoint the boys."

"No problem, stranger," he was told. Figuring his cut of what Butch had just lost, the saloon man could afford to be generous. He wrapped up three bottles of Old Crow. "Take 'em with my compliments."

"No, mister, I ain't asking for charity; just credit till tomorrow."

"Okay, if that's the way you want it. You can stop in some time and pay me if you're passing this way."

The train from the east was on time the following morning. The paymaster, carrying two leather bags, stepped down on the platform. With his armed guard beside him, he started across the street. Miners lined the sidewalk, but they were so intent on watching the man carrying the leather bags containing their wages that they failed to notice Butch and Bob Leigh, who had slipped down from the saddle and leveled their guns at the paymaster and his guard.

"Hands up!" Cassidy ordered.

As the guard and paymaster stood with uplifted arms, Bob Leigh secured the money bags and tied them over his saddle horn. Butch backed to his bronc and swung up. From a second-story window a clerk began firing at them. A good-looking saddled horse

179

began pitching at the tie rack. Butch got control of the bronc and galloped away with it.

Just beyond the town limits, half a dozen members of the gang were waiting to discourage pursuit. Collectively they formed the inner circle of that division of the Wild Bunch who regarded Butch Cassidy as their leader. One of them was swarthy little Harvey Logan, alias Kid Curry, who had been run out of Montana for killing old Pike Landusky on the Musselshell. Because of Logan's swarthy skin, Pike had made the mistake of calling him a Negro. There were also Harry Longabaugh (the "Sundance Kid"), Lonny Logan, Camella Hanks, Flat-nosed George Curry and Will Carver.[2]

Keeping in character, Cassidy got a ten-dollar note out of one of the money bags and wrote on its face "Pay for the Whiskey." Attaching it to the bridle of the saloon man's horse, he sent the animal loping back to Castle Gate. Knowing that the country was being alerted by telegraph of the robbery, they broke their trail by crossing and recrossing little Price River and shaking off pursuit. Two days later they were laughing it up over Matt Warner's bar on Green River.

At the same time, two hundred miles to the north in Brown's Hole, Elza Lay, Bob Kilpatrick, the Tall Texan, and several lesser members of the gang were celebrating the successful robbery of a Union Pacific train west of Wamsutter, Wyoming.

Soon after the United States declared war with Spain, following the blowing up of the battleship *Maine* in Havana Harbor, the newspapers spread the word that several hundred outlaws were gathering in Routt County, Colorado, and undergoing military training in the hope that they might be inducted into Torrey's Rough Riders and shipped off to Cuba, asking in return only that the law drop the charges it had against them. It was a pretty story but proved to be completely fictional. At the time, however, it was considered a serious-enough matter to call for a conference by the governors of Wyoming, Colorado, and Utah. They met in Salt

Lake City. Governor Richards brought John Ward, long-time sheriff of Fremont County, along with him. On the second morning, a stranger stopped the sheriff on the street and conveyed a message to him. It was from Cassidy. "He wants you to take the afternoon eastbound train and meet him at Soldiers' Summit. He'll be waiting for you a couple hundred yards east of the water tank. He wants you to come alone, of course."

Ward nodded. "I'll be there."

Soldiers' Summit was just a speck in a thousand square miles of mountain wilderness: the tiny combination depot and agent's cabin, a water trough, and coal chute. The sheriff walked eastward a hundred yards or more and found a seat on a log. He had been waiting only a few minutes when Cassidy joined him. "We talked for a few minutes before Butch got down to business," Ward told an interviewer the next day. "We had a lot to talk about, cutting up some old touches. We had been acquainted for going on to five years now. When he got down to business he said: 'You can tell the railroad companies they can take their gunmen off the trains. They ain't going to need 'em. As for calling out the militia, that's nonsense. There's some rustlers and horse thieves in Routt County, but there always is. They don't mean a thing. Nothing is going to come off, and you've got my word for that.' "

"And you believe him, Sheriff?"

Ward nodded. "I've always found him a man of his word."

No Wyoming place name is as fearsome to eye and ear and so often encountered as the Hole in the Wall. There, to a generation now long gone, the foulest deeds were believed to have occurred, bringing the sharp finality of death by gunfire to legions of young cowboys and range outlaws. Today it is a handy and beautiful weekend vacation playground for the young people of Casper, the county seat of Natrona County. The famous "Hole" is no hole at all but a break in the beautiful and remarkably circular, thirty-mile-long Red Wall, through which Buffalo Creek, skirting the southern extremities of the Big Horns, flows into Powder River.

There were thousands of acres of extremely rich grazing land in the Hole in the Wall Basin. United States Senator Joseph M. Carey, owner of a cattle empire, claimed grazing rights to it. So did others. By one means or another, Carey usually got what he wanted in Wyoming. In June, 1897, he sent his cowboys and a herd of cattle into the Hole. On July 24, a battle took place in which several fatalities occurred, the CY, the Senator's outfit, losing a man and having several seriously wounded. John R. Smith, the leader of the defenders, was killed. His brother Jim was weeks recovering from a supposedly fatal wound.

Subsequently, the CY outfit, backed up by the Pugsley brothers and the Ogallala Cattle Company, whacked up the Hole in the Wall between them and pushed the little fellows out.

XVII

The Last Hurrah

No MATTER how carefully you read the Wyoming newspapers of those days, you will find no mention of that ferocious organization of bandits known as the Hole in the Wall Gang. In fact, the term was not coined until after the Wilcox train robbery in 1899, when the fleeing bandits crossed the Hole as they escaped north into Montana. The men who took part in the Wilcox robbery can be identified as members of that loosely held together organization known as the Wild Bunch. But it must have amused them to learn that they were also members of that mythical, nonexistent group the public prints had labeled the Hole in the Wall Gang.

It was just before dawn on the morning of June 2, 1899, when a westbound Union Pacific train was held up as it paused at the little settlement of Wilcox to take on water. Harvey Logan and Flat-nosed George Curry climbed into the cab of the locomotive and with drawn guns ordered the engineer to pull across the bridge that spanned Little Medicine River, and stop. The man did as he was ordered. As soon as the train had crossed, Lonny Logan and Harry Longabaugh, the Sundance Kid, stepped out of the brush and dynamited the bridge, preventing a following train from crossing.

The safe in the express car was blown and the bandits secured

183

more than $60,000, some of it in unsigned bank notes. The bandits then disappeared in the direction of Casper, a hundred miles to the north.

Pursuit was organized by telegraph. In a few hours several hundred men were in the field, and the greatest manhunt in Wyoming history was under way. In a driving rain that continued all day, men turned out to block the trails and cut off escape by way of the Platte River bridge. As yet they were unaware of the identity of the fleeing bandits. Perhaps that was just as well, for they bore established reputations as desperate men.

Harvey Logan was known to have snuffed out the lives of at least nine men, very likely more. His younger brother Lonny had a hardly less vicious reputation. Harry Longabaugh, born and reared in the little Wyoming settlement of Sundance, was a savage young illiterate and an apt pupil of the Logan brothers. Flat-nosed George Curry, a son of a respectable Nebraska rancher and the oldest of the four, was a confirmed rustler, horse thief, and all-around desperado.

Sheriff Oscar Hiestand of Natrona County called in his wet and hungry men, who had been without food for twenty-four hours, and replaced them with newly arrived possemen and detectives. Sheriff Hazen, of neighboring Converse County, took over for a few hours.

On Sunday morning Al Hudspeth, a CY puncher, rode into Casper with news that the outlaws were holed up in a deserted cabin about six miles northwest of town. "No one's been living there for months," he told Sheriffs Hiestand and Hazen. "When I rode up, they stepped out and told me to hit the road and hit it quick."

It was learned later that Harvey and Lonny Logan had ridden into town on Saturday night and purchased food and ammunition. Smarting with the audacity of the bandits, Hiestand and Hazen left for the old cabin with a posse of twenty men. As they had expected, they found the place deserted, but they now had a trail to follow. The rain ended, leaving a gray and sodden world.

Some time after ten o'clock they reached John Devore's sheep camp. A herder told them that four riders had passed within the hour, headed for the Tisdale Mountains, which convinced Sheriffs Hiestand and Hazen that instead of following the creek, which was over its banks in a spring freshet, normally the easiest way out of the Hole in the Wall, the bandits meant to drive through the Tisdale Mountains and escape into the Big Horns.

The possemen were confident that they would be in time to cut off the fleeing men, but they ran into gunfire in the early afternoon. They were crossing a shallow valley when the outlaws opened up on them from behind a waist-high outcropping of rock. Several horses were killed, and Sheriff Hazen was shot in the stomach.[1]

As the posse dropped back, seeking cover, the outlaw gang got into the saddle and disappeared. A week later they were reported to have been seen at a Wild Bunch hangout on Fifteen Mile Creek, west of Worland, where, presumably, they split up the proceeds of the Wilcox robbery.

I have read that Butch Cassidy was present when the swag was divided and that he was either given or he purchased some of the unsigned bank notes taken at Wilcox. However, no evidence to that effect has ever been produced. Until it is, I refuse to accept the story or that Cassidy planned the Wilcox robbery and thereby broke his pledged word to Governor Richards.

When he joined the other leaders of the Wild Bunch at one of the gang's strongholds in the wilds of the Wind River Range later that month, it was his gloomy prediction that the time had come for them to be thinking of getting out of the United States and heading for South America, as many men had done following the Johnson County war. Argentina had no extradition treaty with the United States, and a man could not be brought back to face trial in this country.

The Pinkertons, employed by the American Bankers Association and the railroads, were everywhere. There was an old saying that "a man can't move his feet without stepping on a Pinkerton." Many were brave men; some were shot down in the line of duty. But there was a prerequisite to fleeing to Argentina: a man had to have a stake. Cassidy set out to get himself one. A number of the unsigned bank notes taken in the Wilcox robbery came into his possession. He signed them and put them into circulation. He must have done rather well, because in the fall of 1899 he purchased a saloon in what was then Milligan's Place, hard up against the Arizona line in Catron County, New Mexico, today known as the town of Reserve.

Calling himself Jim Lowe, Cassidy soon became the most popular man in town. With his wit and engaging personality, he made the ideal dispenser of whiskey. But things were not going so well with other members of the Wild Bunch. Lonny Logan was traced back to Dodson, Missouri, on a visit to his home town, and was killed by a posse that had surrounded the house. Bob Leigh was arrested, convicted, and sentenced to fifteen years in the Utah State Prison. A month later, Flat-nosed George Curry was slain on Green River by a Utah sheriff as he was fleeing an attempted bank robbery. Harvey Logan, furious at the killing of his brother, got four members of the Wild Bunch together and held up a Union Pacific train at Como, a flag stop west of Medicine Bow, Wyoming, but when they opened the express safe they found it empty.

When the dire tidings eventually reached Butch, he must have realized that the sanctuary he had found in New Mexico was not permanent; that sooner or later the agents of the big corporations would be closing in on him. Sometime late in August, 1900, he had a visitor who had come a long way to confer with him. It is not known what it was they discussed, but in the weeks that followed there were scandalous rumors to the effect that the subject matter concerned the prearranged robbery of a Nevada bank to cover the defalcations of the cashier.

Supposedly the hour and day of the robbery were set and that, in addition to whatever the bandits could make off with, they were to be given a bonus of some thousands of dollars. If this sounds incredible, so was the robbery of the First National Bank of Winnemucca, Nevada, on September 19, 1900.

It lacked a few minutes to twelve noon when Butch Cassidy, Harvey Logan, and the Sundance Kid jogged across the small wooden bridge that spanned the shallow Humboldt River and proceeded up Bridge Street, then as now busy Winnemucca's main thoroughfare. In two or three minutes they reached the intersection where the First National stood on the northwest corner. To the rear of the bank there was a high board fence and a small building that was used as a coal shed, the narrow space beyond forming an alley.

Apparently following instructions, the men tethered their horses at the rail. Three abreast, they walked to the corner and entered the bank. It being the noon hour, they had only four men to contend with. George S. Nixon, the cashier and future United States senator, was seated in his office, conferring with Will Johnson, a cattle buyer from Reno. A bookkeeper and a teller were standing at the banking counter. At gunpoint they were ordered to throw up their hands and were marched across the room, where they were forced to stand facing the wall.

Producing an old ore sack, Cassidy scooped up the gold coin in the counter drawers and rifled the open safe. It took only a few minutes. Backing to the door, the bandits hurried to their horses and, heading down Bridge Street, got out of Winnemucca without alarming the town. Seizing a rifle, Nixon ran out into the street, only to have the gun jam as he attempted to fire at the fleeing riders.

The bank robbers could be seen as they toiled up the dirt road that curls over the lower eastern flank of Winnemucca Mountain. In the hope of cutting them off, the Sheriff commandeered a Southern Pacific freight locomotive and, putting a score of possemen aboard, steamed eastward. At the Silva ranch, they got horses and began the long, hopeless chase. Toward evening, when they learned at the Rebel Creek ranch that they were being outdistanced, they gave up.

The cashier reported that the desperadoes had made off with some $36,000. If this was an ingenious way of covering up some of Nixon's losing speculations, it was an effective one, enabling him to balance the First National's books. It would have been interesting to have heard from Cassidy how much he, Logan, and the Sundance Kid actually netted from the Winnemucca robbery.

But there are other questions, equally pertinent, that have never been answered. They were experienced bank and train robbers. When they made a strike it was not until they had canvassed the situation and made sure they would have an escape route open to them. This was possible only if they were acquainted with the surrounding country. Cassidy, Logan, and the Sundance Kid knew nothing about Winnemucca and the surrounding mountains and miles of sagebrush. One thing they couldn't have escaped knowing: the distance from any of the outlaw hideouts in Wyoming and northern Utah to the county seat of Humboldt County was at least three hundred and fifty miles. To ride seven hundred miles—there and back—to crack a country bank doesn't make sense, unless some "arrangements" had been made.

That winter, while detectives and law-enforcement officers were tacking up "Wanted" notices for the three bandits, Butch, the Sundance Kid, and Logan were taking their ease in Fort Worth. Having put aside their cowboy regalia, they had donned "city" clothes and hard hats, with gold watch chains spanning their brocaded vests.

In Fort Worth they met Ben Kilpatrick and Will Carver, old members of the Wild Bunch. The five of them had their photograph taken. It shows them in a gay mood and has since appeared in every book and magazine article dealing with the Wild Bunch.

They were in funds, and they agreed that after one more strike they would head for the Argentine.

The following June the five of them rendezvoused in the Milk River country in northeastern Montana. With them was old Camella Hanks. At Wagner, a flag station approximately two hundred miles east of Great Falls, they stopped a westbound Great Northern express. When they blew the safe, they found themselves in clover and rode off with something over $60,000 in bank notes, consigned to a Helena bank.

They now had the stake to take them to South America. Not all of them made it. Ben Kilpatrick was arrested in St. Louis and sentenced to fifteen years in the Missouri State Prison. With time off for good behavior, he came out, but unchanged, and he was eventually killed in Texas as he was rifling an express-company safe. Camella Hanks was captured in Tennessee and escaped, only to be killed in a bloody brawl in San Antonio. Bob Leigh was captured and as the old saying had it, "got the book"—fifteen years at hard labor in the Laramie city penitentiary.

As previously mentioned, Flat-nosed George Curry had been killed in a shoot-out with a Utah sheriff. Will Carver was cut down by a Texas sheriff in the village of Sonora. The disintegration of the Wild Bunch hit bottom when deadly Harvey Logan was captured in Knoxville, Tennessee. Before he could be extradited to Wyoming, which had first claim on him, he bribed a prison guard and escaped. It was his last brush with the law.

Piecing together what evidence time has turned up leaves no doubt that Logan knew how and where to contact Cassidy and Harry Longabaugh, the Sundance Kid. Butch was living quietly in Salt Lake City. Longabaugh, in poor health, was resting in a Buffalo, New York, sanatorium, with his wife in attendance.

Apparently it was at this time, early in 1902, that the trio—Cassidy, Logan and Longabaugh—decided to get out of the United States immediately and meet in Buenos Aires, where a trusted companion would be waiting for them. The identity of this fourth man remains in dispute. Although many knowledgeable writers may disagree with me, I believe he was Elza Lay, a long-time member of the Wild Bunch.

Longabaugh and his wife were the first to go, leaving by steamer from New York. Logan followed them, sailing from Brooklyn. Cassidy took a more circuitous route, crossing the Atlantic on a cattle boat to Liverpool and continuing from there aboard a freighter.

After joining up, they appear to have made a serious attempt to put their outlaw past behind them and go straight. Land was cheap and there was a lot of it. Somewhere on the Salado River, in the province of Santiago del Estero, they bought a ranch. Cattle were cheap and gaucho wages, by American standards, were low. With the foothills of the Andes to the west and the wild mountain streams of Bolivia to the north to turn back straying cattle, they had an empire in the making. But they had been marauding too many years not to realize how easy it would be to run off another owner's herd and dispose of it, no questions asked, at one of the great refrigeration plants on the Bermejo River. So they did. Eventually they were caught at it.

On getting back to the ranch, Logan tried to persuade Cassidy and Longabaugh to make a run for it with him. They refused. Pausing only long enough to stuff some food into a saddlebag, he took off. That's where history leaves him. He was never seen again.

In the morning the little ranch house was surrounded by a company of soldiers. It was shortly after daylight when the shooting began. Cassidy could hear Longabaugh firing from his bedroom. Making his way to him, he found the Sundance Kid dead on the floor.

Snatching up a bag of ammunition, Butch ran across the yard and plunged into a rock cattle shoot, barely wide enough for two men to pass. Time after time the soldiers tried to reach him, only to fall back nursing their wounds.

As the long, hot, smoke-begrimed afternoon came to a close,

Cassidy saw that he had only one live shell remaining in his long-barreled Colt. When the soldiers closed in again, they drew no response. Pushing into the chute, they found him, sitting up, his back to the wall, and quite dead. He had saved his last shot for himself.[2]

Today, three quarters of a century later, without trying to glorify outlawry, one can say that, in his way, Butch Cassidy was quite a man.

XVIII

The Tom Horn Trail

WHEN, on the morning of November 20, 1903, in the jail yard in Cheyenne, Ed Smalley, sheriff of Laramie County, asked the condemned man standing on the trap, the noose already draped about his neck, "Have you anything to say before the sentence of the court is carried out on you?" the answer was a sober, even-toned "No."

So Tom Horn died for the alleged killing of Willie Nickell, the fourteen-year-old son of Kels Nickell, a homesteader and sheepman, on July 19, 1901. Twenty-eight months had intervened between the finding of the boy's body at a stock gate, half a mile from his home, and the hanging of Tom Horn. For two years he had remained a free man. The state had no case against him. But certain "powerful influences," it was said, were determined to keep the matter alive. Who those powerful influences might be, other than the inner circle of the Wyoming Stock Growers' Association, I do not know. However it was, the Cheyenne *Leader*, controlled by the Association, and W. R. Stoll, the Laramie County prosecutor, convicted Tom Horn of the crime and hanged him for it.

It was not until after Tom Horn came to Wyoming, his long career as Apache Indian scout, soldier, cowboy, and rodeo star behind him, that whiskey made a fool and a braggart of him.

192

To go back to the beginning, Tom Horn was born in 1861 of French parents, in the little town of Memphis, in Scotland County, Missouri. It was timbered, rural country, cut up by creeks and small streams through which the Mormons had passed on their enforced exodus from Missouri to their new home at Nauvoo, Illinois.

His biographers describe him as a big, husky boy at fourteen, far more interested in tramping the woods armed with the family shotgun, hunting squirrels and rabbits, than in attending school. When his father caught him shirking his share of the farm chores, he used the strap on him, a recognized parental privilege of those days. One night, after receiving what he considered an uncalled-for licking, Tom did what so many thousands of boys have done: he ran away from home.

Once he had made the break, he kept on going. There is some evidence that he corresponded with Lucy, the eldest of his three sisters, at long intervals. But there is nothing in the record to indicate that he ever saw his family again. The frontier was his goal, and he never changed course until he reached it. Passing himself off for eighteen, doing a man's work and earning a man's wages, he moved on from job to job. Dodge City, the Cowboy Capital, had captured the shifting Texas cattle trade. Tom Horn must have been there, but his name does not appear in the voluminous published material on Dodge.

The Santa Fe Railroad was pushing down through New Mexico in a feverish haste to claim another land grant; it was recruiting men for its work gangs and paying top wages. This was an opportunity for getting ahead made to order for young Horn. Whether he had been hired at Dodge or at some point east is not important. He had a way with horses. Handling a four-horse rig and delivering ties at the railhead became his daily routine. The glare of the white-hot noonday sun did not bother him. The star-filled nights healed a man. For the first time he found himself living and working with Mexicans. He got along well with them and had no difficulty familiarizing himself with their language.

193

With the aggressiveness and self-reliance of most men half again his age, young Horn went to work for the Overland Mail Route, at Santa Fe, as stock tender. A year later he was driving a stage between Santa Fe and Las Vegas, New Mexico. When the Santa Fe completed its eighteen-mile spur into the Territorial capital in 1880, the stage line abandoned the run. Horn moved on westward into Arizona. That he did some cowboying in Yavapai County at this period in his life is evident, for he became recognized as a champion roper and rodeo performer. He made his headquarters at Beaver Head Station, west of the Verde River, the site today of the city of Prescott.

It was there that he became acquainted with Al Sieber, the famous Army scout who had distinguished himself in the campaigns against the Apaches. It was the beginning of a long friendship that was maintained for the rest of Tom Horn's life and bridged the difference in their ages.

Through Sieber, Horn went to work for the government as a paid employee, not as an enlisted man. The War Department had made old Fort Whipple, nine miles north of today's Prescott, a remount facility and had brought in several hundred horses from California. Horn was put in charge of them, breaking and training the animals. A few months later, Sieber asked him to go to the San Carlos Apache Agency with him to act as Mexican interpreter.

"You picked up Spanish easily enough," the old scout told him. "If you live with the Apaches, I'm sure you'll soon be able to speak their lingo."

The hazardous life of an Army scout appealed to young Horn as nothing else had ever done. Responding to the interest Sieber had taken in him, he accompanied Al to San Carlos, where he was lodged with old Pedro, a subchief of the Chiricahuas, who was regarded by the military as a "friendly," a faction that was outnumbered ten to one by the several thousand resentful Apaches who had been forcibly removed from their homelands by the Army and dumped on the new San Carlos Reservation.

Repeatedly large parties of so-called renegades, led by Nana, young Victorio, and old Geronimo, were breaking away from the Reservation to plunder and kill white settlers. When pursued by the military, they found refuge by slipping across the boundary into Mexico, where they were safe from pursuit.

When General Nelson A. Miles succeeded General Crook as Departmental Commander for Arizona, Tom Horn had been on the San Carlos Reservation for over a year. He could understand the Apache language and speak it after a fashion. Al Sieber had taken him on a number of scouting expeditions. Of him, Sieber wrote in later years: "In making my side-scouts, I often needed the help of a man I could rely on, and I always placed Horn in charge, for it required a man of bravery, judgment and skill, and I ever found Tom true to every trust confided to his care. I would always place Horn in charge of all Indian scouts left behind. This required a man who was cool and had good judgment to handle these scouts.

"On other side-scouts, when I took a few pack animals, I made it a point to take Tom with me. Often times I had to split my crowd after being out. I would always put Tom in charge of the set of scouts, tell him where and the time to meet me, and what to do; and I never had him fail to obey my orders to perfection. No matter what came up—rain or snow, clouds or sunshine—Tom was there to meet me."

"High praise from that grim, taciturn old scout," comments Gene Cunningham, himself never one to overpraise.[1]

When General Miles took over, he was expressly ordered to put an end to the raiding that was reducing ranch homes to blackened ashes and wiping out the lives of white settlers. Wily Geronimo, already an old man and the chief offender, retorted that the Apache tribes were only fighting to retain their homeland, from which the white man was dispossessing them, which was not true; it was the Comanches who had pushed them back across New Mexico into the southeast corner of Arizona.

Although the military was watching Geronimo closely, he got away from San Carlos again with half a hundred followers. Relentlessly pursued, the renegades left a trail of burnings and killings behind them before they faded away below the line into the Sierra Madre.

Miles became as devious as the old Apache, causing reports to be circulated to the effect that the chief and his adherents would be granted amnesty if they returned to the reservation and surrendered their arms. Miles was ready to promise almost anything if it enabled him to get his hands on them. Geronimo listened, but he was not fooled; no man appreciated more than he the value of his freedom as a bargaining point.

As soon as the trails had dried out in the spring of 1886, Captain (later Major General) Henry Lawton took to the field with a small force of troopers and scouts. Al Sieber was his chief of scouts. The purpose of the expedition was to contact Geronimo and induce him to agree to parley with General Miles.

A few days later, and for the same purpose, Captain Emmett Crawford and a smaller force, consisting of a pack train and scouts, among whom was Tom Horn, followed Lawton across the border. They encountered a troop of Mexican cavalry and were fired upon. Crawford was killed. Horn and Lieutenant Maus brought Crawford's body back to Fort Apache.

A third expedition, commanded by Lieutenant Charles Gatewood, consisting of two friendly White Mountain Apaches and himself, crossed the border to confer with the shrewd old chief. Gatewood met with Captain Lawton's party. His request that Horn be transferred to his command as interpreter having been granted, they parted.

The Army makes light of the part Horn played in the conferences with Geronimo that followed. But that was standard military practice. It cannot be doubted, however, that Horn was responsible in large measure for the successful conclusion of those talks, the chief agreeing to meet General Miles in Skeleton Canyon.

When the hostiles returned to the San Carlos Reservation, General Miles bundled them and hundreds of other Apaches aboard trains at San Carlos Station and shipped them across the United States to the old Seminole Reservation near St. Augustine, Florida. It marked the end of Apache tribal violence in Arizona.[2]

With the ending of Apache hostilities, the Army dismissed the corps of scouts who had contributed so much to the successful conclusion of the campaign. Cut adrift with the others, Horn divided his time between prospecting—at which he was unsuccessful—and contesting in the rodeos that were becoming increasingly popular throughout the Territory. Men who knew him as he was then —the year was 1887—describe him as a bronzed, burly, fearless six-footer. He was twenty-six.

There is nothing in the record to indicate that he was more than casually acquainted with Sheriff William (Bucky) O'Neil of Yavapai County. Bucky was already well known throughout Arizona, but the career that was to make him famous was still ahead of him.[3] Horn must have impressed him, for he had him appointed deputy sheriff.

The Mogollon Rim (pronounced Moyan) had long been the recognized deadline beyond which sheep could not be grazed, shutting them out of the Tonto Basin and particularly that part of it known as Pleasant Valley. In the late fall of 1887, that ban was put to the test when Daggs Brothers of Flagstaff, the most important sheep outfit in the Territory, drove a band of a thousand head over the Rim into Pleasant Valley.

The three *pastores* who accompanied the sheep were young Navajos. Certainly they must have expected to be stopped, turned back, or killed. That was the overwhelming sentiment of the crowd that had gathered hurriedly at Charlie Perkins' store in Pleasant Valley. If that didn't happen at once, it was due to the coolheadedness of Tom Graham, the leader of the cattlemen. So the first sheep came into Pleasant Valley unopposed. When they were put on range claimed by the fighting Tewksbury clan, it became obvious that the latter had betrayed their neighbors and sold out to the Flagstaff sheepmen.

Thus the celebrated Pleasant Valley war, or Graham-Tewksbury feud, which was to be fought to the last man and take the lives of a reported twenty-six men (I can account for only nineteen), began.

Doubting his ability to remain a neutral, Bucky O'Neil, who was friendly with the Grahams, resigned his commission. Bill Mulvenon, a good man, succeeded him. Horn, disgruntled at being passed over, turned in his badge and moved to the booming copper town of Globe, the county seat of newly organized Gila County.

The notorious Apache Kid, scourge of southern Arizona and reputed killer of a score of men and women, both white and Indian, was taken into custody in 1888 and lodged in the Gila County jail. Sheriff Glenn Reynolds made Horn a special deputy and interpreter, charged with preventing any attempt at escape by the famous prisoner. Horn was given time off to enable him to participate in Globe's first annual Fourth-of-July celebration and cowboy stampede. He won the steer-roping contest handily. A few months later he was in Phoenix, competing in the Phoenix Fair contest and was again a winner.

The Apache Kid had been tried, convicted, and sentenced to life imprisonment in the penitentiary at Yuma. The Territory was shocked by the news that, as he and five other convicted Indians were being taken to Yuma, they had gotten the upper hand of Sheriff Reynolds and his deputy Hunky Dory Holmes, had killed the two officers, and escaped.

Horn was shocked by the news and blamed himself for the killing of his friend Glenn Reynolds and Deputy Sheriff Holmes. "It wouldn't have happened if I'd been there," he told friends. "The Kid and those devils evidently talked over their plans as the stage in which they were riding bumped over the road near Florence. Speaking no Apache, Glenn and Holmes couldn't understand what they were saying. I would have understood and been ready for them."

News of the killing of Reynolds and Holmes and the escape of the prisoners had been brought into Florence by Gene Livingston, the driver of the stage, himself seriously wounded. On the morning of November 1, after crossing the Gila, the sand was so deep on the uphill climb that Reynolds ordered everybody out to ease the load on the horses. The prisoners were handcuffed and shackled in pairs. Reynolds carried a shotgun loaded with buckshot; Holmes was armed with a rifle. In addition, both officers carried .45 caliber pistols. But it being a raw, cold morning, both men were wearing heavy sheep-lined coats, which made it impossible to reach their short guns quickly.

Prisoners and officers had taken only a step or two when the Apache Kid leaped at Reynolds and brought his handcuffs down on Reynolds' head, knocking him unconscious. Two of the other prisoners felled Holmes in similar fashion. Snatching up Holmes's rifle, the Apache Kid knocked driver Livingston off the box. Believing he had killed him, he paid no further attention to him. Whipping around, he sent a bullet crashing through Reynolds' head.

From where he lay, Livingston saw them find the keys and remove the shackles and cuffs. Pulling the harness off the horses, they mounted bareback and struck off down the slope and disappeared after crossing the river.

The Kid's companions were captured a few months later, were tried, convicted, and hanged. But not the Apache Kid. For two years he was the object of the greatest manhunt in Arizona history. He was first in one place and then in another, leaving a red trail behind him. Both as a special deputy and in his private capacity, Tom Horn took part in the long search for the Apache Kid. It was his opinion—and events confirm it—that the Kid spent the winters in Mexico. Certainly there were long stretches of time when the

199

military, the Rangers, and other peace officers, including men who had formerly scouted for the Army, lost track of the Kid altogether.

Down in the Catalina Mountains, some twenty-five miles northeast of Tucson, Wallapai Clarke and John Scanlon, former scouts and old *compañeros* of Tom Horn, were working on some mining claims they had been developing for several years. On a November evening in 1889, Clarke walked down to the corral to make sure that the horses were safe for the night. It was moonlight. When he saw two Indians moving stealthily up the arroyo, he raised his rifle and fired. One of the Apaches toppled over dead, the other turned and ran. Clarke fired a second time and knocked him down. In the morning Clarke followed a bloody trail for a hundred yards or more before he lost it.

The amount of blood the Indian had lost convinced Clarke that the Apache was mortally wounded. But his body was not found. The horse proved to be one that had been stolen from Clarke during the past year. He and his partner Scanlon buried the other Apache. She was a young squaw. It was enough to convince Clarke and his partner that the one who had got away was the Apache Kid. That was the way he often traveled—with a woman at his side. He was never seen again. Among Arizonians, Wallapai Clarke is credited with killing him.

Grubstaked by Al Sieber, Horn had located a mining claim on Cherry Creek in Gila County. It placed him on the fringe of the Pleasant Valley war, which was still being pursued. There is nothing in the record to indicate that he took part in it; although Earle Forrest, its most authentic historian, refers to him as a Graham supporter.

In the mining boom of 1889, Horn and Sieber sold their claim. Horn's share of the proceeds amounted to $8,000, more money than he had ever possessed at one time. He was twenty-nine and still a young man. Foolishly, he began cutting a splurge in Globe:

the wolves were waiting for him. To quote the old song, "whiskey, wimmen and card-playin'" threatened to be his undoing. When Globe became too small a pond for him to swim in, he left Arizona and headed for Denver, then the boom-town capital of the West.

XIX

On the Evidence—True or False —the Verdict Was Guilty

Of Tom Horn's first months in Denver we know very little. By his own admission, made some years later, he went on benders, periods of drunkenness lasting four or five days. I have read that he found temporary employment in one or another of the Larimer Street gambling houses as a "lookout." Perhaps he did, but I have found no hard evidence to confirm the story. His diminishing funds were becoming a problem, and in January, 1890, he went to work for the Pinkerton Detective Agency.[1]

James McPartland, famous for breaking up the Molly Maguire terrorists, was director of the Denver office. He assigned Horn to work with Doc Shores, one of his best operatives. When a Denver and Rio Grande express was robbed at Cotopaxi, between Salida and Canon City, Colorado, Shores and Horn distinguished themselves by tracking down the three guilty bandits and taking them into custody after a chase that took them across Colorado and the Texas Panhandle to Washita, Oklahoma.

Horn found his role as a Pinkerton operative at first both dangerous and exciting, but eventually it became boring. After riding the steamcars back and forth between Salt Lake City and Denver

202

for thousands of miles, he turned in his shield. He headed north for Cheyenne, instead of returning to Arizona, where he was widely and favorably known. It is fair to presume that as a Pinkerton operative he had been in Wyoming on more than one occasion and had some acquaintance with it.

In an attempt to supply a reason for his presence in Wyoming, some commentators have attempted to connect him with the farcical Johnson County Invasion as a hired gunman. As a matter of fact, the so-called invasion had occurred long before he left the Pinkertons. But the problem that had been responsible for it remained—the rustling of range cattle.[2]

The homesteaders who had settled in Johnson, Natrona, and other eastern counties had become so numerous that they elected judges and other officials who could be depended upon to oppose the powerful Stock Growers' Association, which made it almost impossible to convict a man of stealing cattle, no matter what evidence was against him. Big owners, unquestionably supported by the association, were fighting back by hiring so-called stock, or range, detectives to rid Wyoming of rustlers.

It was highly paid but dangerous work, calculated to appeal to a man of Tom Horn's demonstrated fearlessness and intelligence. His days as an Army scout had established him as an expert tracker. That he had the qualifications the cattlemen of Wyoming were seeking in the men they were hiring to curb the rustling that was plaguing them appears undeniable. It is likely that he had come to terms with them prior to leaving the Pinkerton Agency in 1894.

That the deployment of a handful of stock detectives, each working independently of the others, was not going to put down range thievery soon became apparent. They were a deterrent, but the branding of mavericks and the disappearance of branded cattle continued. Some known rustlers left the country for safer ranges, after finding in some lonely canyon the dead body of a man who had refused to heed the warning.

Tom Horn, Charley Siringo, the self-styled "cowboy detective," and Joe Lefors were loners. All three were riding the ranges of Wyoming for the same purpose and drawing their wages from the same men. But they had no good words to say about one another. When Horn was drinking, he boasted of the number of men he had killed or sent hightailing it out of Wyoming. So far as the record is concerned, such tales were figments of his imagination.

Tom Horn had made some substantial friends, among them John C. Coble of the Iron Mountain Ranch, forty miles north of Cheyenne. He made his headquarters at the Iron Mountain.

On the outbreak of the Spanish-American War, Horn sometimes saw in the newspapers the names of men he had known as junior officers in Arizona, now risen to posts of command. They included General Leonard Wood, whom he had known as Surgeon Wood, and who, with General Shafter, was to lead the invasion of Cuba. Horn wrote Wood and was rewarded by being appointed chief packer of all pack trains that were to accompany the expedition.[3]

Horn went ashore in Cuba with the Rough Riders and was giving an excellent account of himself when an attack of yellow fever forced him to return to Wyoming and the Iron Mountain Ranch. He was ten months recovering his health, after which he went back to his role of stock detective.

Horn was well acquainted with both Kels Nickell and Jim Miller, neighbors who had been at odds ever since they had homesteaded their places back in the early 1880's. Miller was the more prosperous of the two. He had a small herd of cattle, honestly come by, it appeared; Nickell depended on his hay crop for a living.

Their smoldering feud broke into flame in the early summer of 1901, when Kels Nickell brought in a flock of sheep and turned them out to graze on his pasture. They were clubbed and a number killed a night or two later.

It was a warning that Nickell did not heed. Instead of disposing of his sheep, he and his son Willie began lying out at night, armed with shotgun and rifle, guarding the flock. Nothing happened, and after several weeks they relaxed their vigil.

On the evening of July 19, 1901, sometime after sunset, the lifeless body of Willie Nickell was discovered a few feet inside the pasture gate. He had been shot twice. Bloodstains on the grass and the gravel adhering to the boy's clothing convinced a coroner's jury that after being killed the body had been dragged inside the gate to where it was found.

"It was the Millers," charged Kels Nickell. "They mistook him for me." But he could produce no evidence to that effect.

Wyoming could take the killing of an adult male in stride and quickly forget it; the slaying of a fourteen-year-old boy was another matter. Certain newspapers kept the case alive as a circulation booster. As speculation widened as to who might shed some light on what had happened, new names entered the case. They included Victor Miller, Jim Miller's son, a boy of approximately the same age as Willie Nickell. The two boys had often fought, with the advantage usually going to the heftier Miller boy. Gossip widened to include Gwendolin Kimmell, invariably referred to as "the pretty young schoolteacher," who was residing temporarily at the Miller ranch as she moved about the district, the school board being obligated to provide her with bed and board. She was from the East and undoubtedly had come to Wyoming seeking adventure as well as a living.

She was the reason, it was said, that Tom Horn was so often seen at the Miller ranch. Undoubtedly she was attracted to him. And why not? He was big and handsome and had barely turned forty. She was still in her twenties. She was to prove herself a courageous young woman, stepping forth in his behalf despite the slurs and innuendos leveled at her.

Although he always came to her sober, she was undoubtedly aware of his drinking sprees. When he was liquored, he told hilarious tales of the men he had gunned down and even hinted that he knew more about the killing of Willie Nickell than he cared

205

to say. As the result of his loose talk, he suddenly found himself without a job, the stockmen who had employed him fearing to become involved in the numerous killings he spoke about so glibly. The Cheyenne *Leader's* suddenly revived interest in the Nickell killing was another indication that something was afoot. In stinging editorials it demanded that the mystery be solved and the guilty party be brought to justice.

Laramie County prosecutor W. R. Stoll, under fire, got very busy and reassembled the coroner's jury that had sat on the Nickell killing, for the announced purpose of discovering new evidence. Nothing came of it. But Stoll had other weapons in his arsenal, and he proceeded to use them.

Joe Lafors, former stock detective and now deputy United States marshal, became his principal conspirator. From among the three or four men, including Jim Miller and Tom Horn, they settled on Horn as their most vulnerable target. Stoll, with his superior intelligence, directed the attack, but court records reveal that Lafors supplied the evidence required for a conviction.

Horn was in Cheyenne, out of work and drinking. Lafors got him in tow by holding out the hope of getting him a job with a Montana cattleman who was on his way to Cheyenne for the purpose of hiring a reliable stock detective. Having won Horn's confidence, he proceeded to keep him drunk. And that brings us to the celebrated "confession."

On the pretext that he had more to say about the Montana job, Lafors sat down with Horn in the United States marshal's office in the State House on the morning of January 12, 1902. In an adjoining office, unknown to Horn, were Deputy Sheriff Les Snow and Ohnhaus, a court reporter, taking down in shorthand every word that was said. Horn was drunk and, boastfully, made a number of damaging statements.

Tom Horn was arrested the following day and charged with the killing of Willie Nickell. John Coble and other friends put up the money for his defense. The betting in Cheyenne was four to one against his being found guilty. But as the trial dragged on, it became apparent that his lawyers were handling the case ineptly. Gwendolin Kimmell was prepared to testify that young Victor Miller had once confessed to her that it was he who had killed Willie Nickell. The court refused to hear her testimony on the grounds that it was prejudiced.

The trial dragged on for several weeks. When the case finally went to the jury, the jurors were so confused that it took six ballots for them to agree on a verdict of guilty. The verdict carried with it a mandatory sentence of death by hanging.

Horn languished in jail as his case was appealed to the State Supreme Court. That august body was in no hurry to act. Weeks passed. When one of his fellow prisoners, implicated in a train robbery, broke jail, Horn walked out with him, only to be captured before he could get out of Cheyenne.

Triggered into action by the incident, the High Court denied Horn's appeal and sustained the verdict rendered by the trial court. So, at six o'clock on the morning of November 20, 1903, Tom Horn was hanged in the Cheyenne jail yard.

Was he hanged for a crime he had not committed? No one knows. Perhaps Prosecutor Stoll could have supplied the answer. Perhaps he found it difficult to live with, for he died a drunkard and a suicide.

Captain Lee Hall,
the Gate City's First Marshal

Before the coming of the Cherokees and the other so-called civilized tribes, the vast wilderness extending several hundred miles west of the Mississippi had been the recognized homeland of the numerous and powerful Osage nation.

Following the stupid governmental policy that two wrongs make a right, the United States pushed the Osage off their tribal lands to make room for the exiles who had been torn up by the roots from their ancestral lands in the Carolinas and other southeastern states and removed to what was then known as Indian Territory and is now eastern Oklahoma.

The distance from the Kansas line to Red River and Texas was approximately two hundred and fifty miles. It was virgin country, cut up by numerous small streams, limestone hills, and timbered valleys. Even after Fort Gibson, at the confluence of the Arkansas, Verdigris, and Grand (Neosho in Kansas) rivers was garrisoned in 1829, the only military post in Indian Territory, its white and mixed-blood (French-Indian) population of traders, hunters, trappers, and missionaries did not exceed three hundred.[1]

Missouri, itself a recently organized territory, had sovereignty over what was loosely called Upper Louisiana Territory. Its principal business appears to have been the granting of licenses to trade with the Indians. The Chouteaus, Jean, the father, and his son Auguste Pierre, members of the St. Louis Missouri Fur Company, made St. Louis the fur capital of the United States. Politics being then what they are today, they secured the exclusive license to trade with the Osage and Little Osage nations. It was a concession that proved to be priceless.

Colonel Auguste Pierre Chouteau could cut a dashing figure in a St. Louis ballroom and be just as much at home in the smoke-stained lodge of an Indian. The title of colonel was one he had given himself, as there is nothing in the record to show that he ever had any military service.

When young Chouteau built his great trading post at La Grande Saline, on the Grand River, several miles above Fort Gibson, he established the dominance of the family name. There, with his wife Rosalie, an Osage full blood, the convent-educated daughter of an Osage chief and mother of his numerous children, he lived the life of a wilderness potentate.[2]

For as long as the oldest of the longhairs could remember, the Osage had been going down the Osage Trace to La Grande Saline once a year "to make salt," which was accomplished by boiling down water taken from the salt springs and gathering the white crystals that remained. They continued to come, bringing their furs and peltries and other forest commodities to the Chouteaus' trading post to exchange for powder and firearms.

In earlier days it was by way of the famous Trace that Osage war parties raided deep into Texas, returning with remudas of captured horses and mules. From the Neosho River, in today's Ottawa County, the Trace swung eastward across Missouri, opening the way to St. Louis and the French settlements on the Mississippi.[3]

In 1839 the Bureau of Indian Affairs removed the Osage nation from its established tribal homeland in southern Kansas and along the Neosho River basin (without apparent justification) and re-settled them on the Great Osage Reservation in Indian Territory, west of the Cherokees. The net effect of this act was to enrich the Cherokees and impoverish the Osage. Auguste Chouteau at Grand Saline and his competitors who had established themselves at the Three Forks were quick to realize that their trade was shrinking; the Cherokees and the Creeks were not hunters and would have few peltries to sell. Accordingly, traders began hiring wilderness runners to drum up business with the Kiowas and other western tribes.

After a fashion their strategy worked. As the aftereffects of the nationwide panic of 1837 wore off, they resumed dispatching boatloads of furs and forest products down the Arkansas River to the distant New Orleans market. And now—and not appreciated at first—Texas longhorns were driven up the Osage Trace.

The herds were small—three or four hundred head—but they became more numerous as the season advanced. The fur traders gathered at the Three Forks were witnessing the beginning of the fabulous Texas cattle trade, which, in the forty years to follow—with time out for the bitter War Between the States—was to see millions of Longhorns driven north to markets over trails as yet undreamed of.

The Longhorns that passed the Three Forks and Fort Gibson came up through the Nations (the lands allotted to the Choctaws, Creeks, and Cherokees), having crossed Red River at Rock Bluff Crossing, a natural cleavage in the limestone bluffs that led down to the river. They either swam or walked across, depending on the stage of the unpredictable Red.

In the middle 1840's, it was only a matter of weeks after Texas announced a policy of granting free land to prospective settlers that streams of covered wagons were moving down the historic Trace. Born of the disputes for a right-of-way with the trail herds coming north, they renamed the old Trace, and it became the Texas Road. In the War Between the States, it was along the Texas Road that the battles and skirmishes in Indian Territory occurred.

Although as many as four thousand gold seekers crossed the Territory in the rush to California in 1849, they left no mark on the country. The following year the government built a chain of forts in Texas, running southwest from Preston (Denison) on Red River to Dona Ana on the Rio Grande. The Army garrisoned them until the outbreak of the war. It was not the shortest route to the California fields, but the presence of the military offered some protection against Indian attack, which was reason enough for preferring it. It was also the route which the speeding stagecoaches of John Butterfield's Overland Mail traveled.

The isolation that had been imposed on Indian Territory by the legislation that created it was broken on June 6, 1870. The crowd of several thousand whites and Indians who were on hand to witness the event cheered and a band tootled as the first iron horse came steaming down from nearby Chetopa, Kansas, whistle blowing, and rumbled across the border to the end of the track, a matter of a few yards. It was a "Katy" (Missouri, Kansas and Texas) locomotive. In time, the letters that decorated its tender were to become the trademark of one of our great north-south railroad systems.

The Katy had had to overcome some distressing financial problems to get as far as it had. As it pointed down through the Nations, paralleling the Texas Road, where possible, it was beset by countless construction difficulties; half-finished bridges were swept away by rivers on a rampage; a recently graded right-of-way was destroyed by a freshet; horses were stricken with fever and the work gangs bedded with ague. Working in the swamps, waist deep in the stagnant water, harassed by flies and clouds of mosquitoes, men staggered out of the muck and made for the hospital tent.

Colonel Bob Stevens, head of construction for the Katy, needing workmen, turned to the Indian chiefs for help. From them he got a firm no. They feared what the railroad would do to their country. But Stevens received reinforcements from Missouri, and the work was pushed forward.

The only law in the Territory was tribal law, enforced by the

211

Indian police, the best of which were the Chickasaw Light Horse and the Mounted Cherokee Rifles. Rarely did a United States marshal, working out of Fort Smith, Arkansas, make an appearance. The Indian police were not interested in apprehending wanted white men. As a result the Territory was a haven for horse thieves, bank robbers, assorted outlaws, and whiskey peddlers.

By the hundreds they gathered to prey on the Katy's construction camps, tagging along as the rails advanced. The women who plied their ancient trade in the canvas brothels were as vicious as their masters. Killings, knifings, robberies, were a nightly occurrence.

As the railhead advanced, speculation grew as to where the Katy was going to cross Red River. A few miles one way or the other couldn't make much difference to Texas or the Territory, but it was of the first importance to the railroad company. It knew exactly where the crossing and terminus were to be located. For weeks its land agents had been buying cheap Texas land in a confusing pattern. Finally, the cat was out of the bag: the river was to be spanned a short distance above Indian Ben Colbert's ferry and a new town, Denison, on the site of old Fort Preston and named for George Denison, vice-president of the Missouri, Kansas and Texas Railroad, was to be the Katy's Texas capital.

Shortly after five o'clock on the afternoon of December 25, 1872, Christmas Day, its whistle tied down and screeching, the first "official" train, with company bigwigs and assorted dignitaries aboard, including Ben Colbert, rolled across the Red River bridge. Rumbling through the squatter settlement of extravagantly named Red River City, it steamed into hilarious, wholly railroad-owned Denison.

Denison made a commendable effort to escape the evils that had surfaced in similar towns. The Denison town board had received a charter that appeared to be a formidable weapon for combating sin. Under its provisions it had the authority to "license, tax and regulate billiard tables, pen alleys, ball alleys, disorderly houses, tippling shops, barrooms, dramshops, or other places wherein liquors were sold or dispensed, bawdy houses, houses of prostitution or assignation, gambling and gaming houses, lotteries, and all fraudulent devices and practices, and all kinds of indecencies."

The charter sufficed to keep Main Street, Denison's principal thoroughfare, fairly respectable, but Skiddy Street, which took off down the ravine to the south, became the almost nightly scene of a stabbing or killing. The canvas and tar-paper shacks that lined both sides of Skiddy formed an unbroken line of saloons, gambling "parlors," and brothels. By the time the Houston and Texas Central, building up from south Texas, reached Denison, in March, 1873, between three and four hundred assorted desperadoes, outlaws, rustlers, horse thieves, and frontier scum were gathered in Skiddy. Deputy United States marshals, whose business took them there, described it as the "toughest spot on the frontier." [4]

Rowdy Joe Lowe, saloonkeeper, dance-hall proprietor, and whoremaster, late of Delano, the scabrous settlement across the Arkansas River from Wichita, had arrived in Skiddy and opened its gaudiest establishment, the Crystal Palace. Needless to say, it was an extravagant misnomer, crystal being as impossible to find in its environs as virtue.

Joe Lowe, a short, stocky man, had a fearsome reputation as a barroom brawler. Several killings could be traced to him, but he was not a gunfighter. He had arrived in Denison with a comfortable bankroll and was prospering. Formerly a shabby dresser, he strutted about Denison in a Prince Albert and silk hat. He was bucking to make himself boss of the district and he achieved his goal when he induced the Denison Town Company to grade Skiddy Street and install plank sidewalks. Formerly it had been a sea of yellow mud after every heavy rainfall.

If Denison was lawless, it was also prosperous. Before the year's end, an estimated thirty thousand head of beef cattle were shipped north. They were mostly longhorns from east Texas. To attract cattle from the Southwest, a modern stockyard had to be built.

213

Joseph G. McCoy, the originator of the Kansas Cattle Markets and builder of the Abilene, Newton, Wichita, and Caldwell stockyards, was engaged to build the Denison facility.

Progress was indicated in other directions. Bill Munson, the Katy's general land agent, and Indian Ben Colbert formed a partnership to span Red River with a wooden toll bridge. When completed, it represented an investment of $40,000.

By act of the Texas legislature, Denison became an incorporated town on March 7, 1873. Less than two weeks later, on March 18, the spur of track connecting the Houston and Texas Central was completed and a train of loaded stock cars steamed across Red River bound for the north. It was a doubly notable day for Denison, for it marked the formal opening of the famed Alamo House, for years the finest hostelry in northern Texas. A group of Katy officials had arrived by special train from Sedalia for the ceremonies. Strings of lighted Chinese lanterns lent a holiday air to the outdoor banquet, where a large crowd was treated to broiled quail, roast venison, and champagne.

Colonel Bob Stevens was the principal speaker. He predicted that Denison, the Gate City, would become one of the great cities of the West; that "the Katy will not be halted until it has connected the Gulf Coast of Texas with the Great Lakes of the North."

Instead of being built around a central, four-sided plaza, in the pleasant Spanish manner, like so many other Texas towns, Denison was built on northern lines with an oversize main street, eighty feet wide. Given the most obvious of names—Main Street—it began out in the sagebrush to the west of town and lost its identity in the opposite direction when it converged with the cattle trail that led down to Rock Bluff Crossing.

For a distance of several blocks it built up quickly and became in fact, as well as name, the town's principal thoroughfare, graded and embellished with sidewalks. Briefly it became the scene of what the *Denison News*, tongue in cheek, labeled "our Sunday afternoon sporting event."

To anyone acquainted with the history of harlotry in the United States, Ada and Minna Everleigh and their fabulous Everleigh Club on Chicago's South Dearborn Street are familiar names. At the height of their success as the queens of the town's whoredom, it was Ada and Minna's custom on their trips to the bank, or when shopping, to set out in an open barouche, a liveried coachman on the box and accompanied by several of their prettiest young bawds, giving the gawking males along the way a look at the young lovelies whose favors were for sale at the Everleigh Club.

Undoubtedly this form of advertising proved profitable. But Ada and Minna Everleigh did not originate it. That distinction goes to Millie Hipps, the rough, tough, overripe queen bee of Skiddy Street's madams, thirty years earlier. Renting a carriage and team of high-stepping horses at Farmer's Livery—she did her own driving—she filled the two-seated rig with the prettiest of her powdered and painted frails.

To the raucous applause of the growing crowd of amused males who lined the sidewalk, Millie drove up and down Main Street for several hours. The afternoon had been such a success that she at once engaged the barouche for the following Sunday to head off her competitors. Since there were no other two-seated rigs available in Denison, several were brought up from nearby Sherman during the week.

The following Sunday the rival madams of Skiddy and their followers were out in full force. Hundreds of others were on hand to observe the excitement. Minor accidents occurred when the inexperienced drivers failed to resist the temptation to race. The participants screamed unladylike threats back and forth. The climax came when Frankie Greene, Rowdy Joe's inamorata of the moment, which gave her special privileges on Skiddy, drove her horses into Millie Hipps's speeding team. The wheels locked and two of Millie's girls were pitched into the road, both suffering multiple bruises and one a fractured arm.

The following morning the town board passed an ordinance banning such exhibitions. But to put ordinances on the books without being able to enforce them was an exercise in futility. What Denison needed was a peace officer with the clout to whip the town into line and keep it there. Due to the cooperation of the superintendent of the Texas Rangers at Austin, Denison found the man it needed in the person of ex-Ranger Captain Lee (Red) Hall.

I don't know who (very likely it was Gene Cunningham) first told the story of the Texas Ranger who was responding to an urgent wire for help from the mayor of a Texas town where a riot was taking place. As he stepped down from the train on arriving, he found his honor waiting for him, a troubled look on his face. "There's only one of you?" exclaimed the mayor. "You've got only one riot, haven't you?" returned the Ranger.

Better than anything else, that incident has always typified Lee Hall to me. The spotlight of publicity has seldom focused on him, but on his record he must be included in the galaxy of famous Western peace officers. With his fists—or his guns, when necessary —he brought law and order to Denison.

In the July, 1873, issue of *Scribner's Magazine*, Edward King, a well-known magazine writer of the day, described his visit to Denison and his impression of Captain Lee Hall. Judging by the picture that accompanied the article, Hall was then a muscular young man, still in his mid-twenties, handsome and possessing tremendous vitality and alertness.

"He had been impressed by the Town Company to clean up the community," says King. "He did a workmanlike job and did it in a workmanlike way.

"It is exceedingly remarkable, that in a community one-half of which is undoubtedly made up of professional ruffians, 'verminous' types and gamblers, and the off-scourings of society . . . that there is not more of terrorism. Every third building in the place is a drinking saloon with gambling appurtenances, filled after nightfall with a depraved, adventurous crowd, whose profanity is appalling, whose aspect is hideous."

King does not mention the women, or perhaps the editor of fastidious *Scribner's Magazine* blue-penciled his references to them.

"Red Hall," continues King, "seems to bear a charmed life. He moves about every day in a community where there are a hundred men who would be delighted to shed his blood. . . . He has been ambushed and shot at, and threatened times innumerable, yet has always . . . ended in forcing them to admire him."

Rowdy Joe Lowe warned him to keep his hands off the Crystal Palace. Hall realized that the man was dangerous, but he pulled Lowe's teeth by holding him up to ridicule for the airs he was giving himself. With Skiddy enjoying a laugh at his expense, Joe put aside his silk topper and frock coat. He disposed of the Crystal Palace a few months later and left Denison. For a year or two he is known to have bobbed up in Leadville and other Colorado mining camps before reaching the end of his trail in Denver, where—according to conflicting reports—he died in 1889.

This is not the story of the Katy Railroad and should not be regarded as such. Nor is it important to this narrative that the Katy became the prize for which Jay Gould and the other robber barons of American railroading contended. Times have changed, but the indelible fact remains that it opened the commerce of the Southwest with the North. Twenty-one months after it crossed the Kansas line and began laying its rails down through Indian Territory, it had crossed Red River and established itself on Texas soil.

On September 18, 1873, Jay Cooke and Company of Philadelphia, America's leading banking house, closed its doors. Other banks were dragged down in the resulting crash. Panic spread across the nation. Right and left, railroads went into bankruptcy. The year 1874 took its place in history as "the Year of the Great Depression"—which it was, up to that time.

But as other railroads went into the hands of receivers, the Katy continued to prosper, its freight and passenger revenue increasing from month to month. Work on the bridge that Ben Colbert and

Bill Munson were building was progressing at a satisfactory pace. Munson had his hand in other enterprises; he had opened a real estate office on Main Street and in partnership with the Katy Railroad was promoting the erection of the biggest cotton compress in Texas. The tonnage of cotton carried by the Katy was third only to the hard grains (wheat and corn).

With the country wallowing in the depths of the depression, the free-spending underworld area of most Western towns felt the pinch of hard times. Being by nature birds of passage, the pimps and their chattels, the gamblers and the criminal fringe pulled up stakes and began looking for greener pastures. Many of them headed for still-prosperous Denison, where they were not wanted, neither by the town government nor by the "native" residents of Skiddy Street. Ironically, in light of what had been, Captain Lee Hall became the Skiddy Street spokesman and led the fight to have the newcomers removed.

He is reported to have given the town board the choice of authorizing him to deport the undesirables or requesting his resignation. "This morning," reported the *Denison News* of June 19, 1874, "the Deportation Special pulled out for Sedalia. Captain Hall and his constables managed the departure with their usual efficiency."

A new industry, still in its experimental stage, which was to change the whole concept of shipping dressed beef by rail, was underway in Denison. The cat was out of the bag when the Texas Refrigerator Car Company was incorporated.

Previous experiments with icing cars had been modestly successful but too expensive to be commercially feasible. Employing the improved insulating material coming on the market and by making it possible to ice and re-ice a car by means of airtight openings in the roof, the Denison company produced a refrigerator car that bore a close resemblance to the thousands of "reefers" in use today.

On February 1, 1874, the Katy-sponsored Texas Refrigerator Car Company dispatched a train of ten cars, carrying the dressed carcasses of four hundred beeves, which steamed out of Denison for New York City's Washington Market. On arrival, the beef was found to be in perfect condition.

Refrigeration guaranteed the growth and prosperity of the town, but with the Katy its only outlet to the north, Denison could not wrest the beef market away from Kansas City and Chicago.

Today, Indian Ben Colbert is forgotten, and Lee Hall nearly so. Fourteen years have passed since the July morning when I tramped over Ben's old headright with one of his relatives. The big house he built there was destroyed by fire in 1888. Only the ashes remain. We found Ben's costly headstone in the family burying ground, the only one still standing. Rooting hogs had toppled over the others. Years ago it was said that he had died wealthy and buried his money. If so, none of it has ever been found.

Of the men who graduated from D Company, Frontier Battalion, Texas Rangers, none walked taller than Lee Hall. He convinced the frontier outlaws and criminals of Indian Territory, who had flocked to Denison with the expectation of finding easy pickings, that they would have to move on. Several refused to heed the warning and went for their guns. Unfortunately for them, their shooting was as poor as their judgment.

To use the old phrase, Lee Hall brought "law and order" to Denison. Today, you don't hear his name mentioned. If a street sign, "Chestnut Street," catches your eye, take a second look at it. You are standing on old Skiddy.

Notes

CHAPTER II

1. At first, a herd of longhorns, bound north, was reckoned to have reached the Chisholm Trail when it had been put across Red River at Red River Station. Soon, however, a herd that had been shaped up as far south as Williamson County or Matagorda was regarded as having reached the Chisholm Trail, or one of its branches, almost as soon as it began moving. In like fashion, the Abilene Trail, between the future Wichita and Abilene, became the Chisholm Trail.

2. Car loadings reveal that not more than 60 percent of the cattle received at Abilene were shipped out by rail; the rest were purchased by government agents for the beef issue at the various Indian reservations and by Army contractors to supply the forts with beef.

3. How well he was being paid can be judged by comparing his salary with the $60 a month that Wichita paid Earp in the year that he served on its police force.

4. W. D. Stambaugh, *Kansas State Historical Collections*, Vol. IX.

5. J. B. Edwards, Abilene *Chronicle*, Nov. 1870.

CHAPTER III

1. Wild Bill Hickok was thirty-three, born at Troy Grove, LaSalle County, Illinois, in 1837.

2. Strawhorne's name is also given as Strawhan and Strawan.

3. One of his deputies was the cowardly Jim McDonald. The others were James Gainsord and Tom Carson, the latter the nephew of the famous scout Kit Carson.

4. See *Wild, Woolly and Wicked*, by Harry Sinclair Drago.

5. See *Conquering Our Great American Plains*, by Stuart Henry.

Notes

CHAPTER IV

1. Major William Walton was Ben Thompson's friend as well as his attorney and biographer. His *Life and Adventures of Ben Thompson*, although heavily slanted in Ben's favor, remains the basic book on the Thompsons.

2. See Eugene Cunningham's *Triggernometry*.

3. Henry Fraker, Beebe's clerk, dug the slug out of the doorjamb. Although it had missed Morco's head by only an inch or two, Major Walton calls it "one of the worst exhibitions of shooting ever charged to Ben Thompson."

4. Billy Thompson was removed from the Ellsworth jail to Salina, where he was held three days, awaiting information from Leavenworth.

CHAPTER V

1. The yards had a capacity of 125 carloads a day. Meeting that figure became more or less routine in the four years that followed.

2. See Chapter XXI of the author's *Wild, Woolly and Wicked*.

3. Bessie Earp's closest friend and possibly her partner was her next-door neighbor, a madam known professionally as Dixie Lee. They had grown up together in Lamar County, Missouri.

4. Although the Mennonites who soon settled in Harvey County arrived from Russia, their homeland was Germany, from which they had migrated to Russia in the reign of Catherine the Great to escape religious persecution. They were excellent farmers, who built their own mills and ground their own grain.

CHAPTER VI

1. Whether Caldwell was in Kansas or in the Cherokee Strip was debatable until the federal government conducted a new survey of the boundary in 1872 and awarded an additional 2.47 miles of land to Kansas.

2. A state quarantine law, prohibiting the entrance of longhorn cattle into Kansas between March 1 and December 1 was enacted into law on March 7, 1885.

3. Talbot had quarreled with a neighbor near his home at Covelo, in Mendocino County. The man had waited until after dark at Talbot's gate and shot him. This killing was in no way connected with the events that had occurred in Caldwell.

4. Ben Wheeler, born Ben Robertson, was a native of Rockdale, Milam County, Texas. He had only recently escaped from the Huntsville Penitentiary when he appeared in Caldwell.

5. He was indicted, along with Billy the Kid and several others, in the ambush slaying of Sheriff Brady, on the main street of Lincoln. He never was brought to trial, however, being covered by the general amnesty that followed the killing of the Kid.

CHAPTER VII

1. Dodge City's first jail was a covered eight-foot-deep hole on the plaza. Wyatt Earp's biographer relates how the assistant marshal arrested Bob Wright

and shoved him into the pit for the night for disturbing the peace. No mention
of this incident occurs in the newspapers. Of course it never happened.

2. The modern town hall now occupies the Boot Hill site.

3. For years an award of $100 was offered for an authentic photograph of Dora
Hand. Many pictures were submitted, but none was acclaimed a winner.

4. James Earp, the eldest of the Earp brothers, had a crippled foot and was
not, as has often been said, "a fighting man."

Chapter VIII

1. Jefferson C. Dykes, the noted writer and bibliophile, has listed 155 books
devoted in whole or in part to William Bonney, the notorious Billy the Kid.

2. See *Tales of the Old-Timers*, by Frederick R. Bechdolt.

3. Catron was elected to the United States Senate in 1912 and died a wealthy
man. As someone has said, "Tom Catron always knew where the money was."

Chapter IX

1. Governor Axtell promptly disqualified Squire Wilson and removed him
from office.

2. Wallace had been second officer of the court inquiring into the assassination
of President Lincoln, and president of the commission that awarded the electoral
vote of Florida to Rutherford B. Hayes, which made possible his inauguration as
President of the United States.

3. The horse on which the Kid escaped from Lincoln belonged to Billy Burt
and was found tethered to a post in front of Burt's house the following morning.

4. The Kid's gun was not found in Maxwell's bedroom. Garrett says the Kid
was armed. Others say he was not.

Chapter X

1. For three quarters of a century, the disappearance of Colonel Fountain and
his nine-year-old son has continued to be New Mexico's greatest unsolved mystery.
On January 31, 1896, they left Lincoln for Las Cruces, in a buckboard drawn
by a span of horses. Within hours they disappeared. Their bodies were never
recovered, and no clue ever turned up to explain their disappearance.

2. Logan was serving his second term as United States Senator from Illinois.
He was defeated for the vice presidency in 1884.

3. Luke Short died of natural causes in a Kansas City, Missouri, hospital in
1916. Bat was the next to go, suffering a heart attack as he sat at his desk in the
editorial rooms of the *New York Morning Telegraph* in 1921. Wyatt died in his
sleep at his home in Los Angeles in 1929.

Chapter XI

1. The always financially shaky Atlantic and Pacific Railroad succeeded in
putting its rails as far west as the Colorado River before it was taken over by the
Atchison, Topeka and Santa Fe.

Notes

2. The Southern Pacific built on eastward through Bowie and Wilcox and in 1881 connected at Deming with the Santa Fe, which had built south through New Mexico, thus opening the American Southwest market to the Tombstone mines.

3. John P. Clum, editor and publisher of *The Epitaph* and staunch supporter of the Earps, had begun his career in Arizona as United States agent at the San Carlos Apache Indian Reservation. His greatest achievement was getting the military police replaced by an all-Indian Apache police with noteworthy success.

4. George Whitewell Parsons was a staunch supporter of Clum and the Earp faction. His frequent letters to *The Epitaph*, always signed "An Average Citizen," won him the sobriquet "Of Average Citizen Parsons."

Chapter XII

1. See *The Last Chance: Tombstone's Early Years*, by John Myers Myers.

2. This brief narrative makes no attempt to explore the private lives of the Earp brothers, as that distinguished writer Frank Waters has done in his controversial *The Earp Brothers of Tombstone*.

3. Tombstone survived the demonetizing of silver, but when in 1886 subterranean water flooded the mines and could not be controlled, the "jig was up." Tucson began its ascendancy to the metropolitan city it is today.

4. Among the boxers he managed was a young lightweight named Jack Kearns, who was to win enduring fame as the manager of Jack Dempsey.

Chapter XIII

1. I am informed that in the Deep South the nickname Cooney was given to young hunters who had distinguished themselves in trapping or shooting raccoons, and was bestowed as a compliment.

2. Owens was pardoned on January 11, 1890. Shaw died of natural causes while a prisoner at Huntsville on October 31, 1876. It is agreed today that neither man was guilty of any crime and that it was a gross miscarriage of justice to sentence them to prison.

3. Samuel Tucker Lanham became the twenty-second governor of Texas in 1903.

Chapter XIV

1. This version of how Baldy Russell learned that his father had been hanged for his part in the violence that occurred in the Mambrino Road affair in 1874 was given to me many years ago by Eugene Manlove Rhodes, the celebrated cowboy writer. Although others have told it differently, I accept Rhodes' version as factual. Gene knew Baldy Russell and was well acquainted with what transpired on the flatlands and desert reaches of lower New Mexico.

2. Spradley manufactured a reputation for himself as a great manhunter, but his little paperback, published in 1931, is so filled with errors and exaggerations that it is impossible not to question whatever he has to say.

224

3. Spradley says that the stranger stopped at the roadside smithy to have the shoes reset the following morning, which must be doubted, since a set of new shoes would hardly have needed resetting after having been used only a few miles on a dirt road.

4. Frank Knight, a blacksmith by trade, had married Baldy's stepdaughter Belle, and shortly thereafter had deserted her. He held Baldy responsible for his marital troubles. Beyond question he was the informer.

CHAPTER XV

1. Among the noted gunmen of the Southwest, the practice of drawing from vertical, leather-lined hip pockets was fairly common, the conviction being widespread that when a man became proficient at it, he could fade an opponent drawing from a holster.

2. Selman, ex-rustler and desperado, was killed by Deputy United States Marshal George Scarborough. In turn, Scarborough was killed at Sonora, Texas, by Will Carver of the Wild Bunch.

CHAPTER XVI

1. This meeting is one of the pegs on which the story of the Cassidy years hangs, and was sufficiently dramatic to require no fictional embellishment.

2. In addition there was a score or more of shadowy men on whom they depended to keep the trail open and who lived on their bounty.

CHAPTER XVII

1. Hazen was brought to Casper by wagon and from there by special train to Douglas, where he died in the Converse County Hospital about daylight the following morning. His passing occasioned a widespread outpouring of grief, for at a time when many Wyoming sheriffs were the creatures of the powerful Wyoming Stock Growers' Association, he was the friend of the "little fellers" who had only a handful of cattle on the range.

2. Following the rubbing out of the Sundance Kid, his widow and Elza Lay are alleged to have married. Leaving Buenos Aires, they holed up in La Paz, the capital of Bolivia, where their trail fades out.

CHAPTER XVIII

1. See *Triggernometry* by Eugene Cunningham.

2. Geronimo spent the last years of his life as a prisoner at Fort Sill, Oklahoma, and was buried on the Apache Reservation on Cache Creek.

3. In the Spanish-American War, Bucky O'Neil was killed in a Rough Rider charge up San Juan Hill. An equestrian statue of Bucky, in bronze, executed by the noted sculptor Solon Borglum, stands at the north entrance to the court house in Prescott.

Chapter XIX

1. For an informative account of the Pinkerton Detective Agency, see James D. Horan's *Desperate Men*.

2. Helena Huntington Smith's *The War on Powder River* should be read by anyone interested in an unbiased account of conditions in Wyoming in the 1890's.

3. After steaming up and down the Cuban coast for several hours, unable to find a place where he could land his five hundred mules, Horn requested and received permission to push the animals overboard and let them swim ashore, which they did with only several exceptions.

Chapter XX

1. For a colorful account of the country in its primitive state, see Washington Irving's *A Tour of the Prairies*.

2. Chouteau later took a second wife, a cousin.

3. The southern third of the Osage Trace was known as the Shawnee Trail, but Texans seldom alluded to it as such.

4. Named for Francis Skiddy, the effete Easterner who was president of the Land Grant Railroad and a Katy director. He is said to have shuddered whenever Skiddy Street was mentioned in his presence.

A Selected Bibliography

Adams, Ramon F., *The Rampaging Herd*. Norman, University of Oklahoma Press, 1959.

Aikman, Duncan, editor, *The Taming of the Frontier*. By ten authors. New York, Prospect Press, 1925.

Bartholomew, Edward, *Western Hard Cases, or Gunfighters Named Smith*. Ruidoso, New Mexico, Frontier Book Co., 1960.

Bechdolt, Frederick R., *Tales of the Old-Timers*. New York, The Century Company, 1924.

Beebe, Lucius, and Clegg, Charles, *U.S. West, the Saga of Wells, Fargo*. New York, E.P. Dutton & Company, 1949.

Breakenridge, William M., *Helldorado*. Boston, L.C. Page Company, 1929.

Buell, James, *The Border Outlaws*. Chicago, Regan Publishing Co., 1892.

Burns, Walter Noble, *Tombstone: An Iliad of the Southwest*. Garden City, N.Y., Doubleday, 1927.

Canton, Frank M., *Frontier Trails*, Edward Everett Dale, ed. Boston, Houghton Mifflin, 1930.

Clum, Woodworth, *Apache Agent: The Story of John Clum*. Boston, Houghton Mifflin, 1936.

Coolidge, Dane C., *Fighting Men of the West*. New York, E.P. Dutton, 1932.

Cox, William R., *Luke Short and His Era*. Garden City, N.Y., Doubleday, 1961.

Croy, Homer, *He Hanged Them High*. New York, Duell, Sloan, and Pearce, 1952.

——, *The Last of the Great Outlaws*. New York, Duell, Sloan, and Pearce, 1962.

Cunningham, Eugene, *Triggernometry*. New York, Press of the Pioneers, 1934.

Dalton, Emmett, and Jungmeyer, Jack, *When the Daltons Rode*. New York, Doubleday, 1930.

Dillon, Richard, *A Biography of James B. Hume*. New York, Doubleday, 1968.

Drago, Harry Sinclair, *Road Agents and Train Robbers*. New York, Dodd, Mead, 1973.

——, *Wild, Woolly and Wicked*. New York, Clarkson Potter, 1961.

A Selected Bibliography

Dykes, J. C., *The Bibliography of a Legend*. Albuquerque, University of New Mexico Press, 1956.

Eye Witness, *The Anonymous Account of the Dalton Raid on Coffeyville*. Chicago, Laird and Lea, 1892.

Faulk, Odie B., *Tombstone, Myth and Reality*. New York, Oxford University Press, 1972.

Foreman, Grant, *Down the Texas Road*. Norman, University of Oklahoma Press, 1936.

Forrest, Earle R., *Arizona's Dark and Bloody Ground*. New York, Appleton, 1951.

Haley, J. Evetts, *Charles Goodnight, Cowman and Plainsman*. Boston, Houghton Mifflin, 1936.

Hardin, John Wesley, *The Life of John Wesley Hardin. As Written by Himself*. El Paso. Published by the author.

Horan, James D., *Desperate Men*. New York, G.P. Putnam Sons, 1949.

Horn, Tom, *Life of Tom Horn: Government Scout and Interpreter. Written by Himself*. Denver, no imprint, 1904.

James, Marquis, *The Cherokee Strip*. New York, Alfred A. Knopf, 1962.

Keleher, William A., *Turmoil in New Mexico*. Albuquerque, University of New Mexico Press, 1952.

Krakel, Dean F., *The Saga of Tom Horn: The Story of a Cattlemen's War*. Laramie, Wyoming, Powder River Publishers, 1954.

Lake, Stuart N., *Wyatt Earp: Frontier Marshal*. Boston, Houghton Mifflin, 1931.

McCarty, John L., *Maverick Town: the Story of Old Tascosa*. Norman, University of Oklahoma Press, 1946.

Masterson, V. V., *The Katy Railroad and the Last Frontier*. Norman, University of Oklahoma Press, 1952.

Mercer, Asa Shinn, *The Banditti of the Plains*. Norman, University of Oklahoma Press, 1954.

Metz, Leon Claire, *Dallas Stoudenmire: El Paso Marshal*. Austin, Pemberton Press, 1969.

Miller, Nyle H., and Snell, Joseph W., *Kansas Cowtown Police Officers and Gunfighters*. Topeka, Kansas, 1964.

Mokler, Alfred James, *History of Natrona County, Wyoming*. Chicago, Lakeside Press, 1923.

Monaghan, Jay, *The Last of the Bad Men*. Indianapolis, Bobbs-Merrill, 1946.

Myers, John Myers, *The Last Chance: Tombstone's Early Years*. New York, Dutton, 1950.

Parkhill, Forbes, *The Wildest of the West*. New York, Henry Holt, 1937.

Penfield, Thomas, *Western Sheriffs and Marshals*. New York, Grosset and Dunlap, 1955.

Prassel, Frank Richard, *The Western Peace Officer*. Norman, University of Oklahoma Press, 1972.

Raine, William McLeod, *Famous Sheriffs and Western Outlaws*. New York, New Home Library (a reprint), 1944.

Rascoe, Burton, *Belle Starr, the Bandit Queen*. New York, Random House, 1941.

Rosa, Joseph G., *They Called Him Wild Bill*. Norman, University of Oklahoma Press, 1964.

A Selected Bibliography

Shirley, Glenn, *Law West of Fort Smith*. New York, Henry Holt, 1957.

Siringo, Charles A., *Riata and Sours: The Story of a Lifetime Spent in the Saddle*. Boston, Houghton Mifflin, 1931.

Sonnichen, C. L., *Ten Texas Feuds*. Albuquerque, University of New Mexico Press, 1957.

Spradley, A. J. (with Henry C. Fullar), *A Texas Sheriff*. Nacogdoches, Baker Printing Co., 1963.

Streeter, Floyd B., *Prairie Trails and Cow Towns*. Boston, Chapman and Grimes, 1936.

Sutton, Fred E. (with A. B. McDonald), *Hands Up!* Indianapolis, Bobbs-Merrill, 1927.

Tilghman, Zoe A., *Marshal of the Last Frontier*. Glendale, Arthur H. Clark, 1936.

Vestal, Stanley, *The Old Santa Fe Trail*. Boston, Houghton Mifflin, 1939.

Walton, W. W. (Buck), *The Life and Adventures of Ben Thompson*. First published in 1884. Latest reprint, New York, Devin-Adair, 1964.

Waters, Frank, *The Earp Brothers of Tombstone*. New York, Clarkson Potter, 1961.

Wellmann, Paul I., *A Dynasty of Western Outlaws*. New York, Doubleday, 1961.

Wright, Robert M., *Dodge City: The Cowboy Capital and the Great Southwest*. Wichita, Beacon Press, 1913.

Index

231

Index